TOWARD A
PHILOSOPHY OF SPORT

TOWARD A
PHILOSOPHY OF SPORT

HAROLD J. VANDERZWAAG
University of Massachusetts

ADDISON-WESLEY PUBLISHING COMPANY
Reading, Massachusetts · Menlo Park, California · London · Don Mills, Ontario

This book is in the
ADDISON-WESLEY SERIES IN THE SOCIAL SIGNIFICANCE OF SPORT

Consulting Editor
JOHN W. LOY

To the "last of the Mohicans":
John, Carol, George, Charles

Contents

Foreword

The magnitude of sport in the mass media of the Western world attests to the fact that modern man is deeply engrossed in sport as an actual or vicarious, voluntary or conscripted participant. Moreover, the constant outcropping of sport in several institutional sectors of society such as economics, education, and politics strongly suggests that sport permeates and effects many aspects of American life. In short, the pervasive presence of sport forcefully indicates that it has become a social institution in its own right.

In view of its ubiquitous presence, it is rather startling that only a handful of scholars in diverse disciplines have seriously studied the role of sport in society. Despite its manifold expressions, many of the manifest and most of the latent functions and dysfunctions of sport have gone unexamined. A detailed description, let alone an adequate explanation of sport as a social phenomenon, is virtually nonexistent. In sum, little knowledge has been established concerning the social import of sport.

The purpose of the *Social Significance of Sport Series* is to provide an initial understanding of the many meaningful interrelationships between sport and society. This purpose is to be fulfilled by the publication of several books examining the social phenomenon of sport from different theoretical and methodolog ical perspectives. The core of the series consists of a set of books covering such general areas as the history, philosophy, and sociology of sport. The common analytical thread running through each of these books is the shared considera- tion of sport as a social institution, and its interaction with other societal in- stitutions.

As physical education is the only academic field which focuses upon sport as its major substantive concern, the primary function of the core volumes is to serve as basic textbooks for upper-division, undergraduate, and lower-level graduate courses in physical education. A secondary function of the core vol- umes is to provide stimulating collateral reading for a variety of courses in related fields. For example, a book in preparation entitled *A Cultural History of Sport in the U. S.: 1850–1970* by the late John R. Betts, of Boston College, should be of interest to a number of social and intellectual historians as well as numerous sport historians. Another title in the series is the *Sociology of Sport*. It is being coauthored by Gerald S. Kenyon, University of Waterloo, Canada, and John W. Loy, University of Massachusetts. Its audience of interest will undoubtedly be found in departments of sociology, as well as in Schools of Physical Education. This series, then, is truly interdisciplinary.

The general nature of the books constituting the core of the series, of course, precludes in-depth analyses of the relationships between sport and any given social institution. Thus, a second set of books presenting detailed analyses of the relations between sport and such   specific social institutions as economics, education, and politics is to be prepared. These latter volumes are designed for upper-level courses in physical education and should serve as useful supplementary texts for advanced courses in related fields. Hopefully, the two sets of books planned for the series will lay the foundations for a full understanding of the interrelationships between sport and society.

For a number of reasons, it is particularly appropriate that the present volume by Professor VanderZwaag be the first text to appear in the *Social Significance of Sport Series*. First, the book briefly describes the nature of the several subfields to be dealt with in the series, including the history, philosophy, psychology, and sociology of sport. Second, the volume raises critical questions which are to be answered from different theoretical perspectives in the course of the series. These questions include: *who* is involved with sport, *when* and *where* they are involved, *how* they are involved, *why* they are involved, and *what* are the personal and social consequences of their involvement? Third, the text affords analyses of several substantial issues surrounding the nature of sport and thus prepares the groundwork for a full-blown philosophy of sport. Fourth, and perhaps most important, this volume presents a significant conceptual analysis of the key construct underlying the series, namely, *sport*.

November, 1971   John W. Loy
Amherst, Massachusetts   Professor of Physical Education
                                            University of Massachusetts

Preface

The *Time* Essay of June 2, 1967, was entitled "The Golden Age of Sport." The thought exhibited in that title has been expressed by other writers in various books and periodicals in which they attempt to point out that sport is an extremely important factor in this culture. Such an appraisal is usually presented in glowing appreciation of the benefits of sport, although Arnold Beisser follows a different tack in his book, *The Madness in Sports.* He suggests that the American boy is prepared, through adult pressures, for a life of dedication to sport. In most cases, he is being prepared for a role he will never realize. Consequently, he is a "has-been" by his teens, and he then joins the "army of spectators."

The idea that sport has a negative effect on a culture tends to cast a shadow of doubt on many current sport emphases in the United States. Yet, it is entirely possible that one should not proceed with either the plaudits for sport or adverse criticism until he more carefully determines the nature of what he is talking about. What is it that is golden, or what is this area of madness?

For example, the *Time* Essay leaves one wondering about the scope of sport as viewed by the writer. Within two pages, the topics covered run the gamut from record-breaking performances in track and field, to the huge payroll of a professional football team, to the use of "Gatorade" by Florida's Graves, to Bill Bradley's signing with the New York Knickerbockers. It is clear, for the most part, that this discussion centers around professional sport. Interestingly, Beisser seems to imply that it is this drive toward professionalism which partially accounts for the madness in sports.

Efforts to analyze the concept of sport are not entirely new. For instance, an article written by H. Graves entitled "A Philosophy of Sport" appeared in the December 1900 issue of *Contemporary Review.* Nevertheless, such pioneer academic efforts in analyzing sport went relatively unnoticed, at least in this country, and Americans proceeded to be guided in their notion of sport by sportswriters who tended to take a speculative and descriptive point of view. One of the interesting developments of the past few years is that there appears to be a keen interest in the concept of sport among certain philosophers in the United States.

James Keating, a philosopher at DePaul University, wrote an article entitled "Sportsmanship as a Moral Category," which was published in the October 1964 issue of *Ethics*. In this article, Keating makes a primary distinction between the concept of sport and the concept of athletics. He contends that the dominant motive in athletics is to win, whereas sport is pursued for purposes of pleasure and enjoyment. He also relates athletics to professionalism and sport to amateurism. Two other articles, published by Keating in 1965, are extensions of this same general theme. These are "The Heart of the Problem of Amateur Athletics," *The Journal of General Education*, January 1965, and "Athletics and the Pursuit of Excellence," *Education*, March 1965.

Perhaps the most highly publicized of the philosophers' study of sport is the work of Paul Weiss. His scholarly interest in sport was first brought to public attention through the Sunday New York *Times* of September 18, 1966. His approach is basically speculative, although it represents a pioneer effort in the direct application of philosophic thought to the concept of sport.

Weiss was also instrumental in planning for the American Association for the Advancement of Science Symposium on "Sport and Its Participants," which was held in Dallas, Texas, December 1968. Two of the papers presented at this symposium focused on the philosophy of sport.

Robert Fogelin, philosopher at Yale University, presented a paper entitled "Sport: The Diversity of the Concept." He takes the overall position that one cannot arrive at a neat, well-organized definition of sport which will fulfill all conditions surrounding sport. Likewise, he assumes that it is a mistake to rush to "certain paradigm cases," such as football, basketball, and baseball, in attempting to describe sport. Rather, he suggests that we should "look for occurrences and omissions that are somehow surprising." For instance, he suggests that "dog shows are worth studying *just because* they constitute a peripheral or intermediate case." His main plea centers around the need for an analysis of the language of sport which should be concerned with the conventions that are used when thinking and speaking about sport.

Kenneth Schmitz, a philosopher at The Catholic University of America, delivered a paper entitled "Sport and Play: Suspension of the Ordinary." He begins by suggesting that "sport is primarily an extension of play, and that it rests upon and derives its central values from play." However, he adds that there are "three abuses which can kill the spirit of play within sport." These are "exaggeration of the importance of victory," excessive rationalization of techniques, and overdue attention to the presence of spectators.

Schmitz's pivotal attention to play points to another consideration before one embarks on a serious observation of sport. The well-known sociologist, David Riesman, has suggested that we might do well to forego scientific investigation of play.

Admittedly, we know very little about play, partly as the result of the cultural definitions that give priority to work . . . we have still to discover the player. Yet is it sensible to suggest research into play when it is possible that it would lead to increasing public and systematic interference with an area that ideally deserves privacy and lack of system? Perhaps a conspiracy of silence about leisure and play is its best protection?[1]

Of course, one can also take the position that sport should not be confused with play. There obviously are many common denominators between sport and play, but the differences should also be noted. Play is a much broader concept than is sport; there are many varieties of play extending from the simplest form of children's play (frolic) to the complexities and intricacies of adult play in several forms. Sociological factors have a marked influence on the type of play as the human being moves from infancy to late adulthood. Sport is a direct reflection of these sociological factors. In contrast to most varieties of play, sport tends to be more highly structured. To this extent, sport mirrors those cultures which are also more highly organized and complex. No one can deny the fact that sport is an extremely big business in the United States today. Because sport has become very institutionalized, we feel that it is necessary to analyze the nature of this institution. This can be accomplished, in part, through examination of the conceptual framework which is associated with sport.

Athletics is the one concept which probably has been most closely associated with sport. In fact, many people are inclined to speak of sport and athletics interchangeably or synonymously. On the other hand, as noted earlier, Keating contends that sport represents a radically diverse activity in comparison with athletics. Professional physical educators have used a more moderate distinction in suggesting that athletics involves interschool contests in sport. Superficially, such contrasting claims may seem to be relatively harmless. But this could also represent the source of much confusion and be the basic explanation of inconsistency among those who conduct programs in sport and/or athletics.

Sport also relates to physical education in one way or another. Spokesmen have defined physical education as consisting of sport, dance, and other forms of physical activity. This would imply that sport is part of physical education. Yet, from another standpoint, sport is a much broader concept. One could scarcely classify a professional football game or a weekend of recreational skiing as physical education, whereas sport within the schools properly falls under that banner. But this is also contrary to much of contemporary thought which asserts that education is as broad as life itself and should not be confined to the boundaries of the school.

Perhaps the most interesting point regarding sport is the wide acceptance of sport by the public, contrasted with the reluctance and skepticism with which

---

[1]David Riesman, *The Lonely Crowd* (New Haven: Yale University Press, 1961), pp. 276–277. Reprinted by permission of the publishers.

many physical educators assess sport. One is sometimes led to believe that either physical educators have lost their focus or sport is not an important part of physical education.

Paradoxically, certain physical educators are now attempting to rid themselves of association with the concept of physical education. The problems inherent in this concept have been evident for some time. First and foremost among these problems is the obvious implication of a mind-body dichotomy. The resulting controversy regarding education of the physical vs. education through the physical is a concomitant which lends little to serious study and improvement of programs in sport, dance, and other forms of human exercise.

Another reason for rejecting the concept of physical education is the apparent identification with a profession and nonacademic work, contrasted with a discipline and scholarly endeavor. Certain educational "essentialists" have caused physical educators to become defensive regarding the nature of their work. The response of many is to attempt a new identification with the concept of human movement. The latter concept is proposed as an appropriate umbrella to describe disciplinarylike study of sport, dance, and other forms of human exercise.

Even though it is an umbrella term, it does not take one very long to realize the difficulties encumbered with "hanging your hat" on the concept of human movement. How broad can a field be? Much of life is concerned with human movement in some form or another. Certainly physical educators are not about to propose that the entire realm of human movement is their special province. The most serious difficulty with so labeling an area of study or a program is that it lacks the necessary focus for in-depth preparation. We have reached a degree of specialization wherein no individual or group of individuals can purport to make a substantial contribution toward a concept as abstract and elusive as human movement.

In the cold light of analysis, it is sport and sport alone which provides the concreteness and meaningfulness for disciplinarylike study of those activities which have commonly been associated with programs of physical education. This can be partially supported by comparing activities and programs with the characteristics of sport. Loy has provided a succinct description of these characteristics.[2]

According to Loy, the characteristics of sport are essentially the characteristics of games more generally. There is one marked exception to this similarity. Sport demands demonstration of physical prowess in some form or another. This physical prowess may be physical skill, physical fitness, or any combination thereof. The same cannot be said for all games. Aside from that, the characteristics of sport are those of games. Sport is playful; sport is competitive; and sport involves various combinations of skill, strategy, and chance.

Even the peripheral cases among the activities commonly included under the banner of physical education square quite well with the characteristics of

---

[2]John W. Loy, "The Nature of Sport: A Definitional Effort," *Quest* X, May 1968, pp. 1—15.

sport. We noted earlier that physical education has been defined as consisting of programs in sport, dance and other forms of human exercise. One can make a case for the idea that dance and other forms of human exercise also approximate the characteristics of sport. Dance is playful; it can be and frequently is competitive in some manner; it definitely requires physical skill; dance also requires a demonstration of physical fitness to some degree.

Exercise programs per se can be playful. One of the characteristics of play is that it has no object other than itself. This is the one factor which precludes many exercise programs from being play. Yet, the possibility still exists that exercise can be playful. Exercise is also not always competitive. But there is a greater possibility that exercise is more competitive than playful. Actually, competition is also a most elusive concept. One need not compete only against an individual or a group of individuals. He can also compete against a standard. Many people who exercise are competing against some kind of standard. Individuals may also compete against each other through the medium of exercise. If I attempt to do more push-ups than you do, there is no doubt that I am competing. Exercise also requires some degree of physical skill, be it minimal, and, of course, physical fitness is the name of the game in exercise.

Thus, we are led to conclude that sport is the most meaningful concept to describe those playful, competitive activities which also require physical prowess. When we consider sport from this frame of reference, we are no longer restricted to a discusssion of school programs. In fact, sport programs in the shools are only a small part of the broad realm of sport. This points to another difficulty which is inherent in the concept of physical education. For the most part, physical education has been narrowly conceived and limited to school programs.

In attempting to set forth the framework for a philosophy of sport, it seems logical to begin with a brief treatment of the nature of philosophy. There is probably no field of inquiry more elusive than philosophy. From one standpoint, philosophers are better understood for what they do not do than for what they do. The subject becomes particularly confusing when one moves over to what might be called "applied philosophy," such as suggested by investigations into the philosophy of art, philosophy of music, philosophy of education, and philosophy of sport. These investigations are somehow or other based on the assumption that "philosophy bakes bread." There are those who would argue that philosophy bakes no bread. We must take the contrary point of view, or we would not proceed with an analysis of the nature of sport as we do in the remaining chapters of this book.

Philosophy receives its impetus through the raising of questions. More particularly, the question of "why" has been fundamental to philosophical thought. However, in order to probe the "why" of something, it is frequently desirable and sometimes necessary to begin with other basic questions, namely who, what, where, when, and how? These questions provide the structure of our philosophical analysis of the nature of sport.

Among these questions, we will begin with the question of "when" because this question is largely historical. By itself, the question of "when" is rather insignificant from a philosophical standpoint. However, if we can determine when sport emerged as a significant concept, it may assist us in arriving at answers to the more basic philosophical questions. As an example, we need to know more about the conditions which linked sport with physical education. When did this occur? And, what conditions tended to cause this linkage at that time and place?

The question of "when" is inextricably connected with the question of "where." The latter is also a significant contemporary question. However, an analysis of the current scope (where) of sport is almost certain to cause one to probe into the matter of where sport was found and prospered in the past.

Who participates in sport and who promotes sport? These questions also have historical antecedents. Nevertheless, the historical answers to the "who" of sport or the "who" of anything can cause serious philosophical problems if we fail to see beyond the historical "who." As a case in point, sport has flourished more among men in the past than it has among women. This might lead one to conclude that sport is more important for men than for women. Yet, such a conclusion hardly seems justifiable from other standpoints.

What is sport? This is a question of great philosophical import. In fact, next to the question of "why," the question of "what" is probably the most significant philosophically. If we can determine what sport is, we may have taken a major step forward in analyzing why sport occupies that status which it has. The question of "what" offers the best example of a close bond between science and philosophy. We must explore the "what" through scientific investigations. Sociology of sport and psychology of sport will tell us much about the question: what is sport? But certain problems will remain unsolved. At this point, the philosopher suggests possible solutions and poses new ways of looking at these problems.

How is sport conducted? This is largely a question which must be answered in a descriptive manner. The philosophical counterpart is: how should sport be conducted? Unfortunately, many position statements on how sport should be conducted are for the most part limited to a presentation of the status quo as to how sport is conducted. This is a classic example of the confusion between description and philosophy.

We have reserved the question of "why" to conclude this book for more than one reason. As noted earlier, this tends to be the most significant philosophical question. In addition, all of the earlier questions lead up to the question of "why." We may know much about the where, when, who, what, and how of sport. But burning questions always remain: Why do people participate in sport? Why is sport significant for the individual, the group, or a culture? The philosopher's analysis and/or speculation regarding these questions should also pave the way, or stimulate further scientific inquiry, into the theory of sport.

Amherst, Massachusetts   H. J. V
November 1971

Acknowledgment

As is true of any published work, many people have either directly or indirectly contributed to the writing of this book. I give special thanks to Mrs. Hanna Hopp for her careful typing of the original manuscript, to Addison-Wesley for promoting "the social significance of sport series" and guiding the completion of this work, and to Professor John Loy for his excellent counsel as the editor of the series.

Among those who have contributed more indirectly but also significantly, three other colleagues deserve particular mention. Professor Earle Zeigler has continued to be a most highly respected consultant through his broad insight and interest in the humanities and social science aspects of sport. Professor James Keating has made a fine contribution in stressing that athletics is markedly different from play or sport. He initially prompted several of the thoughts which are expressed in this book. Professor Guy Lewis has also had an influence in at least two respects. First of all he has assisted in convinving me that the focus should be on sport, not on physical education. Secondly, he has stressed that sport must be studied, it is fine to talk about sport, but it is high time that we convert some of our talk about sport to a scholarly study of sport. Other colleagues and students have also been of great assistance in stimulating many of the thoughts which are expressed in this book.

The motivation to complete the work I largely attribute to the continued encouragement of my wife and four children. Without that encouragement and cooperation which they displayed in so many ways, it is extremely doubtful that the book would have been written.

The author

Biographical Sketch

Harold J. VanderZwaag was born in Spring Lake, Michigan, on June 26, 1929. His early exposure to sport was primarily in football, basketball, and baseball on the sandlots of Spring Lake prior to the time when the Little League establishments were firmly entrenched. He was graduated from high school in the neighboring town of Grand Haven in 1947 after "lettering" in basketball and baseball.

In 1951 he received his A.B. degree from Calvin College. At Calvin he majored in history and minored in physical education and political science in addition to "lettering" in basketball. His intention at that point was to teach history and coach basketball in a high school. However, through the positive influence of his college basketball coach, he decided to continue his studies in physical education. The following year, Mr. VanderZwaag received his M.S. degree from the University of Michigan.

The years 1952–59 were spent on active duty with the United States Coast Guard. This experience included a variety of shipboard assignments as well as three years at Coast Guard Headquarters in Washington, D.C., where Lt. VanderZwaag headed the Enlisted Training Section. From 1957 to 1959, he was an instructor at the Coast Guard Academy in New London, Connecticut, where he taught history and English in the Department of Humanities in addition to serving as coach of the tennis team.

In 1959 Mr. VanderZwaag returned to the University of Michigan to pursue doctoral studies in physical education. Through the influence of his adviser, Professor Earle Zeigler, Mr. VanderZwaag took his cognate work in the Department of Philosophy. During his three years at Michigan, he also worked as graduate assistant in the Intramural Sport Department. He received his Ph.D. degree in 1962.

Dr. VanderZwaag's first full-time position in physical education was assistant professorship at DePaul University. From 1962 to 1964, he taught courses in the undergraduate majors program and was appointed chairman of the department in 1964. His next position was at the University of Illinois where he was the Undergraduate Professional Program Director in the Department of Physical Education for Men. He also taught a graduate course in the philosophy of physical education and sport and was promoted to the rank of associate professor in 1966.

Since 1967 Dr. VanderZwaag has been Professor and Head of the Department of Physical Education for Men in the School of Physical Education at the University of Massachusetts in Amherst. He teaches graduate courses in the philosophy of sport and athletics. Under his leadership a masters specialization in sport administration was implemented at the University in the fall of 1971.

Professor VanderZwaag has made several contributions toward the theory of sport and physical education. He is the coauthor of two other books: *Physical Education: Progressivism or Essentialism*? with Earle F. Zeigler, and *Foundations and Principles of Physical Education* with Karl W. Bookwalter. He has been particularly interested in the conceptual analysis of sport and related concepts as they influence the conduct of sport. He has contributed several articles and presented papers at professional meetings which are directed toward that interest.

The author has also maintained his affiliation with the Coast Guard Reserve. He has been the commanding officer of two different Coast Guard Reserve units and presently holds the rank of Commander. In 1967 he received a commendation from the Coast Guard Commandant for a study of the Officer Candidate School in Yorktown, Virginia. Among the recommendations of the study was a peer evaluation procedure which has been implemented with considerable success at the Officer Candidate School.

Professor VanderZwaag is married and has four children. His wife is the former Jane Elizabeth Barker of Detroit, Michigan.

Harold VanderZwaag's views on sport are found in the last chapter. He is dedicated to the idea that sport must be more thoroughly studied. His hope is that there may eventually be a theory of sport, based on historical, psychological, sociological, and philosophical investigations, which will improve the arrangements and procedures followed in the conduct of sport.

1/The Nature of Philosophy

THE SCOPE OF PHILOSOPHY

Theoretically, at least, there is virtually no limit to the scope of philosophy. In its broadest sense, philosophy means literally the love of wisdom. However, historically, philosophers have engaged in the systematic study of the facts and principles of reality and of human nature and conduct. These investigations have usually been categorized to comprise studies in logic, ethics, aesthetics, metaphysics, and epistemology.

Of these branches of philosophy, metaphysics would likely be considered the most basic and the most general. From one standpoint, metaphysics includes all of the more abstruse philosophical considerations. More specifically, metaphysics is concerned with such broad matters as fundamental causes, processes in things, and the nature of being. One might say that the metaphysician attempts to answer "first questions." It is quite obvious that metaphysics tends to be speculative in approach.

Epistemology is a logical outgrowth of metaphysics. When one examines the theory of the method and grounds of knowledge, especially with reference to its limits and validity, he is engaged in epistemological thought. It can readily be noted that the nature of being is basic to understanding the nature of knowledge. Therefore, from the standpoint of order or precedence, epistemology might be considered second line, next to metaphysics.

Ethics is inextricably related to another concept: the concept of morals. In fact, ethics is really a treatise or exposition on morals. So, what is a moral? A moral is an established principle of right or wrong in conduct or behavior. Quite frequently, then, one's metaphysical position also precedes or even dictates his ethical position. Ethics or morality deals with that which is virtual rather than actual. The speculative approach also characterizes ethical thought.

1

A fourth branch of philosophy, aesthetics, is also speculative, but in a different kind of way, as compared with ethics. Even more so, aesthetics might be contrasted with ethics; aesthetics deals with that which is beautiful instead of that which is right. In other words, aesthetics treats of the emotions and sensations in a more subjective manner without direct concern with standards of conduct. Aesthetics is especially in conflict with that which is pragmatic or useful, particularly when the latter are employed as the only criteria for arriving at value judgments.

Among all the historical branches of philosophy, the one currently most in vogue among philosophers is logic. Simply stated, logic is the exact relationship of ideas; logic implies formal principles of reasoning; it is concerned with the causes and criteria of validity in thought. Consequently, logic is distinctly more analytical than speculative in nature. There is a tendency to confuse logic with psychological processes. Hirst discusses the differences between logic and psychology in understanding a form of knowledge:

The logic of a form of knowledge shows the meaningul and valid ways in which its terms and criteria are used. It constitutes the publicly accepted framework of knowledge. The psychological activities of the individual when concerned with this knowledge are not in general prescribed in any temporal order and the mind, as it were, plays freely within and around the framework. . . . The logic as publicly expressed consists of the general and formal principles to which the terms must conform in knowledge. Coming to understand a form of knowledge involves coming to think in relations that satisfy the public criteria. How the mind plays round and within these is not itself being laid down at all, there is no dragooning of psychological processes, only a marking out of the territory in which the mind can wander more or less at will.[1]

THE SCOPE OF SCIENCE

Science has theoretical limits which are not found in philosophy. The scientific approach is characterized by observation and classification of facts and with the establishment of verifiable general laws. This is accomplished through the formulation of hypotheses and the process of induction. Generally speaking, science refers to accumulated knowledge. More specifically, science implies such knowledge when it relates to the physical world or in other words, natural science. However, similar methods may be employed to study the elements, relations, and institutions in man's existence as part of human society in the world. Thus, the term "social science" has also gained widespread usage. In a broader sense, then, science is more closely identified with the methodology employed than with the nature of the subject matter. The scientific method implies carefully controlled procedures which are not found in other forms of investigations.

---

[1]Paul H. Hirst, "Liberal Education And The Nature Of Knowledge," *Philosophical Analysis and Education*, ed. Reginald D. Archambault (New York: The Humanities Press, Inc., 1965), p.135. Reprinted by permission of the publishers.

The impact of the scientific method is most observable in the 20th century. As a net result, the scope of science has steadily increased. Those involved with other forms of scholarly investigations have made a concerted effort to become more scientific. In essence, there has been a growing association of science with academic respectability. The study of history might be used as a case in point.

Those who are concerned about this kind of categorization will readily state that history may be classified as either a humanity or a social science, depending on the approach used in research and study of the subject matter. For instance, if one follows the historiographer's approach that history is the branch of knowledge which records and explains past events, he is viewing history as a form of social science. On the other hand, one may focus on a philosophical explanation of the causes of certain events in history. Following this approach, history is more properly identified with the humanities. The latter are akin to the *belles lettres*, which comprise literature of aesthetic value, as distinct from informational or utilitarian value. Poetry, essays, drama, and fiction are all forms of *belles lettres*. When studied as a humanity, history moves closer to this end of the continuum and away from the historiographer's scientific framework.

SCIENCE'S INFLUENCE ON PHILOSOPHY

At least one thing is fairly certain in discussing the relationship between science and philosophy: science has gradually reduced the scope of philosophy and the subsequent emphasis in philosophy. Some scholars have gone so far as to suggest that philosophy is dead.

Because of the uncertainty and skepticism surrounding anything which is not truly scientific today, philosophers have assumed the position that there are no real answers to life's larger problems. They have more or less internalized their concerns by concentrating on clarification of problems which are raised by other scholarly pursuits.

This movement away from the traditional philosophical stance has been spearheaded by the analytic philosophers, who have particularly made an impact in British and United States universities. Many of these philosophers are content to engage only in analysis. More than that, they purport to claim philosophical analysis as the only defensible academic approach amidst the scientific bent of the mid-20th century.

Interestingly enough, one cannot help but note that science was at one time part of philosophy. This is subject to debate, depending on what one calls science, but, at least philosophy preceded science as a discipline. Gradually, various parts of science broke away as the body of knowledge expanded.

What is left for the philosopher? As noted earlier, the most obvious remainder is analysis. Philosophers have become increasingly absorbed with the question: what does it mean? Possibly, the only marked exception is to be found in the influence of existentialism. But even existentialism represents an interesting kind of exception. Existentialism cannot be considered as a systematic philosophy; in fact, it is a rejection of systematic philosophies which are grounded in metaphysical propositions. An existentialist is committed to the idea that the individual, with his decision-making ability, should be free to choose from a variety of possibilities and work out his own position based on the experiences at hand. The method employed by the existentialist is know as phenomenology. Through this method, the existentialist arrives at his own, unique approach to the question of meaning. He attempts to block out any speculation regarding past or similar experiences. Existentialism is firmly grounded in the individual's reaction to the here and now. Thus, analysts and existentialists share a common bond in shying away from classical philosophical propositions. The impact of science has caused them to substitute critical examination for speculation.

RECIPROCAL RELATIONSHIPS BETWEEN SCIENCE AND PHILOSOPHY

In light of the previous discussion, one may conclude that philosophy is not dead; it has merely emerged in new forms. Furthermore, the new philosophy has offered increasing possibilities for association and mutual benefit between science and philosophy. What are these possibilities?

With the realm of speculation eliminated, or at least seriously reduced, the philosopher is dependent on the data provided by the scientist. Scientific facts become the launching point for philosophical analysis. A philosopher cannot tie together the many loose ends until he has some loose ends with which to work. Scientific findings are the raw material for clarification, explication, critical assessment, and synthesis by the philosopher. Without these facts, he tends to cast a shadow of doubt on the validity of his enterprise.

On the other side of the coin, the scientist can also benefit from the work of the philosopher. Basically, the philosopher points out vistas which can be investigated by the philosopher. We should hastily add that the philosopher has no peculiar right or special insight into vistas. But the philosopher has the advantage of assessing the facts from a more detached, objective point of view. A scientist may well be able to criticize his own work and embark on new frontiers without the assistance of the philosopher. Nevertheless, there may be profit from what might be called the "outside" look. If no other purpose is achieved, the critical appraisal of the philosopher will certainly influence the scientist to present his findings in a way which has meaning for other scholars and in a manner in which the applicability can be seen.

PHILOSOPHY CONTRASTED WITH ART

THE SCOPE OF ART

Somewhat by way of contrast with philosophy, there is a theoretical limit to the scope of art, but such a limit is not readily definable. An artist is first and foremost recognized for the product of his endeavor; yet, there is no predetermined goal or patterned methodology which guides these efforts. This much the philosopher and artist have in common: neither is restricted in terms of how he goes about pursuing his creative enterprise.

Possibly the number-one characteristic of art is its basic symbolic nature. Art is usually representative, although there may be nothing to be represented in the art form. Under these conditions, art may be only expressive. Philosophy may also be representative and/or expressive, but, in either case this appears more indirectly through the medium of art.

The subject of art form leads to other interesting problems in attempting to determine the scope of art. We rather superficially recognize that there are several art forms, but we are never exactly certain about the main characteristics of any particular form. Even more so, we have difficulty in pinpointing the thread which runs through all of the various art forms. In this respect, art may be much like both sport and philosophy in that the thread or threads may be more easily discovered by examining the peripheral cases instead of focusing on the obvious considerations.

Philosophy and art have at least one other common characteristic. Both are frequently approached with the idea that the thoughts they express will be of universal significance. On the other hand, interpretations of philosophy and art tend to be distinctly individual. This is a paradox which seems inescapable for both philosophy and art.

What, then, can one say about the scope of art? Aldrich broaches the question by rejecting the standard approaches. As with many analyses of philosophy, he leaves one with a clearer understanding of what is not than what is art:

Logical analysis of the use of "art" reveals, therefore, that it is inept to treat the word as if it generally stands for an essential quality or set of such, presumed to belong definitively and objectively to all works of art. The ineptitude of this treatment is revealed by the discovery that no necessary and/or sufficient conditions can be found for the application of "art."

This is the short story of the shift among recent philosophers of art from the question, what is the essence of art and its real definition? to the question, how is the term "art" used? Such a transition does not abandon the notion of there being good, objective reasons for recognizing something as a work of art. Indeed, it stresses this idea as against emotivism. Something's being expressive in a certain way, or its exhibiting significant form, is a good reason for calling it a work of art. The traditional mistake occurs only when one or another of these characteristics is alleged to be the defining property of all works of art, and denoted by the term "art."[2]

For further insight into the scope of art, or lack of it, the reader is urged to consult Aldrich's book. His work will also assist in arriving at a clearer under-

---

[2] Virgil C. Aldrich, *Philosophy of Art* © 1963, p. 83. Reprinted by permission of Prentice-Hall, Inc., Englewood Cliffs, New Jersey.

standing of the nature of philosophy. In brief, his approach reflects the contemporary, analytical temper in philosophy.

AN ART VS. A KNACK

The nature of art may be partially understood by contrasting an art with a knack. Through one of his dialogues, *Gorgias*, Plato presented his viewpoints on the difference between an art and a knack. The person who performs only a knack is unable to render an account of the nature of the method which he applies. A knack lacks a deep-seated basis for understanding. Through the words of Socrates, Plato rejects rhetoric as an art in *Gorgias*: "Well then, to me, Gorgias, rhetoric seems not to be an artistic pursuit at all, but that of a shrewd, courageous spirit which is naturally clever at dealing with men; and I call the chief part of it flattery."[3]

Flattery was classified as a knack because of its irrational nature. Plato felt that flattery—consisting of such things as cooking, "make-up," sophistic, and rhetoric—was aimed primarily at pleasure without considering that which is actually best for man. The arts, according to Plato, can essentially be divided into those involving care of the body and those which are concerned with care for the soul. Gymnastics was included under the first grouping and thus was considered to be an art. However, Plato continued that gymnastics loses its artistic characteristic when dominated by "make-up." The latter manifests itself in various deceptions which detract from the natural beauty of an art.

Reference to gymnastics could lead one to hastily conclude that Plato considered sport to be an art. Such a conclusion cannot be validated if Paul Weiss[4] is correct in his assumption. Weiss states that Plato and the other Greek philosophers ignored the topic of sport because of their more general avoidance of all common concerns. They dealt mainly with "the genteel and the respectable." Sport was considered to be something in which the "common" man could participate and do quite well. Therefore, Weiss attributes the general neglect by philosophers in studying sport to the early predisposition of the Greek philosophers. This may or may not be a correct assumption. But, at least, it raises an important point of caution.

There is a common tendency on the part of many physical educators to suggest that Plato and other Greek philosophers provided strong philosophic support for programs of physical education. If Weiss is correct in his assumption, Plato would not have classified sport as an art. Obviously, only the arts were considered to be of esteem. If sport is an integral part of physical education, it is difficult to follow the line of reasoning which would place physical education among the elite areas with the Platonic frame of reference. All this may seem to

---

[3]W. C. Helmbold, *Plato's Gorgias* (New York: The Liberal Arts Press, 1952), p. 23.

[4]Paul Weiss, *Sport: A Philosophic Inquiry* (Carbondale, Ill.: Southern Illinois University Press, 1969), pp. 5—8.

be merely a fruitless, intellectual exercise, but it does point out the pitfalls which may be encountered in attempting to set forth historical, philosophical support for any contemporary program.

PHILOSOPHY OF ART

The comparison between philosophy and art seems to become clearer when one considers the philosophy of art. For instance, it is more common to speak of the philosophy of art than the art of philosophy. The latter is not improper, but it does lack significant meaning. One would not call philosophy a knack; philosophy is also more than a science; it could be considered an art. But more than that, there is a philosophy of art. Similarly, there is a philosophy of science, a philosophy of religion, a philosophy of education, and a philosophy of sport, among other possibilities. Schematically, the arrangement might be as follows:

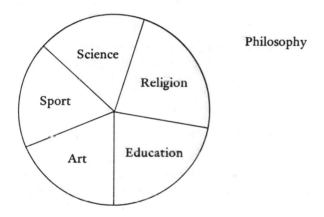

Of course, one need not and should not stop with the divisions noted above. One could add music, government, business, and other practical concerns which are somehow or other influenced by what we call "philosophy." All this is predicated on the idea that "philosophy bakes bread." Everyone is not willing to accept that assumption. There are those who remain firm in their conviction that philosophy must remain in the realm of abstract theorizing, without direct attention to practical endeavors. We obviously reject this line of thinking, or we would not concern ourselves with the philosophy of sport.

PHILOSOPHY CONTRASTED WITH RELIGION

FAITH VS. REASON

The classical distinction between philosophy and religion is that the former involves reason whereas the latter relies on faith. There is some basis for making such a distinction, particularly when comparing the Hebraic-Christian tradition with the Greek philosophic tradition. However, the matter is not quite as simple as it first appears. As with the concept of art, religion is also an abstract construct. Religion might be defined as the worship and adoration of a God or gods. However, some religious groups (Unitarians, as an example) find their faith distinctly more rooted in the here and now, as contrasted with traditional doctrine. Under these circumstances, the gulf between faith and reason narrows rather than widens.

Abraham Kaplan succinctly points out the problem of oversimplification when one attempts to sharply contrast philosophy with religion from the reason vs. faith frame of reference. He describes the pragmatic conception of faith as follows:

In this conception, faith is not the evidence of things unseen, but it is the substance of things hoped for. Such a hope serves as a unifying principle providing drive and direction to all of life's efforts. In this way, pragmatism makes room for religion, as I believe every mature philosophy must; only, it must be a correspondingly mature religion.[5]

On the other hand, the pragmatic view of faith does represent a marked variance from traditional, religious faith. So, it is possible that philosophy may still be differentiated from religion in a rather general way by using the faith-reason dichotomy as a point of departure.

INCREASING GULF BETWEEN PHILOSOPHY AND RELIGION?

The "revolt of the logicians" has had a paradoxical effect on the relationship between philosophy and religion . From one vantage point, analytical philosophy has caused philosophy to be almost entirely divorced from religion because they no longer have common concerns such as those embedded in the study of metaphysics. Formerly, philosophers were men who attempted, through reasoning, to arrive at a knowledge of the ultimate nature of the world. The results of such endeavors frequently clashed with expositions of religious faith. Now the analysts have retreated to more tractable territory in which they merely clarify, explicate, and elucidate the thoughts of others.

From another standpoint, religion and philosophy are now closer bedfellows because they no longer clash head-on over such fundamental considerations as the nature of the universe and the nature of man. Each is now free to go its separate way without getting directly involved with comparisons and points of conflict. The analyst may choose to criticize the theologian's assumptions. On the other hand, and this probably occurs more frequently, he may confine his analysis to those matters which are more empirically rooted in the material world. So, it is difficult to generalize today concerning the relationship between

---

[5] Abraham Kaplan, *The New World of Philosophy* (New York: Random House, 1961), p. 51. Reprinted by permission of Random House, Inc.

philosophy and religion. They represent separate domains, but, at the same time, the change in philosophy's focus enables each to exist without mutual contradiction.

PHILOSOPHICAL METHODOLOGY

RESEARCH IS RESEARCH IS RESEARCH?

We have frequently heard the above slogan uttered as though it were the panacea for all those who desire to embark on a research endeavor. The slogan should not be completely rejected or cast aside. In fact, it does convey an aspect of truth. The value of the slogan lies in the idea that one must proceed in a systematic, disciplined manner if he is to engage in what can be called research.

Nevertheless, the matter is not quite that simple. There are several forms of research even though all research may have certain common denominators. To begin with, there are differences between research in the so-called "hard sciences" and the "soft sciences." These differences are even more evident when one moves over to philosophy. Some people would even suggest that there is no such thing as philosophical research. This could be true, but it is probably more a matter of semantics than anything else. At least, there is scholarly investigation in philosophy which may or may not be called research.

One thing can be said for certain regarding philosophical research or scholarly investigation in philosophy. There is no clear-cut methodology such as employed in the sciences. Philosophy offers more latitude for the scholar; his tools are not ready-made. Fogelin brings out this point very well:

Where do we begin in developing a philosophy of sports? What methodology is appropriate? What data are appropriate? And, finally, what is such an inquiry intended to establish? To borrow a phrase from someone else, these are large questions to which I can give only small answers. (1) Where should we begin? I suppose that just about anywhere will do, for if sports constitutes an area capable of philosophical investigation, it will form a more or less tight network, and wherever we begin, eventually we will be led over the entire terrain. (2) Methodology? Again I think that almost anything goes provided that we do not engage in *a priori* empiricism. *A priori* empiricism can operate in at least two ways: we can make up our minds about how things are without bothering to look, and, more dangerously, we can make assumptions about how things must be, and thus make looking quite beside the point.[6]

By now, the would-be philosopher may view the matter of philosophizing as a hopeless task and throw up his hands in despair. But all is not as futile as it

---

[6]Robert Fogelin, "Sport: The Diversity of the Concept," Unpublished paper presented at the 13th Annual Meeting of The American Association for the Advancement of Science, Dallas, Texas, December 28, 1968. Reprinted by permission of the author.

first appears. There are some guidelines, be they general and indirect, which can assist the student of philosophy in embarking upon the task of contributing to the scholarly production in his field.

SPECULATIVE—NORMATIVE—ANALYTICAL

The entire content of the Spring 1956 issue of the *Harvard Educational Review* is devoted to means of proceeding with educational philosophy. The effort was to assist those who wish to formulate a "philosophically respectable" philosophy of education. In so doing, the writers offer assistance for any who are in doubt concerning where to begin and how to proceed in philosophizing. Frankena,[7] in particular, comes the closest to setting forth concrete guidelines. He suggests that philosophy can be approached speculatively, normatively, and analytically.

A philosopher tends to be speculative in his approach when he ventures to set forth more-or-less questionable hypotheses to fill in gaps in knowledge. As noted in the preface, Weiss is inclined to be speculative in his assessment of sport. Philosophers have also sought to provide wisdom for the conduct of human affairs. Such guides to action fall under the banner of normative philosophizing. This will readily be recognized as a popular approach in education and physical education wherein the "principles" form of philosophizing has been utilized.

Finally, Frankena indicates that a philosopher can and should be analytical. This might also be referred to as the "critical" method. It involves a critical evaluation of the assumptions, slogans, and concepts used by others. The analyst does not attempt to tap virgin territory; he begins with the work of others; his intent is to clarify, elucidate, and explicate the thoughts of scientists, speculators, and those who have contributed normatively.

Frankena recognizes that these are not entirely "pure" categories. A philosopher might engage to some extent in all three. One might expect that the emphasis will be in a certain direction; yet, the three approaches are not mutually exclusive. More importantly, there is need for all three forms of philosophizing, regardless of who does the work. For this reason we are using more analysis in this book because previous contributions toward the philosophy of sport tend to be more speculative and/or normative.

Assuming one wishes to be analytical in his philosophical study of sport, an important question still remains: how does he proceed with his analysis? We offer the following as subareas which may guide the would-be analyst.

---

[7]William K. Frankena, "Toward a Philosophy of the Philosophy of Education," *Harvard Educational Review*, XXVI, No. 2, Spring 1956, pp. 94–98.

HISTORICAL BACKGROUND

To a certain extent, philosophy grows out of history. Some people are inclined to exaggerate this point by suggesting that all of philosophy can be determined by studying history, but we feel that can be challenged. There are those individuals who "ground" their philosophy in the here and now; on this basis, the all-inclusive historical explanation tends to lose its validity. Nevertheless, history is an important determinant for philosophical thought, be the influence direct or indirect.

An analyst will soon recognize that the concepts, clichés, slogans, or assumptions which he is criticizing did not arise spontaneously for the most part. To put it succinctly, they have a history. A given concept, such as sport, may have undergone radical changes in interpretation over the years, but this does not negate the idea that a complete study of the history of the concept may assist those who wish to clarify contemporary usage.

For those who would utilize history to assist in philosophical analysis, one important caution should be added. Too often we are inclined to look for only those threads or elements of continuity in history. The exception, marked departures, contrasts, and deviations may actually shed more light on the problems of today. This is not to suggest that we should forget about those strands of enduring significance, but a focus on common denominators only can lead to a myopia which precludes an analysis of the critical problems.

We would suggest that historical investigation is a logical means for beginning many kinds of philosophical analysis. At the same time, the analyst must beware that he does not confine his criticism to the historical. This is almost certain to lead to a limited perspective. Things are happening just too fast today to permit a focus on historical events only. The contemporary scene also offers fertile ground for analysis.

VARIED INTERPRETATION

A philosophical analyst enters the picture where matters are not clear-cut. That is why analysis is necessary. A concept defies precise definition. Similarly, a cliché, slogan, or assumption may lead to straying conclusions. Philosophical analysis, hopefully, will shed light on the variety of possibilities, while pointing out the implications of each.

An example may further serve to illustrate the manner in which varied interpretation dictates analysis. We will use a cliché as our specific example. "Sport is a laboratory for democratic living." This, or a similar cliché, has been uttered time and time again. One cannot simply accept or reject this cliché as being valid. In fact, it cannot even be tested as a hypothesis until we arrive at an understanding of what is involved. What is sport? What is democratic living? There are many answers to each of these questions, resulting from varied interpretation. An analyst may assist by offering a possible frame of reference for those who wish to test the hypothesis.

VALUE JUDGMENTS

Value judgments may be considered as the raw material for philosophy. The speculator presents philosophical postulates which are based on value judgments. The normative philosopher sets forth principles which are formulated from value assessments. The analytical philosopher looks for and criticizes the value judgments which have been proposed or which are inherent in certain propositions.

A value judgment is really nothing more nor less than an evaluation. One should logically begin with the facts at hand. But there is always the need to interpret the facts and often the tantalizing urge to move well beyond the facts. One important role of philosophical analysis is to determine whether value judgments have any scientific basis whatsoever. In this connection, the analyst would do well to keep in mind that value judgments are not the exclusive province of philosophers. Stevenson brings this point forcefully across, while at the same time stressing that a value judgment must be distinguished from a scientific conclusion:

I think it would be a great pity, then, if those studying education should become so enamored of pure science that they should suppose that value judgments were only for "others." But at the same time, I think it would be a great pity to fail to distinguish between value judgments and scientific conclusions. When a man goes from a scientific conclusion to a value judgment it seems to me that he should carefully give notice that the value judgment is *more* than a scientific conclusion, and that his repute as a scientist does not entitle him to an evaluation that purports to be the last word of adequacy. For the reasons that back up evaluations are not only less than logically related to the evaluation, but are often rebellious of being limited to any special field of science.[8]

Thus, it would seem that the philosophical analyst should look for and criticize value judgments wherever they may be found. He should be careful to point out those value judgments which evolve from scientific conclusions. He will also be interested in comparing value judgments which arise from different sources. However, in all cases he will be guided by Stevenson's warning that a scientific basis does not warrant one moving far out on the limb in setting forth value judgments which might be viewed as the ultimate in authority.

MAIN ISSUES

Varied interpretation and/or conflicting value judgments lead to the main issues which surround a concept. Sometimes these main issues are fairly obscure; they lie hidden beneath lesser problems which engross people on a superficial level. Again, the analyst can provide a valuable service by calling attention to those matters which seem to represent the core of the conflict. At the same time,

---

[8]Charles L. Stevenson, "The Scientist's Role and the Aims of Education," *Harvard Educational Review*, 24:238, Fall, 1954.

he should feel an obligation to explicate and elucidate those factors which have caused the conflict and subsequent issue.

The concept of athletics may be used as an example of the manner in which main issues tend to be obscured by superficial, everyday problems. Particularly at the college level, one can almost constantly hear educators and lay people debate such matters as athletic scholarships, recruiting practices, curricular and grade requirements for athletes, and problems relating to the relationship between athletics and other sport programs in the schools. These do represent points of controversy, but, all too frequently, the arguments ensue without recognition of the core issue which leads to these problems. In the case of athletics, one major question must be raised and answered: what is the purpose of athletics? If the dominant motive in athletics is to achieve excellence, that is to win, many subproblems can be resolved. On the other hand, if the compelling reason for the existence of athletics is to provide maximum participation and fun for all, a different set of postulates prevails.

There has been far too great an inclination to speak of athletics as being an educational experience and leaving it there. The truth of the matter is that athletics may very well be an educational experience, but that does not solve anything as far as issues in athletics are concerned. An educational experience is in itself a very broad concept. Some people go so far as to suggest that education is as broad as life itself. Should that thesis have any merit whatsoever, it really does not shed much light on the subject to suggest that athletics is or should be an educational experience. There are many kinds of educational experiences. Winning or losing can be educational. Likewise, it can be educational to have fun or attain pleasure.

Thus, the analyst must be willing to probe those elements which undergird the superficial issues surrounding a given concept. He may not be prepared to solve the issue; in fact, he may even prefer to stay away from posing a solution; but, hopefully, his analysis will lead to further reflective thought by others if nothing more is accomplished.

RELATIONSHIPS TO SIMILAR CONCEPTS

One aspect of philosophical analysis can appear to be only semantical. This is the analysis which explores and points out the relationship between a given concept and similar concepts. But in many cases there really is much more than semantics involved. Whether we like it or not, our conceptual framework determines much of what occurs with respect to various programs. In short, concepts are symbols of circumstances and events. So, it is not simply a matter of what you name or call something.

The broad field of sport dramatically portrays the need to analyze the relationship between related concepts. Concepts such as sport, athletics, physical education, physical fitness, exercise, human movement, recreation, play, and health have something in common. Yet it would be most difficult, if not impossible, to pick out the one, central thread which runs through these concepts. Furthermore, the attempt to arrive at *the* common denominator could prove quite fruitless.

Nevertheless, there are various kinds of interrelationships which evolve from the above concepts. Professionals and lay people are often confused and misled by the jargon. Many of the conflicting value judgments, points of varied interpretation, and main issues can be traced back to confusion regarding the conceptual apparatus.

The concept of physical education represents a classic case in point. We really don't know what physical education is, even though programs are labeled by that name. Physical education apparently has some kind of relationship to each of the above concepts, but it may well be a more restricted concept than most of them. Need we say more about the need to analyze the relationships among similar concepts?

BIBLIOGRAPHY

Aldrich, V. C., *Philosophy of Art.* Englewood Cliffs, N. J.: Prentice-Hall, Inc., Foundations of Philosophy Series, 1963.

Alston, W. P., *Philosophy of Language.* Englewood Cliffs, N.J.: Prentice-Hall, Inc., Foundations of Philosophy Series, 1964.

Archambault, R. D., ed., *Philosophical Analysis and Education.* New York: The Humanities Press, 1965.

Black, M., ed., *Philosophical Analysis.* Ithaca: Cornell University Press, 1950.

Broudy, H. S., "How Philosophical Can Philosophy of Education Be?" *The Journal of Philosophy*, LII (October 27, 1955), pp. 612−622.

Elton, W., *Aesthetics and Language.* New York: Philosophical Library, Inc., 1954.

Fogelin, R., "Sport: The Diversity of the Concept." Unpublished paper presented at the 13th Annual Meeting of The American Association for the Advancement of Science, Dallas, Texas, December 28, 1968.

Harvard Educational Review, XXIV, Fall, 1954.

Harvard Educational Review, XXVI, Spring, 1956.

Kaplan, A., *The New World of Philosophy.* New York: Random House, 1962.

Langer, S. K., *Philosophy in a New Key.* Cambridge: Harvard University Press, 1957.

Plato, *Gorgias*, trans. Helmbold. New York: The Liberal Arts Press, 1952.

Weiss, P., *The World of Art.* Carbondale: Southern Illinois University Press, 1961.

Weiss, P., *Sport: A Philosophic Inquiry.* Carbondale: Southern Illinois University Press, 1969.

Wittgenstein, L., *Philosophical Investigations.* New York: The Macmillan Company, 1953.

Ziff, P., "The Task of Defining a Work of Art," *Philosophical Review*, LXII, 1953.

2/Sport: When and Where?

HISTORICAL RELATIONSHIPS BETWEEN THE CONCEPTS OF SPORT AND PHYSICAL EDUCATION[1]

Sport and physical education are two widely used and, yet, grossly misunderstood concepts. There is obviously some kind of relationship between the two, but one can never be certain as to exactly what are the ties. The reason for this uncertainty should be readily apparent. We don't really understand either concept. So, how can we hope to determine much in the way of connection between sport and physical education?

This we do know. Sport is a very widely accepted concept. At least, programs and activities associated with the idea of sport have gained considerable approval in terms of participation and other forms of support. The skeptic on this point is referred to the *Time* Essay of June 2, 1967. Data presented there leads one to believe that we are indeed living in "The Golden Age of Sport."

Physical education has also gained a degree of acceptance. It has been customary during the 20th century to speak of programs in sport, dance, and other forms of physical activity in the schools as being physical education. Thus, physical education has emerged as a kind of umbrella term in the educational setting.

One could, of course, take the position of: who cares? Is it necessary to explore the relationships between what we call sport and physical education? Those who assume such a position seem to feel that the whole issue is largely one of semantics. Would that it were that simple! Whether we like it or not, even if we wish to ignore it, there are programs and activities which fall under the varying labels of sport and physical education. Furthermore, even those who are most intimately involved seem to be confused and bewildered by these concepts

---

[1]This topic was first published by the author in *Proceedings*, 73rd Annual Meeting, National College Physical Education Association For Men, 1970 pp. 83–89.

as they relate to purposes which they wish to achieve. Perhaps some of the confusion can be eliminated by looking at the historical relationships between sport and physical education.

Of the two, sport appears to be the older concept, although it, too, may not be as antiquated as some people would believe. In the western world, educators, generally, and physical educators, more specifically, are inclined to cite the ancient Greeks as the ultimate source of theoretical support for contemporary programs. Physical educators particularly identify Plato as the fountainhead of their theory. It is true that Plato freely discussed what he called "gymnastics." However, one must proceed with caution in extending Plato's conception of gymnastics to "modern" ideas regarding physical education.

As a case in point, Paul Weiss states that the Greek philosophers, as a group, more or less ignored the subject of sport:

We will find in the Greeks some good historically grounded explanations for the neglect of sport by philosophic minds, then and later. Despite their evident enjoyment of athletics, and their delight in speculating on the meaning of a hundred different human concerns, the Greek thinkers never dealt extensively with the nature, import, and reason for sport. Since Plato and his fellows formulated most of the issues that have occupied philosophers over the centuries, the Greek failure to provide a philosophical study became a norm for the rest.[2]

If the Greeks did not provide philosophic support for sport as a concept, the question is this: when and where did sport emerge as a theoretical construct? One can go back at least as far as 1900 and find a thoughtful discussion of sport. An Englishman, H. Graves,[3] philosophically analyzed the concept of sport. Sport, as a term, is an abbreviated form of an old noun and verb, *disport*. The latter was derived from the medieval word *disportare*, which meant to move from one place to another or to divert or distract. Thus, sport, in its inception, conveyed the meaning of diverting oneself, that is engaging in amusement or recreation. This thought is reinforced by James Keating's work in which he contrasts sport with athletics.[4]

Graves continued by noting that dictionary definitions of sport will only reveal the contradictory senses in which the term is used. These definitions run the gamut from the idea of amusement to pursuits of killing (field sports) to games in which stakes of money are involved. He suggested that the dictionary meanings should be tested through comparision with usages of the concept in activities and programs. Such a test would reveal that physical recreation seems

---

[2]Paul Weiss, *Sport: A Philosophic Inquiry*. (Carbondale: Southern Illinois University Press, 1969), p. 5.

[3]H. Graves, "A Philosophy of Sport," *The Contemporary Review*, 78, Dec., 1900, pp. 877—893.

[4]James W. Keating, "Sportsmanship as a Moral Category," *Ethics*, Vol. LXXV, No. 1, Oct., 1964, pp. 25—35.

to be essential to the notion of sport. Competition is another likely ingredient in sport, although Graves noted the difficulties which ensue when competition is considered within the framework of sport. Competition frequently leads to various forms of moneymaking which cause sport to lose its important characteristic of being recreative. In summary, one could say that Graves analyzed those ambiguities regarding the notion of sport which continue to provide the focus for present-day theorists on the subject.

By comparison, the concept of physical education is of even more recent origin than sport. Of course, one could take the position that the Greeks were actually talking about that which we call physical education today. However, as we will note later, the historical record does not really indicate this to be true.

We will begin with the broad generalization and assumption that physical education is really a 20th century concept. The skeptic on this point will immediately jump to the foreground and suggest several documented instances wherein the term physical education appeared in the literature and programs prior to 1900. This we will acknowledge and accord. The following might be cited as cases in point. Benjamin Rush used the term as early as 1772 in an article entitled "Sermons to Gentlemen Upon Temperence and Exercise." In 1790, Noah Webster referred to physical education in his "Address to Yung Gentlemen." Heinrich Pestalozzi wrote an article in 1807 which, in translation, is entitled "Concerning Physical Education." A book with the title *The Importance of Physical Education* was published by J. C. Warren in 1831. Another book, by A. L. Pierson in 1840, was entitled *On Physical Education.* Among the more familiar names in the history of physical education is Edward Hitchcock, who in 1881 wrote "A Report of Twenty Years Experience in the Department of Physical Education and Hygiene in Amherst College to the Board of Trustees."

Other references could also be cited. But the aforementioned should suffice to establish the fact that the term physical education was at least coined prior to the 20th century. Now, to coin a term or even to use it repeatedly is one thing; to have a term develop into a concept is something else. A concept is an abstract notion or idea which combines elements into the construct of one object. In other words, a concept is not something which arises spontaneously and without thought; a concept is a configuration which defies precise definition.

Physical education actually emerged as a concept somewhere around the turn of this century with the advent of the so-called "new" physical education. The concept developed from a merger of programs in physical training, gymnastics, sport, and athletics. Proponents of the concept were quick to recognize that changes which were taking place in American education generally opened the door for the inclusion of physical education as part of the school curriculum; thus, the education part of the term physical education took on a new significance.

It has been customary to identify the "new" physical education with the slogan "education through the physical." Nobody seemed to know exactly what that meant, other than it being a reaction to the more restricted idea of "education of the physical." The latter concept, of course, was largely associated with the earlier programs of physical training and gymnastics. The inclusion of sport under the umbrella of physical education added a new dimension. Somehow or other sport did not seem to be quite as physical as gymnastics or physical training, even though it has been suggested in more recent years that physical prowess is the one characteristic that distinguishes games in general from sport in particular as a game occurrence.[5]

Sport also seemed to broaden the scope of physical education by offering new avenues for social experimentation. The element of competition was readily recognized as another important characteristic of sport; this, in turn, provided the stimulus for many of the fantastic claims which were derived from the concept of "education through the physical." Jesse Feiring Williams symbolized these lofty assumptions with his classic statement:

Education through the physical will be judged, therefore, even as education for life will be judged by the contribution it makes to fine living. The ability to punt 60 yards is on a par with some of the esoteric emphases in genereal education. It should, therefore, be declared that physical education seeks to further the purposes of modern education when it stands for the finest kind of living.[6]

Therefore, we find that sport emerged or was submerged in the concept of physical education early in this century through the paradoxical attempt to make physical education more educational. One might suspect that the change occurred only at the abstract level of theory, but the facts indicate that the content of programs and activities was also affected. Hackensmith[7] notes the changes which took place during the first quarter of the century. From 1900 to 1917 gymnastics continued to dominate physical education programs in the public schools. During the same period interscholastic athletics flourished at the high-school level as a program which was distinct from physical education. In 1922, Williams stated that athletics should be conducted as an educational project, "not as a side show, extracurricular affair, or student amusement activity." Surveys conducted in the 1920s revealed that sports were occupying more time in physical education class periods and that efforts had been made in many places to administratively combine athletics with physical education. Thus, the theory of Hetherington, Williams, Wood, Cassidy, and others did not merely remain on the shelf; actual changes took place even though, as is customary, there were noticeable gaps between the theory and practice.

---

[5] John W. Loy, "The Nature of Sport: A Definitional Effort," *Quest*, X, May, 1968, p. 6.

[6] Jesse Feiring Williams, "Education Through The Physical," *The Journal of Higher Education*, Vol. I, May, 1930, p. 281.

[7] C. W. Hackensmith, *History of Physical Education.* (New York: Harper & Row Publishers, 1966), pp. 379—434.

Some people went so far as to suggest that sport was actually the essence of physical education and that physical education should be renamed accordingly. The most vocal spokesman of this position for the college level was Seward Staley. In 1931 he set forth a classic statement of his position.[8]

Needless to say, Staley's ideas on this subject did not exactly fall on fertile ground. On this point, Staley was kind of a lone voice in the wilderness. The concept of sports education never really took hold. Professional physical educators continued to view sport as one part of the concept of physical education. Likewise, programs in physical education were generally organized and conducted to reflect the idea that there is more to physical education than sport.

Paradoxically, while sport was submerged within the concept of physical education, sport has flourished both within and without the schools in a way which would be the envy of any educator, let alone a physical educator. This generalization is so obvious that it scarcely needs elaboration, but we will cite a few points of documentation in an effort to reinforce our major hypothesis. To begin with, we concur with the Keating thesis that sport should not be confused with athletics. We prefer to consider athletics as an extension of sport. The rapid increase in popularity of athletics, especially in the United States, is readily apparent. But that which we call "sport" has also flourished in many ways. The number of people who ski, bowl, swim, play golf, tennis, badminton, handball, and other sports has been steadily increasing. There are many reasons for this such as increased leisure time and more available money, but this is aside from the point that sport has attracted more and more participants regardless of the reasons behind such participation.

This noticeable acceleration in sports participation has also been reflected in school programs. Since its organized beginning in 1914, intramural sport has witnessed a marked growth in many ways. There are more participants, more facilities, more activities, and better organized programs than ever before. Surveys reveal that intramural sport has prospered most at the college or university level, but in some places junior-high and high-school programs have also flourished. Where good programs have been found, they may usually be attributed to the enthusiasm and ability of one or more individuals who have worked in and promulgated intramural sport as their specialized area.

Theoretically, 20th-century physical educators have generally espoused the idea that both athletics and intramural sport are part of the concept of physical education. For many years now, undergraduate major students have been sufficiently brainwashed to accept the following triangle as a panacea for all organizational structure problems within the field:

---

[8]S. C. Staley, "The Four Year Curriculum in Physical (Sports) Education," *Research Quarterly*, II, No. 1, March, 1931, pp. 76–90.

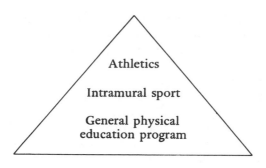

The base of this triangle is also referred to by other names such as the basic instruction, required, or service program in physical education. Regardless of the specific name, this has generally been considered *the* physical education, as contrasted with athletics and intramural sport. In other words, physical educators have been inclined to accept the triangle on the one hand and reject it on the other.

We cannot help but reflect on an event in recent history which dramatically revealed the dispersed thinking which pervades when the idea of the triangle is challenged. At the 64th Annual College Physical Education Association Meeting held in Washington, D.C. in 1960, Donald Mallett, Executive Dean of Purdue University, delivered a provocative speech on the subject of intramural sport.[9] Essentially, Mallett took the point of view that the service or basic instruction program as such was about to be replaced on American college campuses. Although he expressed a strong belief in the importance of physical activity, he did not deplore the trend which he observed. Instead, he suggested that an expanded intramural sport program could more than fill the gap. He depicted a sport program which would encompass instruction, competition, and relatively unorganized activity, such as commonly called "free play." Mallett further suggested that physical educators should stress the instructional phase of physical education at the elementary-school level. Aside from the consideration of athletics, which Mallett considered to be a peripheral program in the sense of the meaning of physical education, he actually came the closest to supporting the blend represented by two parts of the physical education triangle.

There is an interesting paradox here. Mallett's remarks were interpreted by many of those in attendance as being hostile to the cause of physical education. Yet, from another standpoint he offered a framework within which sport and physical education might actually achieve the kind of union that had been envisioned for 50 years. More recently, Thomas Sheehan also saw sport as the focus of physical education, but from a somewhat different frame of reference: "What is there within the total physical education environment which is not

---

[9]Donald Mallett, "An Educator Views the Contribution of Campus Intramural Sports Programs," *Proceedings*, 64th Annual Meeting, College Physical Education Association, 1960, pp. 95—96.

the proper concentration of some other area of study? Is there a phenomenon currently within our interest which may be afforded identification as a social institution? There is. This phenomenon is sport."[10]

Sheehan, of course, was considering sport from the standpoint of an area of study as well as a program of activities, but he would appear to share one thing in common with Mallett: both would attempt to elevate sport from its submersion within the concept of physical education.

Thus, as a concept, sport has had an unusual history. It arose outside the context of physical training, as a more-or-less parallel concept. It was incorporated within the concept of physical education early in this century. Meanwhile, sport continued to flourish outside the context of physical education, while being somewhat submerged within. Physical education has struggled for existence; sport has emerged to a point where it is one of the significant institutions in this culture. Certain physical educators are now questioning the concept which identifies their work. What will the future bring? Will sport eventually replace the concept of physical education?

POINTS OF SPECULATION

This analysis of the the historical relationships between the concepts of sport and physical education leaves us with at least two major points of speculation which extend beyond the facts.

First of all, it appears that the concept of physical education arose out of a pragmatic need, and the concept may very well have fulfilled its purpose. We are not knocking the efforts of Williams, Hetherington, Wood, Cassidy, et al. They were opportunists in the best meaning of that term. In recognizing the weaknesses and limitations associated with the concept of physical training, they seized the opportunity to bring their work under the educational banner. The door was opened for this sort of transition when Dewey and his disciples set forth their "progressivistic" ideas which widened the scope of education.

In recent years, the term physical education has fallen into disfavor among certain scholars within the field for several reasons. Zeigler has summarized these reasons in a humorous, clever, and yet truthful manner.[11] There is no doubt that part of this skepticism in "hanging your hat" on the concept of physical education stems from the attack which has been made on graduate study in the field as being nonacademic. To be nonacademic is akin to being unholy. James Conant lit the fuse which triggered an interesting chain reaction.

Since 1964 there has been a wild and scrambling search to identify the disciplinary nature of our field. Human movement has emerged as the favorite concept because it represents another umbrella, even though it is woefully

---

[10]T. J. Sheehan, "Sport: The Focal Point of Physical Education," *Quest*, X, May, 1968, p. 65.

[11]E. F. Zeigler and H. J. VanderZwaag, *Physical Education: Progressivism or Essentialism?* (Champaign, Ill.: Stipes Publishing Co., 1968), pp. 9—11.

deficient in concreteness. That brings us to point of speculation number two.

Physical education should not and will not be replaced by the concept of human movement. There has been a tendency to contrast the profession of physical education with the discipline of human movement. The net result is a comparison of one abstract entity with another. Both abstractions have arisen from the search for appropriate umbrellas. In this search, concrete components have been overlooked. These components are sport and exercise. Interestingly enough, many of the organizational problems in relating the discipline to the profession could also be eliminated. Sport and exercise would provide the focus for both the profession and the discipline.

STAGES IN THE DEVELOPMENT OF SPORT AS A CONCEPT

Having briefly explored the historical relationships between the concepts of sport and physical education, we might find it beneficial to focus more directly on sport per se in terms of its developmental stages. We speak of developmental stages because the net result seems to be one of a development at this point. A development often is but should not be confused with change or progress. A change is any difference in form, disposition, or quality in comparison with that previously observed. Development is a series of changes in a continuous direction. Progress is a development favorably evaluated from the standpoint of an ideal. When one designates a development as representing progress, he is waving the ethical flag; value judgments are involved.

In this development at least seven stages deserve consideration. Sport appears to have had its genesis with the British "field sports." More specifically, we refer to the interest of the English aristocrats and gentry in shooting and hunting. Such activities were considered the prerequisites of a gentleman. The origins of shooting and hunting as sport can be traced back many centuries, but 17th-century England seemed to highlight its organized emergence. This may be partly attributed to a law of Charles II which stated that persons who were permitted to shoot game must be either freeholders or large leaseholders. One of the characteristics of sport, which we will elaborate on later, is that it tends to be governed by rules. During the 17th century, the British moved toward certain restrictions in their hunting activities. This marked the initial departure toward hunting as sport as contrasted with work (hunting for sustenance) or merely hunting in a more spontaneous manner (play).

The 18th century has been singled out by many scholars as the most comfortable century in English history. At least it was extremely comfortable for those who benefited from the "new wealth." The latter has been identified with the agricultural, industrial, and communication revolutions which were touched off in the 1700s and which, of course, have since continued almost unabated. Few groups in history have been born into more pleasant surroundings than those English peers and country squires of the 18th century.

Historians have also observed that these English aristocrats utilized their leisure relatively well. There was the usual gambling and heavy drinking associated with affluence, but the wealthy also sought out and developed other leisure-time pursuits. As one aspect, the old law of Charles II was held in great favor by those whom the "new wealth" had enriched. The sport of shooting game held more interest than ever before. "Gamekeepers" were even employed to provide a ready source for the sportsman. Likewise, "poaching" became both a necessity for the peasant in search of food as well as a sport for the English schoolboy.

These privileged Englishmen of the 18th century did not merely confine their sporting interests to the field or hunting variety. Several other organized forms of play with a physical dimension were established during this time. As one example, the Marylebone Cricket Club of London was formed in 1788. Although cricket matches were held in England during the preceding century, it was not until the late 18th and early 19th centuries that cricket assumed the more organizational stature which is associated with sport. Additional sporting activities such as archery, bowls, rowing, and track and field were also emerging as popular events.

The English "public" schools also played a prominent role in the 18th-century sport developmental picture. It was customary for the elite to send their sons to Eton, Harrow, or Winchester. From there the normal course of events took them to Oxford or Cambridge. Generally speaking, these young aristocrats were relatively uninterested in learning, but they did enter school with a passion for sport. This sporting interest eventually expanded to the form of interschool competition. Among the earlier examples of this was a boat race held at Winchester in 1818 and a cricket match between Winchester and Eton in 1746.

The English interest in sport continued to increase during the 19th century, but parallel developments in the United States during the same period mark the third important stage in the evolution of sport as a concept. Similar to the situation in England, sport emerged on two major fronts in the United States. These were the sport clubs and interschool sport.

Although Americans had participated in various forms of sport since colonial times, it was not until the mid-19th century that sport emerged as a concept in the form by which it is now recognized. Dulles describes the transformation as follows:

All this took place in the late 1860s and the 1870s. Previously the country had had virtually no organized sports as we know them today. Neither men nor women played outdoor games. Alarmed observers in mid-century had found the national health deteriorating because of a general lack of exercise more widespread than among the people of any other nation.... No transformation in the recreational scene has been more startling than this sudden burgeoning of an interest in sports which almost overnight introduced millions of Americans to a phase of life shortly destined to become a major preoccupation among all classes.[12]

This thought has been reinforced by Betts who attributes the emergence of sport in the United States to the Industrial Revolution:

The roots of our sporting heritage lie in the horse racing and fox hunting of the colonial era, but the main features of modern sport appeared only in the middle years of the nineteenth century. Organization, journalistic exploitation, commercialization, intercommunity competition, and sundry other developments increased rapidly after 1850 as the agrarian nature of sport gave way gradually to the influences of urbanization and industrialization. Just as the Industrial Revolution was to alter the interests, habits, and pursuits of all classes of society, it was to leave a distinct impress on the development of sport.[13]

Thus, it can be noted that 19th-century sport developments in the United States were very similar to those found in England a century earlier. Sport began to take the organized form by which we customarily know it today.

Many points of documentation can be cited in support of the above hypothesis. We will mention only a few to support the general idea. The game of baseball became popular between 1850 and 1880 both at the collegiate and professional levels. Cycling was one of the leading sporting events in the 1880s and 1890s. By 1900, bicycling had emerged as one of the most highly discussed activities in the United States. The first intercollegiate football game was played between Princeton and Rutgers in 1869, and after 1876 there was a steady development of the game as we know it today.

Roller skating was another of those sporting activities which soon became popular among the masses. It was introduced in New York in 1863 as a sport for the elite. By the end of the century, rinks could be found in almost every town. During roughly the same period, archery, lawn tennis, and croquet were other activities which came into prominence and contributed to the collective motion of sport during this third stage of development.

The next significant advance in the conceptualization of sport is related to the organization of intramural sport in the schools and colleges. As noted earlier in this chapter, this began around 1914. Of course, intramural sport, in its broadest sense, can be traced back almost three centuries in this country. Harvard admitted its first class in 1638; William and Mary was chartered in 1692 although the college did not open until 1712; Yale was the third college to be established, receiving its charter in 1701. Many accounts refer to the informal ball games and other kinds of sporting activities in which the students participated on a

---

[12] F. R. Dulles, *A History of Recreation: America Learns to Play*, 2nd edition. The Meredith Press. Reprinted by permission of Appleton-Century-Crofts, Educational Division, Meredith Corporation.

[13] John R. Betts, "The Technological Revolution and the Rise of Sport, 1850—1900." *The Mississippi Valley Historical Review*, 40: 1953, pp. 231—256.

spontaneous basis. Nevertheless, during the long interim, until the early 1900s, there was no real effort to organize sport for all students in the school such as we have come to accept in the United States today.

"Sports for all" was a concomitant of educational changes which affected American schools during the first quarter of this century. Administrators and teachers began to realize that a structure must be established to facilitate and promote the recreational activities of students. In short, the school commenced to assume responsibilities beyond the narrow scope of the curriculum. Considering the characteristics of sport, which we will note later in this book, one would conclude that the organized intramural sport program market another rung in the ladder toward the realization of sport as it is accepted today.

Another 20 years brought about the next major breakthrough in what might be called sport. "Little league" baseball had its inception at Williamsport, Pennsylvania, on June 2, 1939. Actually, precedents for this sort of thing had been established earlier. American Legion baseball was started in 1929 and "Pop Warner" football originated in Philadelphia in 1936. However, "little league" baseball came to symbolize something new on the American sporting scene. Similar organizations, such as "Biddy" basketball, emerged in the 1950s. In short, boys in the United States were gradually enticed from spontaneous participation in these activities (play) to the more formal structure (sport).

These changes, of course, did not occur overnight. There has been a gradual evolution toward organized sport for young boys. Our purpose here is not to place a value assessment on this change, at least for the present. But it is an indisputable fact that the American boy in the 1970s is generally deterred from spontaneous participation in favor of belonging to a sport group with the associated sponsorship, coaches, codification of rules, and other aspects which characterize sport and/or athletics.

The sixth stage in the development of sport as a concept is somewhat more difficult to pinpoint, but it is epitomized in the data found in the *Time* Essay, "The Golden Age of Sport," which was mentioned in the Preface. While the focus there is on the extensive spectator involvement with athletics, the writers also document the increase in active sport participation among the American people as a whole. "In an affluent society, one out of every five Americans is a steady customer at the local bowling alley; one out of 20 plays tennis or golf." To this could be added impressive data regarding the number who swim, ski, water-ski, play badminton, and partake in other sporting activities.

Reasons behind this acceleration in sport participation, both actively and as spectators, are many and varied. Certainly increased leisure time and the availability of money would have to rank near the top in attempting to explain the current situation. Golf is a classic example of the changes which have occurred during the past 30 years. Prior to World War II, golf was still a game that was largely reserved for the country-club set. Granted there were some fine municipal courses, found principally in the large cities. However, since World War II, golf courses have mushroomed all over the country. It is not unusual today to find public golf courses in towns of any size. The net result is that golf is no longer viewed as a sporting activity for a select few. The doors have been opened for the "blue collar" worker and those in a similar economic status to play golf. Factory leagues are a common element on almost every public golf course.

Swim clubs and skiing represent two other interesting kinds of development which epitomize the "golden age" of sport in which we are living. Not everyone can afford to belong to a swim club and to ski, but it is amazing to observe how many people can find money for these activities today. Swim clubs have also sprung up everywhere since the late '50s. Fees largely restrict membership to families of the upper middle class, but the economic structure is such that many fall into this category.

Skiing is a story in itself. It has become a billion dollar a year business in the United States. It has been said that people will even incur large debts to go skiing. Not too many years ago, skiing was more or less limited to wealthy, young people. Now it also is a family activity. People of all ages ski in large numbers. As with golf courses and swim clubs, ski areas have mushroomed in quantity. For many people in northern climates, skiing has become a way of life from December through March. Because of the relatively high cost of skiing, it is a long distance away from being a sport for the masses. Yet, at a time when there is greater affluence in America than ever before, skiing represents another part of the total picture which characterizes the "golden age" of sport.

The most recent stage in the development of sport as a concept is interesting for two reasons: (1) it is still very much in its genesis; (2) it has the potential to provide crystallization for the concept of sport. We are referring to the current interest in sport as an area for scholarly inquiry.

The impetus for this came from outside the field of physical education. We alluded to this earlier in this chapter. In 1963, one of James Conant's[14] books was published. Among the recommendations of Conant was one which stated that graduate preparation in physical education was not necessary. An interesting chain reaction set in. Leaders in physical education began to seek a focus which would legitimize graduate study in physical education even in the minds of educational essentialists, such as Conant. The answer seemed to be the discipline approach, as contrasted with the profession of physical education.

In 1964, Franklin Henry presented his conception of what the discipline of physical education might be.[15] Later that year a national design conference was held in Chicago under the auspices of the American Academy of Physical Education. The conference was called for the expressed purpose of attempting to further pinpoint the nature of that discipline. From this gathering, human movement apparently emerged as the focus for those who would pursue the discipline.

---

[14] James B. Conant, *The Education of American Teachers* (New York: McGraw Hill Book Co., 1963).

[15] Franklin M. Henry, "Physical Education: An Academic Discipline," *Journal of Health, Physical Education, and Recreation*, XXXV, No. 7, Sept., 1964, pp. 32—33, 69.

A short while later, Arthur Daniels set forth his ideas regarding that which might be studied under the disciplinary banner.[16] He suggested the following areas for scholarly activity: history of sport, sport as an element of the culture, biomechanics of human movement, exercise physiology, motor learning, and international studies.

The sport studies aspect was given further impetus the same year when Kenyon and Loy published their article which laid out a framework for the sociology of sport.[17] They pointed out that although the idea of sport sociology was not entirely new, most of the works have been largely descriptive.

Following these articles of 1964 and 1965, there was considerable discussion among physical educators as to the nature of and the means of pursuing the discipline. Some of the thinking was manifested in two issues of *Quest.* The entire issue of Volume IX was devoted to "The Nature of a Discipline," published in December 1967. Then, the May 1968 issue, Volume X, was entitled "Toward a Theory of Sport."

Support for the scholarly study of sport has also come from outside the field of physical education during roughly the same period of time. James Keating's articles were published during a two-year span from 1963 to 1965. Arnold Beisser's book, *The Madness in Sports,* came out in 1967. One of the more significant steps occurred in December 1968 when the American Association for the Advancement of Science, at its 13th annual meeting, sponsored a symposium on sport. This was largely attributable to the efforts of Paul Weiss, who published his book, *Sport: A Philosophic Inquiry,* early in 1969.

It should be noted that physical educators and other academicians have cooperated in working toward sport studies. The symposium noted above included philosophers, sociologists, psychologists, physical educators, and a clergyman. Two cooperative efforts are most noteworthy in terms of potential for continuing contribution. These are found in "The International Committee for the Sociology of Sport" and "The International Society for Sport Psychology." Each of these originated within the past few years. They symbolize the world-wide interest in sport today and the determination by certain academicians to study sport in quantitative terms.

Another form of cooperative effort also deserves special mention. The Committee on Institutional Cooperation (The Big 10) has co-sponsored with The Athletic Institute symposia which are directed toward "the body of knowledge" or discipline approach. The first two symposia, held at the University of Wisconsin in 1968 and the University of Iowa in 1969, resulted in the publication of *Sociology of Sport* and *Psychology of Motor Learning.*

---

[16]Arthur S. Daniels, "The Potential of Physical Education As An Area of Research and Scholarly Effort," *Journal of Health, Physical Education, and Recreation,* XXXVI, No. 1, Jan., 1965, pp. 32–33, 74.

[17]Gerald S. Kenyon and John W. Loy, "Toward a Sociology of Sport," *Journal of Health, Physical Education, and Recreation,* XXXVI, No. 5, May, 1965, pp. 24–25, 68–69.

SUMMARY

Before moving more directly into the philosophical aspects of sport, we have examined the concept of sport from the standpoint of a historical overview. This results largely from the questions: when? and where? These questions cause one to first consider the historical relationship between sport and physical education, because, rightly or wrongly, these two concepts have somehow been linked together. Secondly, we have traced the stages in the development of sport as a concept. This development obviously extends beyond the scope of any relationship to physical education.

Sport and physical education are two abstract terms. Of the two, sports is most widely used and accepted by the public in general. Both concepts are also of fairly recent origin, at least in terms of the constituents of each which we accept today. Sport appears to have originated as a concept in 17th-century England. Physical education is actually a 20th-century concept that emerged in the United States. With the advent of the so-called "new physical education," sport was combined with or submerged in the concept of physical education. A paradox has developed. Sport has flourished both within and without the schools while being somewhat restrained by the concept of physical education. There are those who argue that sport is the focus of physical education, but the professional party line has more frequently suggested that there is much more to physical education than sport. Now even many of the more orthodox physical educators are questioning the concept which identifies their work. Sport may be on a new threshold as a configuration for programs and a field of study.

We basically recognize sport today for what it is even though we may have difficulty in defining or even describing it. Many changes have occurred in sport over the past 300 years. Collectively, these changes constitute a development. They may or may not represent progress, depending on one's value orientation.

As a concept, sport seems to have arisen with the British field sports. In contrast with earlier sportinglike activities, shooting and hunting became more organized and structured during the 17th-century. While interests in field sports continued, several other forms of games requiring physical prowess were organized as sports in England during the following century. These were organized in the private schools and clubs. The 19th century brought similar changes to the United States. Although new sport forms were evident, the parallel was evident. It was not until after 1900 that "sports for all" became a partial reality. This was manifested in the United States through the advent of intramural sport in the schools and colleges, both public and private. Then, sport for boys began to extend beyond the schools through the medium of organizations such as "little league" baseball. More recently, there are further evidences of mass sport participation by adults in activities such as bowling, skiing, tennis, and golf. There is now the recognition that we should also study this thing called sport. A disciplinelike area of sport studies is at least in the genesis stage.

What will the future bring? The development may still have further stages. At some point, we may be in a better position to assess or reject the label of progress.

BIBLIOGRAPHY

Beisser, Arnold, *The Madness in Sports.* New York: Appleton-Century-Crofts, 1967.

Betts, John R., "The Technological Revolution and the Rise of Sport, 1850—1900," *Mississippi Valley Historical Review*, 40: 231—256, 1953,

Conant, James B., *The Education of American Teachers.* New York: McGraw Hill Book Co., 1963.

Daniels, Arthur S., "The Potential of Physical Education as an Area of Research and Scholarly Effort," *Journal of Health, Physical Education, and Recreation*, No. 1, 32—33, 74, January, 1965.

Dulles, F. R., *A History of Recreation: America Learns to Play.* New York: Appleton-Century-Crofts, 1965.

Graves, H., "A Philosophy of Sport," *Contemporary Review*, 78, 877—893, December, 1900.

Hackensmith, C. W., *History of Physical Education.* New York: Harper and Row Publishers, 1966.

Henry, Franklin M., "Physical Education: An Academic Discipline," *Journal of Health, Physical Education, and Recreation*, XXXV, No. 7, 32—33, 69, September, 1964.

Keating, James, "Winning in Sport and Athletics," *Thought*, XXXVIII, 149, 201—210, Summer, 1963.

Keating, James, "Sportsmanship as a Moral Category," *Ethics*, LXXV, No. 1, 25—35, October, 1964.

Keating, James, "The Heart of the Problem of Amateur Athletics," *The Journal of General Education*, 16, No. 4, January, 1965.

Keating, James, "Athletics and the Pursuit of Excellence," *Education*, 85, No. 7, 428—431, March, 1965.

Kenyon, Gerald S., and John W. Loy, "Toward a Sociology of Sport," *Journal of Health, Physical Education, and Recreation*, XXXVI, No. 5, 24—25, 68—69, May, 1965.

Mallett, Donald, "An Educator Views the Contribution of Campus Intramural Sports Programs," *Proceedings*, 64th Annual Meeting, College Physical Education Association, 95—96, 1960.

Psychology of Motor Learning. Chicago: The Athletic Institute, 1970.

Quest IX, "'The Nature of a Discipline," December, 1967.

Quest X, "Toward a Theory of Sport," May, 1968.

Sociology of Sport, Chicago: The Athletic Institute, 1969.

Staley, S. C., "The Four Year Curriculum in Physical (Sports) Education," *Research Quarterly*, II, No. 1, 76—90, March, 1931.

Weiss, Paul, *Sport: A Philosophic Inquiry.* Carbondale: Southern Illinois University Press, 1969.

Williams, J. F., "Education Through the Physical," *The Journal of Higher Education*, I, 279—282, May, 1930.

Zeigler, Earle F., and H. J. VanderZwaag, *Physical Education: Progressivism or Essentialism?* Champaign, Illinois: Stipes Publishing Co., 1968.

3 / Sport: Who?

In considering the subject of the "who" in sport, we are moving closer to the important philosophical questions. The question of "who" may also be viewed historically, but that is less significant for our purposes here. We are concerned with the past and the present only insofar as they shed light on the range of possibilities. The focus will be on what might be called the "ideal who."

At least three aspects of this question are readily apparent. The first involves the subquestion: who is the sportsman? A most obvious answer is that a sportsman is one who participates in sport. However, the matter is not quite that simple. Webster gives the following as the earliest ascertainable meaning of a sportsman: one who pursues sports, especially of the field. This is not the meaning which causes the above question to be significant. The second meaning, in chronological order, does present problems: one who in sports is fair and generous; a good loser and a graceful winner. Such a definition smacks of the amateur spirit and leads directly to the related question: who is the amateur?

Whether we like it or not, we also cannot avoid the fact that sport is a result of promotional efforts of some type or another. This may be largely attributed to the organized nature of sport. However, promotion is also a vague term. For instance, promotion can vary considerably in terms of its directness. This leads one to the question: who promotes sport? The answer is obviously not a simple one involving an individual or a group. Sport is promoted from many sources, some of these being much more remote than others. At the same time, not all these promotional sources may be equally desirable when the nature of sport is considered from the standpoint of an ideal. Then, too, sport itself may also serve as an instigator or promoter in some way. This is a related matter which should not be overlooked in considering the question at hand.

One of the most intriguing aspects of the "who" in sport is that involving men vs. women in sport. Historically, women have not had the same opportunities for sport participation as have men. Reasons for this are many and varied, largely attributed to social standards. However, there are evidences today, at least in this culture, that the situation is changing; increasing numbers of women are participating in sport. Is this a trend in the right direction? Should such participation involve the same activities and standards as for men? These are among the questions which must be answered philosophically.

WHO IS THE SPORTSMAN?

HETHERINGTON'S VIEWPOINT

In 1909, Clark Hetherington published an article called "The Foundation of Amateurism." Although he did not address himself directly to this question, he provided an answer implicitly through his discussion of what constitutes an amateur. The link between the sportsman and the amateur is indicated when he states that amateurism arose with the rise of sports in England. He pointed out that at the time of his writing much of the criticism of the amateur code in the United States seemed to come from those who would equate amateurism with sport conditions in England, at the same time rejecting the concept for the United States. Hetherington was in sharp disagreement with this position because he did not believe that amateurism should be dependent on social conditions.

For Clark Hetherington, amateurism was largely a psychological consideration. The essence of his ideas is embodied in his discussion of why a boy should be attracted to athletics:

His interest in the satisfaction of the impulses and in the pleasure derived reveals the content of those motives we commonly call "sport for sport's sake"; this is amateurism. It is the attitude of mind that determines the root of amateurism. Whoever exhibits this attitude in all his play is psychologically an amateur, no matter what the man-made law or definition of amateurism for social control may be. Here we make a sharp distinction between the principle of amateurism and the law formulated for its administration in practice. Like all human law the principle may be sound, the law enacted may be defective. The principle of amateurism is the concept of the natural mental attitude in play; the law is an enactment for social control. This analysis shows further that nature's aim in play, the boy's pleasure, amateurism as a principle, and educational athletics as an administrative endeavor, have at the root one and the same purpose. Usually the professional interest in athletics is contrasted with the amateur. The amateur motive, however, is the flower of a primary human need and interest; the professional interest is not. This is a secondary interest derived from the spectator's interest which is primary.[1]

The above viewpoint might be considered far too idealistic, particularly in contemporary thought. Since 1909 many people have been faced with the practical problems which surround the concept of amateurism, regardless of any theoretical construct which might be posed. On the other hand, Hetherington

---

[1]Clark W. Hetherington, "The Foundation of Amateurism," *American Physical Education Review*, November, 1909, p. 568.

may well have raised a valid point in stating that "it is the attitude of mind that determines the root of amateurism." The record of the past 60 years would indicate that socially determined distinctions between the amateur and the professional are fraught with all sorts of pitfalls.

At least one athlete has pointed out some of the problems through her "off-the-cuff" remarks:

In any square-off between Avery Brundage and Suzy Chaffee, you have to give Avery a distinct edge in weight and reach. But there his physical advantage ends.

Suzy is prettier. She has a mane of gold hair, a 34—22—34 figure and a deep-seated conviction on Avery's interpretation of amateurism. . . .

"Who does Mr. Brundage think invented amateurism—God? . . . .

"Amateurism is not a religion. It's not an edict of God. It was started in Britain a couple of hundred years ago. A group of wealthy, tuffy lords got together and decided it would be terribly noble if they competed without prizes or remuneration.

"Since then every sport has been tainted with the false notion that there is something sacred about amateurism. It is hypocritical and it is unrealistic.

"The very name Olympics has a beautiful connotation. It should mean the best in any sport. But it doesn't. A bunch of old fuddy-duddies, like Mr. Brundage, are ruining it.

"The Olympics should be open. The man or woman who can run the fastest, throw the farthest, jump the highest, ski the best—no matter what his occupation or financial status   should wear the gold medal."

Suzy's latest ire has been fired by the impending showdown between Brundage's International Olympic Committee and the International Ski Federation on the future of Alpine skiing in the Olympic Games.

Brundage, long a militant champion of purity in amateur sports, is threatening to throw Alpine skiing, the glamor event of the Winter Games, out of the program at Sappora, Japan, in 1972 because of commercialism.

Alpine skiers, particularly those in Europe, are paid tidy sums to endorse skis, boots and other equipment for manufacturers . . . .

"It's ridiculous," said Suzy. "There is no such thing today as an amateur athlete. There is only hypocrisy and under-the-table payments.

"If it were not for these under-the-table payments, the Olympics and all other amateur sports would be restricted to the ultra rich. An ordinary working man or girl couldn't afford to compete.

"I think this violates the spirit of the Olympics."

The blond, leggy Miss Chaffee, from Rutland, Vt., was the United States' top-ranking woman skier in the 1968 Winter Games at Grenoble, France. She placed fourth in the women's world downhill. . . .[2]

---

[2] Associated Press Article, *Daily Hampshire Gazette*, Northampton, Mass., April 6, 1970, p. 20.

A counter argument is that one has to draw the line somewhere. Those on the "firing line" would be inclined to say that employment of Hetherington's concept of an amateur would only add to the confusion; they would say that a concrete distinction must be made to protect the interests of the group as a whole.

Hetherington's conception of amateurism comes into somewhat sharper focus later in his article when he contrasts amateurism with professionalism. His contention was that when an athlete caters to the interest of spectators or seeks a reward for his participation, he is a professional. He concluded that these are legitimate motives, but the acts are immoral when they are performed under false pretenses. In other words, Clark Hetherington would say that a sportsman is one who participates in sport solely for the enjoyment or benefit to be derived from the activity itself without regard to or concern about outside influences.

THE KEATING THESIS

Roughly half a century later, Hetherington's viewpoint was essentially reinforced through the excellent work of James Keating.[3] He added some important dimensions which tend to make the basic distinctions more realistic. According to Keating, there is nothing unique about the amateur's activity or methodology as contrasted with the professional. He concurs with Hetherington in stating that it is the motive which marks the difference; an amateur "participates out of love of the activity itself." However, Keating adds the important limitation that such a motive is not easily determined. The individual himself may have difficulty in assessing his motives, let alone any governing body which may be charged with establishing a distinction.

Therefore, he concludes that it is virtually impossible to identify the athlete with amateurism. He and Paul Weiss are in substantial agreement that an athlete is driven by the pursuit of excellence. The athlete is first and foremost motivated by the desire to win; this automatically forces him toward professionalism. Sport relates very much to amateurism as athletics does to professionalism. In this context, amateurism and professionalism are motives which lead to sport and athletics respectively.

There is no doubt that the Keating thesis has merit. He was really the first to concretely point out a distinction which had been overlooked for years. To this day, his message has not reached as many people as it should. People, even those most intimately involved, are inclined to gloss over the basic issue and speak of sport and athletics in very glib terms. One gets the general feeling that it is really all one large package with the participants motivated by and striving for the same goal. It is no small wonder that we have trouble in determining who is the sportsman.

---

[3] James W. Keating, "The Heart of the Problem of Amateur Athletics," *The Journal of General Education*, 16, No. 4, Jan. 1965.

On the other hand, Keating's strong position can lead one to the same kind of pitfall which permeates much of philosophical, political, and educational thought. It is that which Alfred North Whitehead may well have had in mind when he warned against the "fallacy of misplaced concreteness." To contrast a sportsman with an athlete is not unlike the following commonly accepted sets of polarities: liberal vs. conservative, Republican vs. Democrat, educational essentialism vs. educational progressivism, idealism vs. realism, naturalism vs. spiritualism, genius vs. moron, and introversion vs. extroversion. Whether we wish to accept that fact or not, things are not quite that simple!

Thus, it appears more reasonable and defensible to consider the subjects of amateurism vs. professionalism and sport vs. athletics as being operational frames of reference. They offer a point of departure for organization and general conduct of affairs. One has to start somewhere in describing the overall purpose of an activity; an amateur and a sportsman offer the temper within which the activity may be evaluated.

One of the most interesting and, yet, confusing features which evolves from the Keating thesis is the possible difference between an individual's motives and the orientation, purpose, or structure of the group with which the individual is associated. For example, a given individual may be truly a sportsman in terms of his motive; he participates in the activity first and foremost because he likes the activity; his satisfaction is derived from the nature of the sport. But for all practical purposes he is an athlete and a professional because he is a member of a team which exists for one or more of the following purposes: making money; representing their country, school, or club; achieving recognition and fame.

In this context, it would appear that the group motives may be more readily determined than the individual's motives. The group, at least, is organized and structured with a definite goal in mind. To carry the example further, an individual is a member of a professional football team which exists for one primary purpose—making money. Let us assume that the particular individual does not need the salary which he makes; he has attained wealth from other sources. This individual has already achieved great recognition or fame as a result of past performances. Yet, he continues to participate as a member of the team. What is his motivation? There are at least three possibilities and it might be any combination thereof: (1) he desires to make more money even though he doesn't really require more for an affluent existence; (2) he has a social/psychological need to add to his recognition by remaining in the public limelight; (3) he enjoys participation in football just for the sake of the activity. This example should serve to point out the complexities involved when attempting to determine who is the amateur or sportsman by evaluating the individual's motives. Even self-evaluation would be difficult, let alone an appraisal by another individual or group. So, practically speaking, those involved are usually forced to identify individuals as being amateur or professional according to the purpose of the group with which they are associated.

SOURCE OF THE CONFLICT BETWEEN THE AAU AND THE NCAA

The last premise leads directly into the historical and contemporary problem involving the relationship between the Amateur Athletic Union and the National Collegiate Athletic Association in the United States. Flath[4] has described this relationship from a historical perspective. Basically, the differences of opinion between these two groups revolve around an interpretation of amateurism. The AAU has tended to adhere to a more strict interpretation of amateurism, embodied in the traditional English outlook that an amateur and a sportsman is one who participates in sport for pleasure and inherent interest in the activity without regard for financial gain. Because the AAU was instrumental in reviving the Olympic Games in 1896, this organization has also had a close tie-in with matters of control involving Olympic participation. Jurisdiction of the AAU has been most evident in certain sports such as gymnastics, track and field, and swimming.

As a more recent organization (formed in 1905) and one which has steadily increased in prominence over the years, the NCAA has exercised jurisdiction over collegiate athletic programs. Supposedly, participants in these programs are amateurs. However, the AAU has not always viewed them as such. The NCAA is inclined to recognize the scholar/athlete as a member of a special kind of category; he is not a professional in the usual meaning of that term because he is not employed full time as an athlete; on the other hand, he is also not an amateur and sportsman in terms of the traditional British interpretation of these concepts. In view of these conflicting frames of reference, the two controlling groups have clashed head-on over such matters as standards for Olympic participation and eligibility to compete in various amateur meets which are scheduled from time to time throughout the United States.

From one standpoint the AAU vs. NCAA controversy is primarily a power struggle. However, the struggle is loaded with philosophical overtones. The groups are vying for supremacy in controlling amateur sport in the United States, but they cannot agree on the limits which should be set for the amateur.

ZEIGLER'S IDEA OF THE SEMIPROFESSIONAL

Earle Zeigler has provided what may be considered as philosophical support for the NCAA position. He asserts that it is probably high time that we forget about the sharp distinction between the amateur and the professional. Conditions in the second half of the 20th century necessitate a reevaluation of the concept of amateurism. The essence of his viewpoint is stated in these words:

---

[4]Arnold W. Flath, *A History of Relations Between the National Collegiate Athletic Association and the Amateur Athletic Union of the United States* (1905–1963). (Champaign, Ill.: Stipes Publishing Co., 1964.)

Must we persist in the ideology that in sport and athletics it is a question of black or white—the professional being the black one, and the amateur, the white? Can't we recognize and identify the many shades of "gray" that inevitably exist in between?

What is so wrong with a young sportsman or athlete being classified as "gray" or a semiprofessional? Do we brand the musician, the artist, or the sculptor in our society who develops his talent sufficiently to receive some remuneration for his efforts as being a "dirty pro"? Why must this idea persist in sport—a legitimate phase of our culture? The answer to these questions may well lie in the fact that we are not willing, almost subconsciously, to accept sport as a legitimate and worthwhile aspect of our culture.[5]

In a sense, one could say that Zeigler's position represents a defense of highly organized sport or athletics as we know it today in the United States. Contrasts can also be noted in comparing his ideas with those of Hetherington and Keating. Both of the latter would somehow or another preserve the traditional concept of amateurism. They would also distinguish sharply between amateurism and professionalism even though the distinction lies in a psychological frame of reference. Zeigler is apparently looking at the subject more from the standpoint of financial gain when he refers to the remuneration received. His semiprofessional is one who receives some money for his talent in sport.

Although the NCAA does not use the term "semiprofessional" to describe its scholar/athletes, it appears that is what they are. Thus, in assessing the role of these young men as sportsmen, Zeigler calls "a spade a spade" and, at the same time, finds philosophical support for this intermediary position.

From another perspective, there may not be as much difference between Keating's position and Zeigler's as first appears. Keating says that athletics tends toward professionalism. The college athlete, or semiprofessional, could be viewed as one who is tending toward professionalism. However, in either case, one is still plagued with the problem of the individual vs. the group. Following Zeigler's classification, the group could be considered semiprofessional, such as the large university football team. Within that group, there will be a range, extending from those who are more amateur to those who are more professional.

THE SPORTSMAN ON A CONTINUUM

An analysis of the three philosophical positions which have been outlined in this chapter leads us to conclude that there will never be a simple answer to the question: who is the sportsman? This conclusion is based on the assumption that a sportsman is one who is amateurlike in his motives. The complexity of the question stems from two primary facts. (1) Motives of the individual, would-be sportsman are not readily determined. (2) The motives of the individual may vary considerably from the motives of the group with which he is associated in a sportinglike activity.

---

[5]E. F. Zeigler, *Problems in the History and Philosophy of Physical Education and Sport* © 1968, pp. 113–114. Reprinted by permission of Prentice-Hall, Inc., Englewood Cliffs, New Jersey.

It would appear most defensible to suggest that a sportsman is one who appears somewhere on a continuum between the pure amateur and the pure professional.

Amateur $\longleftrightarrow$ Professional

Sportsman

A second continuum would depict the motives and role of the groups who engage in what we commonly call sport.

Amateur group $\longleftrightarrow$ Professional group

Sportsmen

Assuming that the individual's motives and the group motives can be roughly determined, we could superimpose the first continuum on the second and depict the differences between the individual and the group in relationship to the concept of amateurism.

Amateurism $\longleftrightarrow$ Professionalism

X = The individual sportsman or athlete

√ = The sport group

In the above example, the sport group is structured primarily for the enjoyment which the participants might gain from the activity itself. To carry the example further, the sport group could be a high-school baseball team in this case. The main purpose for organizing the team is to provide competitive opportunities for those boys in the school who enjoy playing baseball and who are among the more highly skilled in this activity. Therefore, the genesis is basically derived from an amateur spirit. However, the team also represents the school; winning assumes some importance. This, in itself, places the team somewhat further along the scale away from the pure amateur point of the continuum.

A particular baseball player is further along to the right on the continuum because his motives are distinctly more professional than the majority of his teammates. He happens to be one of the most highly skilled on the team. In addition, he has objectives other than playing of the game. He has the strong urge to win, entertain spectators, obtain publicity, and hopes to eventually make money by playing baseball. Thus, he is somewhat more of a professional in what is still a basically amateur setting.

There is even more than a continuum involved in evaluating these kinds of relationships between the supposed polarities of amateurism and professionalism. A "normal" curve or bell-shaped curve can be projected above the continuum.

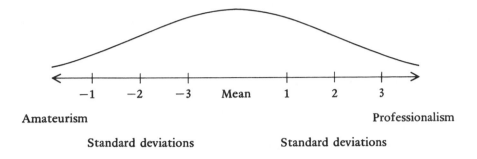

We would hypothesize that this normal frequency distribution can be applied to either individuals or groups in sport. What it implies is that there are relatively few pure amateurs and relatively few pure professionals. Most individuals and groups tend to be more one way than another in regard to their motives for sport participation, but contrary elements can almost always be found.

What, then, can be done to assist those sponsoring or governing bodies who are concerned about delineating the amateur status? Obviously, it will be next to impossible to measure or even evaluate the motives of each would-be participant. About the best which one can hope for is that a governing board will make certain decisions, even though they may be somewhat arbitrary, regarding eligibility. Hopefully, these decisions will be reached with the interests of the majority in mind. The kind of thing we refer to is represented in the recent attempts to determine eligibility of United States basketball players to compete in contests outside the country. As a first evidence of some cooperation between the NCAA and the AAU these two groups have referred the matter to the American Federation of Basketball Coaches. Both the NCAA and the AAU are represented on the Federation. The hope is that this single group will at least be able to establish their eligibility rules for such participation, regardless of whether one wishes to label such participation amateur, semi-professional, professional, or any other name.

WHO PROMOTES SPORT?

THE PUBLIC AT LARGE

One could take the position that the promotion of sport is not primarily attributable to any one kind of group; this position holds that sport is collectively promoted by society; sport is viewed as a societal off-shoot or an arm of society.

This approach is somewhat related to the idea of sport for sport's sake, which we will discuss later in this book. Adherents would argue that sport need not be assessed as a promotional endeavor in the usual sense of that term. Sport has inherent appeal; people will seek or develop sporting activities from what might be called an innate interest. Society, particularly highly organized industrial society, demands its sport. The question then becomes one of: which sports? That is where the business of promotion may enter more directly into the picture.

The problem of who is the public has to be considered. In the United States it is difficult, if not impossible, to only refer to *the* public. The public actually consists of several publics. For instance, there are regional and state conditions which, although diminishing in importance, cannot be overlooked. Sport offers classic examples of variances according to locality. Basketball in Indiana, football in Ohio, Pennsylvania, or Texas, lacrosse in Maryland and New England, soccer in the St. Louis area and New England, are only a starter in supporting the thesis that sports flourish because of promotional efforts. Regional and local demands largely dictate the extent of participation and degree of acceptance. Each of these cases can probably be traced back to and has been promulgated through promotional efforts of some type.

Of course, the promotion of a certain sport does not negate the overall thesis that sport is self-promoting, particularly where leisure and wealth are found, and that the matter of who promotes sport largely reduces to a subsidiary question: who promotes the various forms of sport?

BUSINESSMEN

A strong case can be made for the idea that particular sports are largely promoted by business entrepreneurs. This is especially true of those sport programs and activities which exist outside the auspices of the school. The data for the year 1966 is revealing. Americans spent $40 million for bowling balls, $150 million on golf equipment, and $2.8 billion on boats, including operating costs. Sport is not only promoted by those business people who directly operate the sporting establishment; suppliers of equipment and clothing contribute a great deal to the popularity through their various advertising devices.

Skiing again offers a vivid example of what can be done by those who wish to promote a particular sport for financial reasons. The total situation very much resembles that which has occurred in golf. Clothing, other equipment, and the total setting lend themselves to business promotion from many sources and angles. Skiing not only becomes popular as an activity. Everything associated with skiing is also viewed as the "in" thing. The popularity of skiing as an activity actually mushrooms because of attendant conditions.

In essence, businessmen capitalize on the recognition that sport excites and awes. Sport requires action; most people like action. Sport offers an opportunity for people to test their physical abilities. Some sporting activities also lend themselves to social advantages. These are the ones which are especially capitalized on by business entrepreneurs as a source for financial gain.

We are not making the case that there is anything inherently wrong with this form of sport promotion. It just happens to represent a reason behind sport popularity which may be overlooked. Americans have considerable leisure time today and many have quite a bit of money to spend for leisure in one form or another. Who is to say that those involved in the business of sport do not contribute to the worthy use of leisure time?

EDUCATORS

Educators have been and continue to be among the strongest supporters of sport, but their reasons for promoting sport are often aside from sport itself. In this context, by educators we primarily mean those people who are responsible for organizing and administering the process of education in the schools, such as college presidents, deans, school superintendents and principals. Many of these educators have a firm conviction regarding the importance of sport because they believe that sport offers a wholesome medium for students to "let off steam." Whether they are aware of it or not, they are actually adherents of the "surplus energy" theory.

Of course, there are many educators who also support an extension of sport—namely, athletics. The basic differences between sport and athletics will be discussed in more detail in the next chapter. It should suffice to say here that athletics represents the pursuit of excellence among participants and sport programs in the schools. Educators tend to promote athletics for public relations reasons. Not all school administrators support athletics, but the ones who do not are certainly in the minority in the United States.

There may also be one common reason why educators are inclined to promote both athletics and intramural sports in the schools. The reason can be summed up in the word "identification." Many hold to the value judgment that both sport and athletics are "good" because they offer media for students to identify with the school and their peers in the school.

It should also be noted that educators, as a group, have tended to promote the concepts of sport and athletics to a far greater extent than they have physical education. Often, lip service is given to that which is called physical education. Usually, this implies the inclusion of both sport and athletics. For many educators, sport is a meaningful concept; it is a form of recreation which has a legitimate place in the total program of the school as an extracurricular activity.

PARENTS

In general, parental promotion of sport tends to resemble the support given by educators both in terms of extent and reasons behind the promotion. One could take the position that this is most natural because educators merely reflect the wishes and desires of parents. This is an assumption which could probably be debated endlessly. A case could also be made for the idea that educators influence the parental promotion of sport. Again, it is obviously one of those situations which is not just one way or the other. Both circumstances appear to exist in varying degrees.

There seems to be little question that parents are inclined to be among the most ardent advocates of sport participation for their sons because of such reasons as the surplus energy idea, worthy use of leisure time, and projection of their own ego. The last reason is particularly manifested when sport is extended to athletics.

Arnold Beisser hits at this last point in his book.[6] His work could more properly be titled "The Madness in Athletics," because he is largely writing about highly organized sport where winning assumes much importance. Beisser's basic contention is that the American absorption with athletics is a perpetuating thing because of the paradox of men and boys generally and fathers and sons, more specifically.

When it comes to sport, many adult males do not make a transition from boyhood to manhood. They may have as much interest in softball and touch football when they are in their forties as they did in their teens. Beisser notes that sport is the one thing which many fathers have in common with their sons. These fathers tend to project their interest in sport to their sons. From early years, the boy is prepared for a life of dedication to sport. When he reaches adulthood, he is likely to be faced with the realization that he will not succeed in his hope to attain excellence. He then joins the army of spectators and proceeds to transfer his hopes and dreams to his son or sons.

THE PHYSICAL EDUCATOR

In the preceding chapter we noted that physical education is a 20th-century concept. Professional preparation in physical education is even more of a 20th-century idea. When we use the term "physical educator" we are referring to one who has been directly prepared for the profession of conducting programs in sport, dance, and other forms of physical activity in the schools.

One would logically expect that physical educators are the most ardent promoters of sport. Some are and some are not; the situation is not as simple as it first appears. There are those, such as Thomas Sheehan, who argue that sport is the focus of physical education. These physical educators obviously tend to promote the cause of sport. However, many other physical educators begin with the premise that there is much more to physical education than sport. For some, this has almost become a cliché. They may be hard pressed to specify what the more is, but they cling tenaciously to their assertion. When an outside observer hears the statement that there is much more to physical education than

---

[6]Arnold Beisser, *The Madness in Sports.* Copyright © 1967 by Meredith Publishing Company. Reprinted by permission of Appleton-Century-Crofts, Educational Division, Meredith Corporation.

sport, he cannot help but conclude that sport is not as important as it might be.

There are still other physical educators who go further in minimizing the importance of sport in terms of their work. These people are actually physical trainers; they never made the transition from physical training to physical education. For them, physical education is still largely a matter of education *of* the physical. Although sport has as one of its characteristics the demonstration of physical prowess, these physical educators feel that sport is not as physical as exercise programs which are established for the specific purpose of improving the physical condition of the human body. Therefore, rather than promoting sport, these physical educators are often prone to view sport as something which is a cancer in their programs and which detracts from their primary purpose.

Thus, one would almost have to conclude that the promotion of sport does not necessarily come from what would superficially appear to be the most logical source—physical education. It all depends on who is the physical educator. He is one of several possibilities. With physical education being such a broad, umbrella concept, the physical educator is not easily pinpointed. Some physical educators have a sport orientation; these tend to promote sport. Others actually feel that sport works against their central purposes.

THE COACH

Superficially, this might appear as a repetition of the previous discussion. Are not the coach and the physical educator one and the same? By and large the public would answer "yes," particularly in the United States. A physical educator is commonly asked the question: what do you coach? However, many physical educators are not coaches. As a result, the role of the coach with regard to sport should be a separate consideration.

If anyone were to promote sport, it would appear to be the coach. At least on the surface, this would seem to be the case. Many coaches are strong proponents of sport in the full meaning of that concept. However, the very nature of coaching, the pursuit of excellence, often works at cross purposes to the promotion of sport. The coach may find that he is forced to share personnel, facilities, and equipment with others who are dedicated to sport. Theoretically, he believes in sport and would be inclined to support all aspects of sport, but the practical situation forces him to temper his enthusiasm for sport within his own school or other program. Athletics requires dedication, sacrifice, intensity; one cannot afford to alter one's goal by being sidetracked with the cause of sport.

SPORT AS A CATALYST

Thus far we have merely looked at one aspect of the societal role of sport by considering that matter of sport promotion by society and parts of society. Another facet should also be considered. Sport may serve as its own promoter and a promoter of other causes by being a catalyst or instigator of social change.

The capacity to cut across traditional social barriers through the medium of sport is most strikingly exemplified in observing the play of children of elementary school age. Whether consciously or unconsciously, children frequently enter the sporting activity with a potential social bias, stemming from family and narrow community associations. Nevertheless, in most cases the mere diversion of the sport is enough to at least tentatively eliminate the social bias. A difficulty is encountered in attempting to assess the transfer of this social acceptance to other life situations. It does seem reasonable to assume that a prolonged experience through sport with children from other social backgrounds should have a positive effect on the individual child in shaping the direction of his social philosophy as an adult. Of course, it would be erroneous to assume that sport alone can accomplish this objective. It seems more logical to accept the premise that an individual's social philosophy arises and is developed from a complex of environmental factors without any clear indication of the relative priority among the component factors.

Perhaps too much has been made in certain quarters regarding the social force of sport. Sport does tend to be a very absorbing activity because of the action component. When something is absorbing it will almost always have strong social effects. But one must still proceed with caution in stressing that sport is unique in bringing about social change. Sport does hold a considerable amount of interest for many people; for those who are interested, sport offers a medium which may contribute to their social awareness.

MALE VS. FEMALE IN SPORT

In this culture, when one thinks of sport he will almost invariably turn his attention to the activities of boys and young men. The majority of the American public are inclined to accept this as a fact and the way it should be without giving serious attention to the reasons which lie behind this situation. Reasons for such general acceptance of the status quo are rather apparent. Sport is active and demands demonstration of physical prowess. In our western culture, women have historically been expected to be more passive and less physically active than men. The male is supposed to prove himself in a physical way. A "tomboy" stage may be sanctioned for a girl, but she is expected to grow out of that stage and assume a role of feminine maturity.

Furthermore, the American sporting scene has been very much dominated by team sports such as football, basketball, and baseball. Somehow these sports are viewed as being more masculine than certain others. For example, a woman baseball player is not accepted in the same way as a woman tennis player. Football, basketball, and baseball also lend themselves to the spectator role in which males and females throng to see men and boys display their talents. Thus, the masculine sport image is perpetuated.

Within recent years there have been numerous signs that women are achieving a breakthrough in terms of fuller opportunities for participation in sport. This is to be expected because of broader social trends which gradually but steadily open new doors to women in many walks of life. Also, women, along with men, have more time for sport due to the mechanization of the home which eliminates many time-consuming chores. Generally speaking, the advancement of women in sport is viewed with favor, but there are strong opinions by some males who would continue to resist the trend.

MADLEM'S TRADITIONAL VIEWPOINT

In an address given at the 39th Annual Meeting of the American Football Coaches Association in Chicago, Ill., January 1962, Leo Madlem put it this way from his perspective as a psychiatrist:

The experiential value of athletics, and especially football is that it is an encounter with another and one's self that is real, concrete, naked and out in the open for all to witness. Athletics is one of the few endeavors left where a young man can have an experience in masculinity. As a matter of fact, the word is getting around these days that "the men are getting more feminine and the women more masculine and that probably this is a good thing." I personally feel this is a bad state of affairs because if this trend keeps up—and there is every evidence it will—a young man, when confronted by another, won't know for sure whether to "fight 'em or kiss 'em." As a matter of fact, I'd like to go on record as being against the building up of women's athletic teams to compete with the Russian gals, as my own personal response to the development of athletic females is, "who in the hell wants a bunch of fast running women?"

This is obviously a rather extreme point of view, but it may very well be one that has been and continues to be shared either consciously or unconsciously by many males. It is opinions of this type which probably contribute the most to the explanation of why we find such vast differences in sport participation among women as compared with the man's role in sport.

Of course, there is the usual problem of confusion between sport and athletics. One could very easily take the stance of opposing highly organized, athletic competition for women and yet support the premise that women should have full and equal opportunities for participation in sport.

A TYPICAL POSITION OF WOMEN PHYSICAL EDUCATORS

This represents the position that more or less typifies the ideas of women physical educators on this subject. Forty years ago Mabel Lee stated the case which has since been echoed many times at conferences and through writings of female leaders in the physical education profession:

It is interesting to note the rising tide of condemnation of men's intercollegiate athletics. It has grown from a mild protest, voiced by a few in the study of 1923, to most emphatic statements of disapproval, voiced by a large number in this present study of 1930. There exists a great fear that once intercollegiate athletics for women gain a foothold, college women might become involved in the same predicament as their brothers. The director who replies in the following strain seems to voice the opinion of the great majority when she says "I would approve of a program of intercollegiate athletics for women if it would actually be conducted as amateur sports should be conducted but not as men's intercollegiate athletics are conducted in this country." There is ever present the alarming thought that women might become involved in something equally undesirable. . . .

Many of the suggestions, especially some concerning Play Days, will most probably sound utterly naive to most men and to some women but they prove how absolutely determined are the women of the physical-education profession and, judging from the report of ACACW for 1930, how determined are the women college students of today, not to permit women's athletics to follow in the footsteps of men's athletics. They are determined to keep them free of all taint of professionalization and commercialization — to keep them quite informal, entirely sane, and absolutely wholesome.[7]

Naturally, there is quite a range of opinion among women physical educators, extending from those who would make their athletic programs more like the men's to those who would avoid or eliminate interscholastic and intercollegiate competition altogether. But the kind of position embodied in Lee's statements has been the keystone of the arch in structuring and guiding sport programs for women. This is often attributed as being one of the major reasons why we find so many separate departments of men's and women's physical education, particularly in the larger schools.

Theoretically and superficially there appear to be few, if any, legitimate reasons for administratively separating men from women in terms of the organizational structure in the schools which has commonly been called physical education. However, the splits have developed from practical problems such as this matter of the extent to which females should engage in competitive sport. The women feel that they must preserve their autonomy to avoid the dominance by athletic male counterparts. The men feel that athletics represents the pursuit of excellence in sport, and they do not wish to get entangled in any structure which may detract from their athletic interests.

Zeigler includes this entire situation under his listing and critique of persistent problems in the history of physical education. He discusses the pros and cons of this issue as follows:

There is no doubt that athletic competition for boys and young men has been and is being carried to unwarranted extremes in many institutions. The leading women in our profession reacted violently to many of these excesses by the men, and, to their credit, saw to it that similar problems did not arise in the programs for girls and women. In so doing, they were able to set quite a good, and in many cases an excellent, standard in the

---

[7]Mabel Lee, "The Case For and Against Intercollegiate Athletics for Women and the Situation Since 1923," *The Research Quarterly of the American Physical Education Association*, Vol. 2, May, 1931, pp. 126—127.

other phases of the total program. But in their zeal to meet the needs of the average girl, they have negated one of the basic tenets of our democracy—giving every girl, insofar as possible, the opportunity to develop to the maximum of her potential. The accelerated youngster has been slighted and has turned elsewhere, if possible, for her competitive athletic experience and coaching. In most cases it has not been possible for her to reach her potential. If competitive sport experience in an educational setting has value, and all of the philosophical tendencies grant this to a greater or slightly less extent, then it is the duty of the women physical educator to make these values available to girls and young women, and as soon as possible in the years that lie ahead. The excuse that such a development would immediately place the average woman physical educator in the same untenable position that the average male physical educator is in might be true to a certain extent, but only if the women allow it to develop that way.[8]

The reader will note that Zeigler's analysis is based on the premise that sport or athletics should be organized and conducted under the physical education frame of reference. However, some people, particularly those outside the profession to physical education, assess the role of women in sport without reference to physical education whatsoever. Paul Weiss exemplifies this sort of approach.

WEISS' EXTREME HYPOTHESIS

Most of the discussions of differences in sport participation among women as compared with men tend to be largely descriptive in nature. That is, writers on this subject usually note the differences and then only attempt to account for these differences in a superficial way. Paul Weiss is one of the few if not the only writer who speculates on *why* women have participated in sport in a limited manner.

Men are able to live in their bodies only if they are taught and trained to turn their minds into bodily vectors. And they can become excellent in and through their bodies, only if they learn to identify themselves with their bodies and what these do. Normal women do not have this problem, at least not in the acute form that it presents to the men. A woman's biological growth is part of a larger process in which, without training or deliberation, she progressively becomes one with her body. What a man might accomplish through will and practice after he has entered on his last period of biological growth, she achieves through a process of bodily maturation. By the time she passes adolescence she is able to live her body somewhat the way in which a male athlete lives his.

. . . A woman, therefore, will typically interest herself in sport when she sees that it will enable her to polish what she had previously acquired without thought or effort.[9]

---

[8]E. F. Zeigler, *Philosophical Foundations for Physical, Health, and Recreation Education* © 1964, pp. 270–271. Reprinted by permission of Prentice-Hall, Inc., Englewood Cliffs, New Jersey.
[9]Paul Weiss, *Sport: A Philosophic Inquiry* (Carbondale, Ill.: Southern Illinois University Press, 1969), pp. 217–218.

We would imagine that most people's initial reaction to Weiss' thought would be that this is a wild, far-out idea which would appeal only to speculative philosophers. Yet, his conjecture should not be so summarily desregarded. At least this much can be said: we have little, if any, scientific evidence on the subject. Paul Weiss has ventured to offer something which is thought-provoking. It may well serve to stimulate other people to think seriously about sport participation for women without merely accepting the status quo or deploring the differences which are noted.

Weiss has left himself wide open for criticism, but this was probably his intent. Speculative philosophers are inclined to engage in generalities. He tends to generalize regarding the sexes. It may be that there are differences among the members of a sex which are just as striking in noting their sport participation. Several interesting questions emerge: Are we to assume that those males who are less interested in active sport participation are more like women in that they turn their minds into bodily vectors in a more natural way? If Weiss' last assumption is correct, would not women be first and foremost attracted to highly competitive sport (athletics)? What of the social determinant? Weiss' thesis seems to be entirely based on the biological differences between males and females. Would one have to assume that a male must be a highly competitive athlete, rather than a casual sportsman, in order to achieve bodily maturity?

Regardless of these questions, it is high time that someone began to critically probe the reasons which lie back of the dual standard of sport involvement for men and women. It may take someone outside the physical education profession (such as Paul Weiss, a philosopher) to raise issues which are frequently overlooked amidst the practical problems of an administrative nature. For example, the very fact that we find so many separate departments of men's and women's physical education is almost bound to color some of the professional thinking as to what ought to be and why it is as it is.

THE INTEREST FACTOR AS THE DETERMINANT

We wish to conclude our discussion of the "who" in sport by "going out on the limb a bit" ourselves. Our treatise is built on the proposition that too much has been made of this question. The reader may then ask: why have you devoted an entire chapter to the subject? This has been done to explicate the diversified thinking regarding the "who" in sport. Unfortunately, this split thinking also has the effect of causing this question to overshadow more significant philosophical questions. When we look at organizational structures and read the reports which come from those involved with these structures, we are commonly led to believe that sport must be assessed in terms of amateur vs. professional, promotion vs. nonpromotion, and male vs. female. We are convinced that perpetuation of these concerns can only lead to further confusion regarding the true nature and purpose of sport.

What is there to suggest as a replacement from a positive point of view? Our answer may be rejected as being too elementary, but we suspect that the overriding determinant should be the *interest* factor. How would this interest factor be manifested?

In the case of the professional or would-be professional, let the young man or woman receive money for participating, provided he or she realizes the obligations involved and is interested for reasons other than the game itself. By the same token, an institution should not feel obliged to conduct its business in a hypocritical manner by offering an intense athletic program under the guise of sport. There is nothing wrong with "big time" athletics in college if that is what the institutions involved desire.

As far as sport promotion goes, we are sometimes obsessed with the notion that sport is the special province of certain groups. Physical educators are a dramatic case in point. One can frequently hear a physical educator suggest that some person should not be teaching or conducting a sport program because he has not been professionally prepared as a physical educator. That, in our opinion, is utter and pure nonsense! How can any one group claim sport as only their province? It would seem more reasonable to suggest that sport may and should be conducted and promoted by any group or individual who is interested and qualified. Further, we assume that such promotional efforts will usually fail if the individual or group is not qualified. So, we are again left with the interest factor as the number one determinant.

Above all other considerations, the interest factor should be the guide in organizing and conducting sport programs for women. We basically concur with Zeigler's idea that all persons should have full and equal opportunity for a competitive sport experience, if that is what they desire. We also suspect that for social reasons there will be relatively fewer females who will choose to pursue sport at the level of intense competition. It will probably also prove true that the women will tend to select and focus on somewhat different sport activities than the men, although there will be several common selections. But, above all else, we should fully let interest be the guide. When we continue to require attendance in "gym" classes under antiquated departments of men and women's physical education, we refuse to give the interest principle a chance to be implemented. At such time as men and women, boys and girls, have the opportunity to select and participate in sport according to their interests, we may know more about *why* there are sexual differences in the extent and type of sport participation.

BIBLIOGRAPHY

Beisser, Arnold, *The Madness in Sports*. New York: Appleton-Century-Crofts, 1967.

Flath, Arnold, *A History of Relations Between the National Collegiate Athletic Association and the Amateur Athletic Union of the United States (1905—1963)*. Champaign, Ill.: Stipes Publishing Co., 1964.

Hetherington, Clark W., "The Foundation of Amateurism," *American Physical Education Review*, 566—578, November, 1909.

Keating, James, "The Heart of the Problem of Amateur Athletics," *The Journal of General Education*, 16, No. 4, January, 1965.

Lee, Mabel, "The Case For and Against Intercollegiate Athletics for Women and the Situation Since 1923," *The Research Quarterly of the American Physical Education Association*, Vol. 2, 93—127, May, 1931.

Madlem, Leo, "Athletics In a Young Man's Life," *Proceedings*, 39th Annual Meeting, American Football Coaches Association, Chicago, Ill., January, 1962.

Weiss, Paul, *Sport: A Philosophic Inquiry*. Carbondale: Southern Illinois University Press, 1969.

Zeigler, Earle, *Philosophical Foundations for Physical, Health, and Recreation Education*. Englewood Cliffs, N.J.: Prentice-Hall, Inc., 1964.

Zeigler, Earle, *Problem In The History and Philosophy of Physical Education and Sport*. Englewood Cliffs, N.J.: Prentice-Hall, Inc., 1968.

4/Sport: What?

In the second chapter we noted that sport is a varied and elusive concept in terms of its historical origins and development. Yet, sport is also part of everyday parlance. Most people have some understanding of sport even if they have not analyzed the many ambiguities which are involved with the concept.

Probably the most confusing aspect of sport is its relationship to similar concepts. We noted that physical education is one of these related concepts. Unfortunately, analysis of the concept of physical education only adds to the vagueness which initiates discussion of sport.

There are at least three other concepts, inextricably related to sport, which may be of greater assistance in bringing the concept of sport in clearer focus. These are play, games, and athletics. In fact, it is quite difficult to talk about sport without getting involved with a consideration of play, games, or athletics, either singly or in combination.

Of the four concepts under consideration in this chapter, play is the most general and the most basic. Sport derives its central value from play. Games are a form of play. Athletics is an extension of sport. However, all is not as simple as it first appears. For example, games are found in play, sport, and athletics. From that one could conclude that games are the most basic and general in comparison with the other concepts. We are also faced with the perplexing fact that we are using sport as our focal concept. Therefore, considerable analysis of play, games, and athletics is required before we can begin to determine the nature of sport and the relationships among sport and the other three concepts.

SPORT CONTRASTED WITH PLAY

THE NATURE OF PLAY

But what is meant by *mere play*, when we know that in all conditions of humanity that very thing is play, and only that is play which makes man complete and develops simultaneously his two-fold nature?

For, to speak out once for all, man only plays when in the full meaning of the word he is a man, and *he is only a man when he plays.*[1]

If von Schiller was anywhere close to being correct in his value assessment of play, we are examining a concept of great importance for man's potential in life. What is there about play which makes it essential for a human's well being?

One's initial reaction is to contrast play with work. The latter is usually considered to be a productive enterprise which provides man with a livelihood. Work is customarily considered as a serious endeavor. Likewise, people usually work with an ulterior purpose in mind. Often, the purpose is to make money.

A simple conclusion would be to say that people play when they are not working. But such a generalization is fraught with many pitfalls. Elements of play may take place during the period of time when man is supposedly engaged in work. More importantly, what is work to one individual may be play to another. There is still a further complication which is exemplified in the work of the professional person, who derives considerable pleasure from his work. For this person, his work and play could be virtually the same.

It seems reasonable to suggest that play should not be sharply contrasted with work. As is true with many comparisons, the continuum approach seems more appropriate. Play and work may be placed on opposite ends of a continuum with the understanding that the vast majority of situations lie somewhere between, being neither purely play nor purely work.

$$Play \longleftarrow \hspace{5cm} \longrightarrow Work$$

Under this simple frame of reference, play and work are sharply contrasted but allowances are made for individual differences both among people and situations. For many people there may not always be a clear-cut distinction between their work and their play. Likewise, many situations may contain elements of both work and play found in various combinations.

If play is something which is essentially different from work, what, then, are the characteristics of play? We will begin with the assumption that play is an activity and/or a state of mind which is better recognized or experienced than described. Everyone has observed young children in the spontaneous movements of running, skipping, jumping, rolling, and climbing. They appear to engage in these activities without any particular purpose in mind. Furthermore, the activities seem to be performed without predetermined structure. The word frolic is often used to describe the basic play activities of a child. We also observe that these children are completely absorbed by their play activities. Adults may come and go from the scene but the play continues without interruption and apparently with little conscious recognition that the play has been observed.

---

[1]J. C. Friedrich von Schiller, *Letter on Aesthetic Education*, ed. C. W. Eliot (New York: P. F. Collier & Sons, 1910), p. 266.

As adults, we have also experienced that which we call play. Sometimes when we have decided to play, we find that we are unable to do so. We may be going through the motions of what is commonly considered play, but we find that we are unable to transfer our thoughts to the play spirit. Our minds continue to be occupied with problems and tasks of the work-side of our lives. From this we would have to conclude that play is something more than an activity.

Adults have also found that plans and preparation for play do not necessarily enhance their realizing the potential of playing or increase the values which they derive from the play. To the contrary, planning and preparation seem to serve more as deterrents to play. One can much more easily plan the time to play than he can plan the play. It may be said that true play is unpredictable both in terms of its form and its results.

There is a common tendency to equate play with fun or pleasure. However, if one were to compare play with other activities or states of life, this would assume that only play can be fun or pleasure. Such would not seem to be the case when we observe people who derive pleasure from their work.

Another popular idea has been to search for reasons why people play. Several theories have been postulated and argued over the years. Friedrich von Schiller saw play as being the aimless expenditure of exuberant energy. This has become known as the "surplus energy" theory. Superficially, the theory seems to have merit until one realizes that it implies activity, or perhaps, even vigorous activity. There must be more passive forms of play which do not result in the release of exuberant energy.

The German educator Guts Muths stressed that people play in order to recuperate and revitalize themselves. To him, recreation was play. By contrast with Schiller, he was inclined to view play in a broader context. Although it is a difficult matter to pinpoint, one would almost have to conclude that recreation includes many factors and conditions other than play. It seems more appropriate to say that play is a form of recreation.

One of the most widely discussed theories of play has been the "instinct theory" as presented by Karl Groos. He followed a common pattern early in this century in searching for a biological reason to explain human behavior, at the same time making the comparison with animal behavior generally. In simple terms Groos felt that all animals, including man, play because of natural instincts. These instincts are designed to prepare the young for adulthood. He pointed out the similarities between the play activities of the young and the work of adults. One obvious weakness of this theory is that if fails to account for adult play. In the strictest interpretation, the conclusion could be reached that we arrive at a stage wherein play is no longer necessary.

A closely related theory is G. Stanley Hall's "re-capitulation theory." According to Hall, people play because it is the natural thing to do in light of the activities of previous generations. At one time man hunted for survival. Therefore it is not at all surprising to find children playing hunting games. The oversimplification of this theory resembles the problems inherent in Groos' "instinct theory."

Other explanations as to why people play have also been presented over the years. In general these theories tend to resemble those which have been presented above. The only conclusion which can actually be drawn is that all theories which attempt to explain the basis for play tend to be speculative. We lack scientific evidence in this regard. Furthermore, such evidence may never be attained. If Riesman is correct in his assumption, we should not deplore our lack of knowledge about play. The reader will recall from the statement found in the preface of this book that Riesman feels it may actually be preferable to maintain a "conspiracy of silence" about play. At any rate, the one thing we can say about the nature of play is that it is an activity and/or state of mind which exists without anyone knowing why it exists.

SPORT AS AN EXTENSION OF PLAY

In his excellent paper, Kenneth Schmitz[2] set forth the idea that sport is an extension of play. This is the most succinct and descriptive differentiation between sport and play which we have encountered to date. According to Schmitz, sport "derives its central values from play." This may be interpreted to mean that sport at least has its origins with a playfullike spirit. As sport becomes more organized some of the play characteristics tend to disappear or become less apparent.

When sport is considered as an extension of play, the continuum effect is again evident:

$$\text{Play} \longleftarrow \hspace{4cm} \longrightarrow \text{Sport}$$

Similar to the comparison between play and work, this conveys the idea that many activities cannot be classified as being either purely play or purely sport. To some extent they may be more playlike. On the other hand, they also resemble that which we call sport. At the same time, it must be noted that sport is considerably more similar to play than play is to work. To that extent the two continua cannot be compared.

Later in his paper Schmitz seems to be guilty of internal inconsistency when he discusses the varieties of play as he sees them. The varieties he describes are "frolic, make-believe, sporting skills, and games." A question immediately emerges: if sport is an extension of play, how can sporting skills be a variety or form of play? Examples of sporting skills cited by Schmitz are surf-boarding, sailing, horseback-riding, mountain climbing, and hiking. These examples help to explain why he can at the same time view sport as an extension of play

---

[2] Kenneth Schmitz, "Sport and Play: Suspension of the Ordinary," Unpublished paper delivered at the 13th Annual Meeting of The American Association for the Advancement of Science, Dallas, Texas, Dec. 28, 1968.

and sporting skills as a variety of play. Sporting skills are not the same as sport, in the full meaning of that concept. Schmitz's varieties of play can also be projected on a continuum to show the differences involved between play and sport:

Frolic $\longleftarrow$ ————————————————————————————— $\longrightarrow$ Games
$\qquad\qquad$ Make-believe $\qquad\qquad$ Sporting skills

As we move along this continuum from left to right, the activity tends to be more structured. Frolic is obviously the least formal and most spontaneous. Make-believe, such as found at the costume party, is somewhat less so. Then, in terms of formality, there is quite a jump from make-believe to sporting skills. This formality is found primarily in the fact that there is a standardization of knowledge, skill, and, sometimes, etiquette which is not evident in the same way in frolic and make-believe play.

Games are even more formal because rules predominate. When one reaches the "games" end of the play spectrum, he has moved a far distance along the extension from play to sport. In fact the extension is sufficient enough to cause one to initially believe that games are virtually synonymous with sport. However, John Loy adds an important point of differentiation between games in general and sport as a particular form of game occurrence. He states: "We observe that sports can be distinguished from games by the fact that they demand the demonstration of physical prowess."[3]

The analysis of games cannot be simply dismissed by classifying them as a variety play. Games are fully as complex a concept as play, sport, and athletics. However, we will withhold further discussion of games as a concept at this point because there are still other factors to be considered in contrasting sport with play.

FACTORS WHICH TEND TO DETRACT FROM THE PLAYFUL CHARACTERISTICS OF SPORT

For our frame of reference here we are also indebted to Kenneth Schmitz through the thoughts in his paper. One of the factors which causes sport to be an extension of play is that certain things occur in sport which conflict with the pure spirit of play. Schmitz labels these differences in sport as abuses. He says that they "kill the spirit of play within sport and reduce sport to something less than its fullest human possibilities." We can agree with only part of his evaluation. There seems to be little doubt that these factors do work toward killing the spirit of play within sport. To call these factors abuses and to say that they "reduce sport to something less than its fullest human possibilities" is a value judgment with which we do not concur. Sport may be an extension of play because of these factors, but, at the same time sport can be legitimate in its own right.

---

[3] John W. Loy, "The Nature of Sport: A Definitional Effort," *Quest*, X, 6, May 1968.

The three so-called "abuses" as seen by Schmitz are (1) exaggeration of the importance of victory, (2) rationalization of techniques when promoted by an exaggerated sense of the value of efficiency, and (3) the presence of spectators. Each of these "abuses" or factors requires further analysis, based on both Schmitz's discussion of them and other ideas which seem germane.

It is true that the competition element of sport calls attention to the importance of victory whereas victory and defeat are not even evident in many other forms of play. Thus, there is some direct correlation between sport and victory. But many forms of sport do not manifest themselves in an *exaggeration* of the importance of victory. The exaggeration seems to primarily occur in very highly organized sport, which we prefer to call "athletics." Later in this chapter we will present the case for the idea that athletics is an extension of sport where exaggeration of the importance of victory actually takes place. Even then, such exaggeration need not necessarily be an abuse.

Sport, as a broader concept than athletics, places more of a premium on performance and striving to win when a contest is involved. Intramural sport within the schools affords an excellent example of what we have in mind. These programs offer numerous opportunities for competition. Participants are interested in improved performance, and they strive to win. However, in the vast majority of cases it would be unfair to say that the importance of victory has been exaggerated. If that were true there would be considerably more preparation for the contests. Likewise, the results of these contests would receive much more publicity than is evident.

Other forms of sport even more strongly exemplify the idea that victory is not exaggerated in sport. We will take skiing as an example of another kind of sporting activity in which winning is of even less importance than it is in the intramural basketball program in the schools. Schmitz might argue that skiing is a sport skill, not a sport, and that skiing must be considered as a variety of play. We prefer to take a contrary point of view because of the institutionalization which surrounds skiing. Skiing has its beginnings or inception as a sport skill just as sport, generally, has its genesis in play. After individuals acquire some skill in skiing, they gradually move toward more advanced slopes where they test their ability along with others who have moved beyond the beginner's stage. Frequently, there is no formal competition as such among the individuals who ski. However, the people involved more and more identify themselves with other skiers in terms of comparing levels of performance, equipment and dress, and general, social orientation. A code of etiquette and a particular kind of social structure surrounds the sport of skiing. Skiers have moved beyond the simple sport-skill stage as a variety of play. The vast majority of skiers may never actually compete against others in formal competition. Therefore, it would not be valid to say that there is a premium on victory.

Among the factors under consideration, rationalization of techniques is probably more characteristic of sport than is true of the other two factors. Again, we would not label this factor an "abuse" as Schmitz does. He is primarily referring to coaching techniques in which the athlete is subjected to "an uninterrupted drive for limitless proficiency." Even that may not be an abuse for athletics; it all depends on one's value judgment. But there is another aspect of rationalization of techniques, found in sport, which may more clearly exemplify how this factor tends to distract from the playful characteristics of sport. A true story may illustrate what we have in mind.

Several years ago a friend of mine, who is also a physical educator, played a round of golf with another physical educator who had established quite a name in the profession as a research professor. Among the latter's research interests was kinesiology or the analysis of human movements. My friend had played golf for a few years and was a "good" golfer, regularly shooting somewhere in the '80s. Ostensibly, they went out to *play* golf, that is to engage in a pure form of recreation. All started well on the first tee. Both men were reasonably successful with their drives and played the hole in a standard manner. Beginning with the second tee, the researcher began to analyze his companion's golf swing. This continued more or less for 18 holes. By the time they reached the 18th hole my friend could barely hit the ball. He was thinking so much about the mechanics of the swing that he was unable to employ those techniques which he customarily employed quite well in a "natural" sort of way.

This story, humorous as it may seem to some, reveals a principle which is pertinent to our discussion of sport in this context. One can rationalize himself or literally be rationalized out of playful existence. In the case cited there was no bad intent involved. Also there was no premium or victory, such as if they were playing for money or in a tournament. It was a casual afternoon of golf, but the extension from play to sport was partially manifested.

Similar situations occur everyday in other areas of sport. We may look at "little league" baseball as another example. Most boys learn to play baseball in the backyard or on the neighborhood lot. In a spontaneous and unstructured manner they meet with other boys with only one purpose in mind — to play the game. At that point they are relatively unconcerned about an analysis of the specific skills involved. A couple of years later they may report for their first "little league" practice session. They are told what to do, how to do it, and the key points involved. Frequently, the coach will attempt to modify habits which are not considered to be most efficient for a particular skill, such as hitting. Once again, the transition from play to sport is evident.

We do not mean to infer that such rationalization of techniques must necessarily be viewed negatively. It all depends on the purposes of the individual and the group. The golfer might benefit in subsequent rounds of play from the analysis of his swing even though this temporarily led to frustration because it suspended him from the playfullike spirit associated with his "natural" swing. Similarly, the "little league" baseball player may well improve his hitting by following the kinesthetic cues of his coach. Much of the spontaneity associated with play will be lost, but the boy has made the accomodation to sport wherein he also obtains pleasure from a more structured activity and one where rationalization of techniques occupies some importance.

The presence of spectators is not particularly characteristic of sport if one makes the distinction between sport and athletics. On the other hand, sport activities may be observed by spectators just as the play of children and adults does not always occur in private. We may watch children frolicking in the yard. Such observation may be quite casual, but in the broadest sense of the term we are spectators. Adults may also look on while other adults play a game of cards. Thus, the presence and importance of spectators seems to be one largely of degree. As we move along the continuum from play to sport to athletics, the presence of spectators seems to occupy increasing importance. In play, the appearance of spectators is most incidental. Sport tends to be somewhat more attractive to spectators. Athletics is geared first and foremost to attracting and pleasing spectators.

There is truth in Schmitz's idea that the presence of spectators does tend to distract from the pure spirit of play. This is particularly evident when the participants are adults. Children seem to be relatively less affected in their play when others watch them. Adults are more conscious of social expectations. An example may again assist in illustrating that the presence of spectators does tend to distract from the playful characteristics of sport even though it does not resemble the magnitude and role of spectators in athletics.

Most colleges and universities find that touch football is among the more popular activities in their intramural sport program for young men. Leagues are usually formed, consisting of fraternity, residence hall, or other units of competition. When there are fraternities on campus, the touch football competition among the fraternity teams is likely to be very keen. For this reason, spectators; including fraternity brothers, girl-friends, and others attracted to the contests. When this occurs some of the original play element of the game of touch football had been lost. It is not an abuse; the intramural touch football game is no less significant than the casual playing of touch football on a "pickup" basis; but the game has acquired a new dimension because spectators appeared. The transition from play to sport has been partially accomodated.

SPORT CONTRASTED WITH GAMES

GAMES AS A VARIETY OF PLAY

Loy defines a game "as any form of playful competition whose outcome is determined by physical skill, strategy, or chance employed singly or in combination."[4] In the notes of his article he also states that "this definition is based largely on the

---

[4]*Ibid.*, p. 1

work of Caillois (1961) and Roberts and others (1959). Other definitions and classifications of games having social import are given in Berne (1964) and Piaget (1951)."[5]

There are numerous other ways in which games can be described, and several characteristics of games may be noted. A game is a form of contest. From one standpoint the latter is a broader concept because individuals may also contest through media other than games. In most games rules predominate. Rules are probably the one thing which most clearly distinguish games from other varieties of play and other forms of contests. At some point in time, rules are determined by agreement of those parties who are either promoting the game or participating in the game. Contestants enter the game with a general acceptance of the rules, be this conscious or subconscious. To a certain extent, game rules differ from other kinds of rules which one may encounter in life; game rules exist under the condition that they apply as long as one remains in the game. At any time the participant may leave the game and no longer be subjected to the rules. This is partially due to the fact that the space and time of a game are not contiguous with the space and time of the broader environment in which the game occurs.

Prior to the game, the participants or their representatives may meet to either establish the rules or review the rules. The latter is evident when the managers or team captains meet at homeplate with the umpires prior to the start of a baseball game. This usually amounts to a brief review of the "ground" rules which are applicable to the particular park (a game limitation of space). However, the discussion could also include a game limitation of time, such as no inning will start after a certain time because of a curfew or to permit one of the teams to meet a travel reservation. The participants mutually agree to abide by these rules as a condition of the games.

On a much more informal level the same kind of situation exists each day on the playground when boys and girls organize a "pickup" game. Sometimes they may make up a game, originating the rules right on the spot. Other times they may modify the rules of an established game to meet their own interests or conditions of their immediate environment. At any rate, they either casually or quite directly agree to live by the rules. During the course of the game one of the boys or girls may suddenly and arbitrarily decide to leave the game for any one of several reasons. When this occurs the game may continue, but the player who leaves is immediately freed from any conditions involving the rules of the game.

Schmitz describes very well the structured order of games and how this sets off games from the environment in which they take place:

The structured order of play-space is especially evident in those games in which a single point or double point in the play-space is the key to the contest, the privileged

---

[5] *Ibid.*, p. 14.

space of the goals, target, or finishing line. So, too, play-time is not contiguous with ordinary time, though it must frequently bow to it. In ice-hockey sixty minutes of play-time are not sixty minutes of clock-time, and in baseball play-time is simply nine innings or more. Of course, natural space and time are the alien boundaries that ring about the mark the finitude of human play, but the play has its own internal boundaries set by the objectives and rules of the game.[6]

Although Schmitz is describing play generally, one cannot help but note that his comments particularly apply to games, as a variety of play. The rules of games tend to make them much more structured than other forms of play, not only in terms of space and time but also with regard to the total conduct of the activity.

With regard to structure, a spectrum is also evident within games themselves. An adult game of bridge is an example of one extreme where the entire game is played amidst a series of patterns and predetermined moves. The novice bridge player soon learns that he is handicapped if he departs too severely from those guidelines which have been tried and found true. Generally speaking, children's games are much more pliable. The latitude is manifested in the relative freedom of entry to and exit from the game. Spatial arrangements are not usually as binding, and the rules may not be as restrictive.

Brian Sutton-Smith made some interesting observations on the relationship among games, play, and daydreams. He noted that games are the most formalized of the three. Games are recreative, but they also have rules, sides, competition, and winners. Probably the most significant aspect of Sutton-Smith's work was to call attention to the artifactual nature of games. He found that games are artifacts of human culture; some cultures have no games. In his work with Roberts it was also noted that there are cultural comparisons involving games of physical skill, chance, and strategy:

Briefly what we found was that each of these types of games existed in a distinctive cultural complex. Games of physical skill were essential parts of simple hunting and gathering cultures; games of chance were found in cultures where divinatory procedures were used to overcome basic survival uncertainties; and games of strategy were present in cultures with military classes, complex technology, and diplomacy. It was not hard for us to argue that in each case the game was a model of some of the essential functions in the culture of which it was a part.[7]

Sutton-Smith made the point that games have sides and are competitive. We earlier noted that games are a form of contest. There seems to be little doubt that games and contests share the common denominator of being competitive. One difference between games and other forms of contests may actually revolve around the matter of sides in a game. Needless to say, sides are not a necessary

---

[6]Schmitz, op. cit., pp. 11—12.

[7]Brian Sutton-Smith, "Games-Play-Daydreams," Quest X, 49—50, May 1968.

condition for a contest. What of games? We commonly refer to the game of solitaire. Webster defines solitaire as a game which one person can play alone, applied to many card games. Thus, it seems plausible that solitaire is actually not a game in the precise meaning of that concept.

Games have sometimes been contrasted with contests by suggesting that games are more complex. This complexity includes elements of strategy, deception, and unexpected situations. This kind of thinking could lead one to conclude that something like archery is merely a contest because there is relatively little in the way of strategy and unusual developments. However, when one competes against another in archery it seems more useful to call it a game because sides are involved and there may be strategy employed even though it will seem minute compared to the strategy of other games, such as football. In summary it seems appropriate to say that games are a form of contest involving sides. On the other hand, various forms of contest also take place within and during the period of the game.

SPORT AS A GAME OCCURRENCE

Loy describes very well the idea that sport may be viewed as a particular kind of game occurrence:

Perhaps most often when we think of the meaning of sport, we think of sports. In our perspective sports are considered as a specialized type of game. That is, a sport as one of the many "sports" is viewed as an actual game occurrence or event. Thus in succeeding paragraphs we shall briefly outline what we consider to be the basic characteristics of games in general. In describing these characteristics we shall continually make reference to sports in particular as a special type of game.[8]

Later in this article he proceeds to discuss the other forms of sport as an institutionalized game, a social institution, and a social situation or social system. Although it is useful to consider these other manifestations of sport, the subject of sport as a game occurrence is the one which holds special meaning for our discussion of sport in this context. Earlier in this chapter we noted that he singles out physical prowess as being the one characteristic which distinguishes sport from other kinds of games.

This particular distinction has considerable merit when one realizes that the word "prowess" permits a latitude of interpretation. Physical prowess is not necessarily restricted to vigorous physical activity. In other words, complex physical skills may also be connoted by the term "prowess." This permits such activities as bowling and golf to qualify as games of sport even though they may not be vigorous in the same way and to the same extent that other sports are vigorous.

---

[8]Loy, *op. cit.*, p. 11.

Fogelin discusses the physical dimension of sport in a similar manner:

To put matters simply, bridge and chess seem somehow too cerebral to count as sports. A sport, it seems, must be a contest involving the exhibition of physical strength, speed, endurance, or other forms of prowess. If we dwell upon the physical aspect of sports, we then see why horse racing is closely connected with, say, tennis in a way that chess is not. This brings to the fore a fact that we can easily overlook; a sport need not exhibit the physical prowess of a human body.[9]

His extension of physical prowess beyond the human realm may initially seem strange and even ridiculous to some. However, his further discussion tends to show that the thought has consistency and merits consideration from that standpoint. Horse racing is an interesting kind of case because it demands physical prowess both by the horse and the jockey. Fogelin's example of a dog show is more extreme. Here one would have to stretch his imagination to say that there is any physical prowess displayed by the owner of the dog. But as Fogelin states "if dog shows were simply canine beauty contests, they would not appear on the sports pages." His purpose in using the example of dog shows was really to demonstrate that we cannot easily and simply divide activities into those which are sport and those which are not sport. Nevertheless, the physical dimension of sport emerges clearly and consistently in comparing this enterprise with other kinds of games.

This interest in delineating the characteristics of sport is by no means limited to present-day concerns. Graves commented on this matter more than 70 years ago.

To begin with, we find that one of the commonest meanings of the word is that of a physical, as distinct from a purely intellectual, recreation. In this sense it is held to cover such non-competitive recreations as hunting, fishing, mountaineering, and the like, together with such competitive recreations as horse-racing, running, cricket, football, in fact all outdoor games. But the words "physical recreation" will hardly serve as a definition of sport. For then we should be compelled to include amateur gardening, which I think no one would be sufficiently daring to class among sports, except, perhaps, in its competitive aspect at flower shows and the like—a form of gardening in which the physical aspect of the recreation is most subordinated to the intellectual. Nor do we get any nearer to a solution by adding the word "competitive" to our definition. For this would compel us to exclude hunting, fishing and the like, none of which recreations are essentially competitive.[10]

When we view sport as being a game occurrence it excludes such activities as hunting, fishing, and mountaineering which Graves preferred to

---

[9]Robert Fogelin, "Sport: The Diversity of the Concept." Unpublished paper delivered at the 13th Annual Meeting of the American Association for the Advancement of Science, Dallas, Texas, Dec. 28, 1968. Reprinted by permission of the author.

[10]H. Graves, "A Philosophy of Sport" *Contemporary Review*, 78 (Dec., 1900), p. 878.

include under his broader conception of sport. Games of sport are marked by spatial and temporal limitations; they are controlled by rules; they are competitive; and they do include the demonstration of physical prowess in some form or another. This leads us to a final observation in contrasting sport with games: one should recognize and understand the difference between sport skills and games.

SPORT SKILLS AS DISTINGUISHED FROM GAMES

Earlier we noted that Schmitz made the differentiation between sporting skills and games, while including them both as two of the four varieties of play. The distinction seems to have merit but requires a more careful analysis before it will be meaningful to the casual observer.

We begin with the generalization that most sport skills lead up to one or more games of sport. This is based on the assumption that individuals usually have some practice in the skills of a particular sport before they participate in the sport as a game. Thus, as an example, a boy learns to dribble and shoot the basketball before he plays a game of basketball.

Some variance from this generalization can be noted, depending largely on the nature of certain sports. Bowling may be cited as a case in point. We have observed that people often move directly into the game of bowling without prior exposure to or practice of the skills. Other, less extreme, examples could also be cited. But these appear to be more the exceptions than the rule.

Often it is not merely a matter of either sport skills or the game in the sport. A modified and lesser form of *the* game may be involved. Backyard volleyball could be considered as a minor version of *the* game of volleyball. Halfcourt basketball, frequently involving two or three players on a side, closely resembles but is not the same as *the* game of basketball. People may actually compete against one another in tennis without following the prescriptions of set and match play associated with *the* game of tennis. Many modified forms of *the* game of golf can be observed on the course as casual golfers compete somewhat less formally. Almost every sport offers similar examples. Children, in particular, are frequently engaged in playing these modified varieties of *the* game.

On the other hand, Schmitz's classification seems to imply that certain sport skills are seldom or never found in the game form. Those which he specifically lists are surf-boarding, sailing, horse-riding, mountain-climbing, and hiking. We would agree that these are valid examples because they are not generally manifested in the game form. However, in each case the point could be stretched so that the skill can be observed in a situation which at least approximates a game. Aside from physical prowess, as noted earlier, the characteristics of games include rules, competition, and spatial as well as temporal limitations. With the examples under consideration physical prowess is most evident in one form or another. Each can also be competitive, although hiking looms as the most tenuous in terms of this criterion. Nevertheless, even hiking may be displayed as a walking race in which there is no question about the inclusion of competition. Walking races are not very popular today, but the sport historian, Guy Lewis, has reported that this type of competition was in vogue at the end of the last century, particularly among women.[11]

Spatial and temporal limitations vary considerably in terms of restrictiveness among games. Football offers an extreme with its one hundred yard field and sixty minutes of playing time. Other games tend to be less restrictive either from a time and/or space limitation. On a continuum or relative scale of things we might say that both space and time tend to be less significant in surf-boarding, sailing, horse-riding, mountain-climbing, and hiking. Yet, the reader will also recognize that there is variance even among these activities, and some limitation of space and time may well be prescribed in each.

As far as rules are concerned they tend to go somewhat hand in hand with competition. The latter usually dictates the former; rules offer guidelines for the competition. Therefore, we may also expect to find rules in those sport skills which develop into or at least approximate the game form. The difference, again, will more likely be one of degree. A continuum effect is once more evident when we compare sport skills with games:

Sport skills $\longleftarrow$ ——— Hiking ——— Sailing ——— Golf ——— Football ——— $\longrightarrow$ Games

This continuum implies that there is a wide variance among sport skills in terms of their adaptability to a game format. As we move along the continuum from left to right we noted the probability increase of finding the sport skills in the form of a game. Also, the games on the right tend to be more highly structured than those on the left.

Thus, it would appear that the principal difference between a sport skill and a game is one of degree, with structure being at the core of the difference. *The* game is a structured event which is marked by certain traditions and procedures. What actually happens is that a game becomes more meaningful as a game over an extended period of time. Some games come and go. Others are modified through the years as a result of rules changes. Occasionally, there may be marked changes in the rules which cause the game to assume an entirely different structure. But that which we call *the game* is characterized by a code of conduct, both written and unwritten, which sets it off from other games, be they similar or altogether different.

The game of squash racquets may be used to illustrate this point. To begin with there is an obvious similarity between squash and other racquet games. Common elements can be observed in some of the skills of squash, tennis, paddleball, paddletennis, and badminton. However, part of the uniqueness of squash lies in the fact that there are certain skills which are peculiar to squash.

---

[11]Guy M. Lewis, "The Ladies Walked and Walked," *Sports Illustrated*, 27, Dec. 18, 1967, R 3–4.

Secondly, the rules of squash, although comparable to those of other racquet games, are not identical to those games. A third factor, and possibly the most significant in distinguishing it as a game, is also evident. This factor includes several aspects but can be summarized under what might be called the customs and traditions which surround the game. These customs and traditions evolve partly from the skills and rules, but certain other, less tangible, factors also habituate themselves over a course of time. Part of this is a matter of etiquette; another facet involves the strategy of the game.

To a certain extent strategy is dictated by the rules and skills, but a player may follow the rules, have the basic skills, and still be relatively deficient in strategy in comparison with other players who have more experience and/or possess greater insight into the game. Thus, we can safely say that the game of squash racquets consists of more than skills and rules; it is not rules alone which mark the delineation between sport skills and a game.

Paul Weiss offers a fairly complete and, yet, succinct description of "the game" in Chapter 10 of his book. Those who have carefully studied his work will recall that this is a most significant chapter in his treatise because the game is the one place where the relative excellence of the athlete is tested. Everything else in sport and/or athletics is either preparatory to the game or is an aftermath of the game. We can readily see that many sport skills lack real significance until they are displayed in the context of the game. The aftermath of the game will also reveal that the execution of specific skills tends to be forgotten amidst the total impression of the game. In short, there is a gestalt aspect of the game which defies precise definition.

When Weiss makes the point that the game offers the test he hits at the crux of a major distinction between sport skills and a game in that sport. Numerous examples can be cited of potentially fine athletes who possess all the skills but for some reason or another do not produce in the game. We have frequently heard tennis coaches comment that a certain player possesses all the strokes (has good form) and, yet, does not win consistently because he "falls apart" in the game. This so-called "falling apart" results in some way from being unable to cope with the intangibles of the game which extend beyond the skills and rules. It may be attributed to strategical errors; emotions are often a factor; or it could be that the player lacks the necessary insight which the game demands due to its gestalt nature.

On the other side of the coin we can also observe and encounter the player who seems to be relatively weak in terms of sport-skill ability, but the game is the thing for him. During the warm-up no one may be impressed with the individual, but once the whistle blows everything changes. Similarly, such individuals may appear relatively less capable in practice sessions, and they do not make the starting line-up. The "game" player enters the line-up and immediately responds by reacting to the situation at hand. Each year this sort of scene is reenacted in athletic contests.

To be somewhat more specific on this point each of us has observed a basketball player who seems to be at the right place at the right time. He may not be able to jump as high as others; he may not be as quick and agile; but when the ball comes off the board he is there to grab it. Such a player has a sense of the game which goes beyond sport skills per se. Weiss' discussion of the dynamics of the game offers a description of the area wherein the game is unique as a testing ground:

Each game has its own dynamics. There unit act is followed by unit act. Those acts exist only in the game. The parts of the act are inseparable from it though they can be conceptually separated out, and even learned and practiced as moves and acts having indivisible unities of their own. . . .

In sport the largest present is the present of the game. In this we can isolate plays and moves only conceptually. The bunt and any other play is an organic, integral factor in the present indivisible whole of the game.[12]

SPORT CONTRASTED WITH ATHLETICS

THE COMMON IDEA

No player, manager, director or fan who understands football, either through his intellect or his nerve-ends, ever repeats that piece of nonsense "after all, it's only a game." It has not been only a game for 80 years, not since the working classes saw in it an escape route out of drudgery and claimed it as their own. What happens on the football field matters, not in the way that food matters but as poetry does to some people and alcohol does to others: it engages the personality. It has conflict and beauty, and when these two qualities are present together in something offered for public appraisal they represent much of what I understand to be art.

Arthur Hopcraft, *The Football Man*, 1968.

These thoughts on football, specifically, can be extended to athletics, generally. They are thoughts which suggest that athletics is something more than a game of sport. Yet, as far as we see it, this is not the common or popular idea. In terms of everyday usage there is a definite custom of using the concepts somewhat interchangeably. Generally, people refer to the athlete who participates in a sport. The sport pages in the daily newspapers are filled with accounts of football and other activities which resemble the kind of situation described by Hopcraft. In other words, the sport pages record and discuss the achievements of athletes and not sportsmen.

Perhaps the only thing that resembles a consistent usage between the concepts of sport and athletics is found within the context of the schools. There, under the banner of physical education, it is quite customary to speak of an intramural sport program and an interscholastic or intercollegiate athletic program. However, even that is not done with complete consistency. Some

---

[12]Paul Weiss, *Sport: A Philosophic Inquiry*. (Carbondale, Ill.: Southern Illinois University Press, 1969), pp. 163—164.

departments have a director of intramural athletics. Frequently, one can find references to interscholastic sports.

When we move outside the realm of the schools the situation gets even more confusing. Professional sport is the most vivid example; seldom, if ever, is this referred to as professional athletics. Yet if intercollegiate athletics represents highly organized activities with the purpose of winning, it is hard to imagine that this activity becomes sport at the professional level. At the same time we will also refer with regularity to the professional athlete who competes in football, baseball, or some other sport. So, it is not accurate and safe to say that athletics is a concept which is reserved for school activities.

When we describe the synonymous use of sport and athletics as being the common or popular idea, we are, of course, confining our observation to the United States. The situation is very different when we look to England as another example. There, the concept of athletics connotes something much more definite and concrete; athletics is the name for track and field events. Sport is a much broader concept; it is the title for all other games which have the demonstration of physical prowess as one of their characteristics. In an earlier chapter we noted that the concept of sport had its origins in England. This may partly explain why the English have more carefully distinguished between sport and athletics. At the same time, even though the concept has not been employed with clarity and regularity, athletics has had a broader and, possibly, more significant meaning in the United States. One could almost say that there has been an American emphasis on athletics, compared with the British sporting heritage.

One other idea deserves mention before we move on to another possibility in the relationship between sport and athletics. Not only do Americans use the concepts of sport and athletics synonymously; they would probably prefer it that way even though it is done rather unconsciously. Competition is the name of the game in this country. Therefore, both sport and athletics symbolize something "good" because they offer media for wholesome competition. The athlete is one who competes in sport. It may even sound better that way than to refer to the sportsman who competes in athletics. There may also be another reason why we have popularly shied away from extensive use of the word "sportsman." Generally, this first and foremost connotes one who engages in field sports, especially hunting and fishing.

Even though there is full recognition that some sport organizations are more highly structured than others, any name to differentiate purposes is considered relatively insignificant. The matter is thought to be merely one of semantics. Furthermore, any differences in purpose are largely those of degree. Hovering over the entire climate is the paradox of trying to win and still having fun. There is a tacit awareness that winning requires sacrifice and dedication, but still it is also supposed to be pleasurable and recreative rather than work.

This kind of thinking pervades and prevails in spite of repeated exhortions by athletes and coaches that they are really interested in only one thing—winning. Occasionally, they may lapse into other utterances involving the platitudes of sportsmanship, but these can hardly be taken seriously.

Furthermore, such glib statements do not really concern most people because they just accept the fact that sport is something like athletics, and therefore one would expect athletes and coaches to relate their activities to sportsmanship.

KEATING'S CONTRIBUTION

Earlier we have referred to the works of James Keating, particularly as they relate to the problem of amateurism and professionalism. At the very core of his thinking is the basic contrast which he makes between sport and athletics. In his own words this contrast may be summarized as follows:

Thus we see that historically and etymologically, sport and athletics have characterized radically different types of human activity, different not in so far as the game itself or the mechanics or rules are concerned, but different with regard to the attitude, preparation, and purpose of the participants. Man has probably always desired some release or diversion from the sad and serious side of life. This, of course, is a luxury and it is only when a hostile environment is brought under close reign and economic factors provide a modicum of leisure that such desires can be gratified. In essence, sport is a kind of diversion which has for its direct and immediate end, fun, pleasure and delight and which is dominated by a spirit of moderation and generosity. Athletics, on the other hand, is essentially a competition activity, which has for its end, victory in the contest and which is characterized by a spirit of dedication, sacrifice and intensity.[13]

In our opinion Keating has made a substantial contribution by verbalizing a situation which actually exists and by challenging the popular myth that sport and athletics are somehow or another all part of the same "large ball of wax." Many people are probably perfectly willing to accept his thesis even though they had not thought about the matter in the way in which it is expressed.

Two possible limitations of his position may be noted. First of all, as is generally true of extreme statements, the criticism could be made that his position leads to misplaced concreteness. Some people could infer that it is a simple matter of black vs. white or right vs. wrong. Under such simple thinking one could end up classifying each specific activity as being either sport or athletics. No room might be allowed for an intermediate or gray area. Even worse, the implication could be drawn that the sportsmen are the "good guys" whereas the athletes are the "bad guys." We are quite sure that the latter comparison was not intended, but it nevertheless looms as a possibility for varied interpreters.

A second limitation evolves around the complexity of individual vs. group motives. For instance, could a sportsman exist in athletics; or, could an athlete be found in sport? The answer to each of these questions would appear to be "yes."

---

[13]James W. Keating, "Sportsmanship As A Moral Category," *Ethics*, LXXV, 1:25–35, Oct. 1964.

Yet, Keating more or less conveys the impression that his hypothesis applies to both the individual and the group. The would-be sportsman might find it extremely difficult to maintain his sporting attitudes in an atmosphere which is completely dedicated to winning the game above all other considerations. Similarly, an athlete could become quite frustrated when he attempts to pursue his specialized area amidst the spontaneity and gaiety of sportsmen in the same activity. The complexity of the problem is accentuated when we consider the athlete who participates in a sport which is not his specialized area. For example, what of the professional baseball player who participates in a leisurely game of volleyball? Do his predominant athletic attitudes transfer to the sport of volleyball?

Group motives would appear to be more easily determined than individual motives. However, that, too, requires further explanation. A group can be and often is organized with a definite motive in mind. A professional football team is organized for the purpose of winning and making money. Certain individuals in that group might not share the burning desire to win, but one of two conditions will then likely appear. These individuals will either remain on the team as less effective members, or they will leave the team after a period of time.

Generally speaking, we suspect that Keating's hypothesis will hold up best when considered from the standpoint of the organizational basis for a group. A college basketball team could be and frequently is organized with a single purpose in mind—to win as many games as possible. This will result in attendant purposes for the school, such as making money, pleasing spectators, and obtaining publicity. But all these purposes point to the fact that the activity is indeed athletic in accordance with Keating's conception and should not be confused with the activity of sport. Athletics, in turn, may provide recreation for the spectators, but it is basically neither recreation nor sport for the participants.

In spite of any possible limitations in Keating's approach, he has caused certain people to really think for the first time about the nature of the problem. Frequently, some form of extreme hypothesis is desirable to shake people out of their complacency. For years, many college athletic programs have been shrouded with hypocrisy. On the one hand, all the attributes and values of sport have been claimed; on the other hand, those involved proceed about their usual big business of trying to produce winning teams at all costs.

What Keating seems to be asking for is: let's call a spade a spade. Physical education literature is replete with discussions of what should be the place of athletics in the schools. These discussions usually include one or more of the following clichés: athletics is first and foremost an educational activity; athletics should contribute to the purposes of education generally; athletics is an integral part of physical education; the purposes of athletics should be substantially the same as those of physical education generally. Keating does not even mention the term "physical education." At the same time, he raises some serious doubts concerning the treasured assumptions of physical educators and certain others who follow in that yoke.

WEISS' THEME: ATHLETICS AS THE PURSUIT OF EXCELLENCE

We will begin with the generalization that Weiss' work is basically an extension of one half of Keating's hypothesis. The title of Paul Weiss' book is actually a misnomer; it should read "Athletics: A Philosophic Inquiry." He has proceeded to speculate in more depth regarding the nature of that concept which Keating designates as athletics. Although he consistly refers to the athlete in sport throughout the book, there is little doubt that his whole case in built on the concept of athletics, if one gives any credence to the distinction between sport and athletics. In fact there is only one chapter in the book which appears to be out of context. Chapter 9 is entitled "Play, Sport, and Game." As far as we can see, it could just as well have been omitted. Aside from that, Weiss' treatise hangs together very well from beginning to end.

He sees athletics as one of the areas in life where excellence can be displayed. In that respect athletics is similar to scholarship, art, statesmanship, and religion. One of the unique features of athletics is that it also offers the opportunity for spectators to vicariously identify with the athletes. The athlete's relative degree of excellence is on public display in the game for all to behold. This is a primary reason why boys and young men are readily attracted toward athletics. Athletics demands public attention, and it is an area where excellence is attained at a relatively young age. This is soon sensed by the would-be athlete, and he proceeds to pursue a goal which, hopefully, will make him one of the excellent men in the world, among whom there are not many.

Training is another key concept in Weiss' theme. His description of training for the athlete is more abstract than one would popularly encounter, but there is no doubt that he accords training a high place in the earlier phases of the athlete's preparation. The discussion of training, alone, would be sufficient to convince even the casual reader that he is not really talking about sport. If sport is a form of recreation, one would be shocked to find that such attributes as commitment, intensity, dedication, and "alteration of the vectoral thrust" are essential to sport. On the other hand, he describes the needs and drives of the athlete very clearly.

His keen interest in standardization is another factor which causes one to believe that Weiss is not first and foremost concerned about sport with its leisure nature. The entire business of standardization is extremely important because without it the really excellent cannot be fully determined. No matter how one looks at it, excellence always ends up being somewhat of a relative matter. A few people are considered to be more excellent than others with respect to a selected trait, characteristic, or element of performance. Weiss is very concerned about those measures which are used to compare the top man in one situation with the highest achiever in a similar situation. Who really is the excellent one?

Whether or not one shares Weiss' enthusiasm for standardization, there is no doubt that he follows a consistent theme for those who are impressed with excellence, wherever it is found. Promoters of academic excellence are constantly searching for ways and means to compare a student from one institution with his counterpart at a different school. Such instruments as "college boards" and graduate record examinations are obviously related to the need for standardization.

Probably the closest parallel between the work of Weiss and that of Keating is found in the former's chapter on "the urge to win." Weiss states:

If a player would win, he should try to win, should strive to win, should want to win. To obtain maximum results in a game, he must give himself to it. He can then sometimes come close to getting what he desires. And this he will do if he is a true athlete.

The athlete must have a strong urge to defeat his opponent, and must carry out that urge in the form of actions which will enable him to outdistance all. This requires him to be aggressive.[14]

Neither one leaves any doubt that winning is the name of the game in athletics. As philosophers they share the common advantage of taking a "fresh" look at one of life's activities as they see it. They have not entered the arena with a predetermined bias that athletics must be something different than what it is because it must be first and foremost educational.

As is true of almost any work if one probes deeply enough, certain possible inconsistencies may also be found in Paul Weiss' book. His discussion of the role of the coach is at least confusing, if not inconsistent. Initially he states that: "Coaches, like sergeants, chefs, and teachers of typing and other skills, and of singing, sculpture, and other arts, of chemistry, engineering, and other experimental and applied sciences, mold their charges somewhat along the lines in which they themselves have been molded."[15]

He then proceeds to discuss the limitations of this method, although certain advantages are also noted. Basically, this method is described as the process of training, and there is no doubt that the coach can play an important role in the training of the athlete. However, a few pages later the situation becomes much more complicated:

Ideally, a coach is a model man, a unified whole in whom character permeates the body, and sensitivity is fired with imagination. He inspires his charges to possess something like his spirit, sustained by a self-assurance that is appropriate to one who is at home with his tasks, himself, his fellow man, and his sport.[16]

In view of the limitations of the training method, it is somewhat difficult to imagine that a coach could be described as "a molded man, a unified whole in

---

[14]Weiss, *op. cit.*, p. 44.
[15]*Ibid.*
[16]*Ibid.*, p. 50.

whom character permeates the body." Yet, maybe the word "ideally" is the key; Weiss could be describing what coaches should be rather than what they are. At any rate, he is fully consistent on his major points: excellent men are the exceptions; athletics is one area in which men may pursue excellence; coaches direct athletes toward excellence; the excellence in athletics is manifested in winning in *the* game.

ATHLETICS AS AN EXTENSION OF SPORT

The general distinction between sport and athletics has merit and deserves consideration. However, as is true in comparing the amateur with the professional, it is not a simple case of black and white. It would appear more accurate to say that some activities tend to be more athleticlike whereas others are more sportlike.

Earlier in this chapter we projected the continuum between play and sport. This continuum can be further extended to show the relationships among play, sport, and athletics:

Thus, we seen that athletics is an extension of sport in much the same way that sport is an extension of play. The whole picture would be a nice, neat package if we could also place games somewhere on the continuum, but, unfortunately, that is not the case. Games are a variety of play; they are found in sport; and they are an essential ingredient in athletics. Therefore, it is necessary to project still another continuum of games which parallels the above:

This conveys the idea that games are found in play, sport, and athletics. The nature of the games changes as one moves from play to sport to athletics.

Just as Schmitz noted those factors which tend to detract from the playful characteristics in sport, we can observe certain factors which cause athletics to lose its essential sporting characteristics. One of these is very definitely the presence of spectators.

Although there may be spectators in sport, their presence is likely to be much more incidental. Athletics is structured with the spectators uppermost in mind. Winning is important because the spectators come to the game to see their team win. Furthermore, the various elements of ritual and display are heightened in athletics. This, too, may be attributed to the presence of spectators. From one standpoint the athletic game is one large display to please the spectators. The better the display the greater likelihood there is that more spectators will be attracted to succeeding games, and more money will be made by the promoters of the athletic event. The owners of a major-league baseball team realize that there is no substitute for a winning team as far as their display goes, but they may include fireworks after the game, just to add to the display. Therefore, the purposes of the athletic game of baseball are not substantially different from the fireworks.

Elements of ritual in the athletic game are also closely akin to the business of display. Again, there will usually be much more ritual in athletics than in sport because a large part of the ritual is for the benefit of the spectators. Professional football offers a classic example of this. Team captains meet at the center of the field before the game for the traditional coin-tossing ceremony. However, the actual toss of the coin to determine who receives and who has which side of the field has taken place earlier, before the participants even appeared on the field.

The entire area of promotion and sponsorship is part and parcel of the athletic enterprise. This is another factor which causes athletics to lose some of its sporting characteristics. When John Loy discusses sport as an institutionalized game,[17] he actually points out many of those factors which detract from the sporting nature of athletics. Governing bodies in athletics also go hand in hand with the business of sponsorship and promotion. College teams and little league teams are governed at local, regional, and national levels. Each of these governmental levels also contributes to the sponsorship and promotion of their athletic activities.

In general, probably the one feature of athletics which causes it to be an extension of sport is that athletics tends to be more highly organized and structured all the way along the line. Some manifestations of the emphasis on organization and structure are the following: (1) athletic teams are selected with greater care; (2) more attention is given to establishing and enforcing the rules in athletics; (3) increased attention is devoted to standardization of facilities and equipment; (4) the athletic game becomes more of a science due to the detailed analysis of skills, knowledge, and strategy of one's team plus his opponent's; (5) the entire area of public relations and publicity is extremely significant in athletics.

Rather than sharply contrasting athletics with sport, we prefer to consider athletics as an extension of sport. This follows for the many shades of gray which designate those activities which do not neatly fit the pure categories in terms of characteristics which have been noted. We can take our continuum between sport and athletics; by rather arbitrarily projecting certain activities on this continuum, the extension of sport into the athletic realm should be more evident:

Sport							Athletics
H.S. intramural sport program	College intramural sports	Little league	H.S. inter- scholastic team	Inter- collegiate team	Green Bay Packers		

Above all other considerations, those factors which cause athletics to be less sportlike should not be labeled as abuses. The entire matter is one of value judg-

---

[17] Loy, *op. cit.*, pp. 6—11.

ments. A given individual may not like the organization and structure of athletics; he is certainly entitled to that viewpoint. However, for another athletics may offer a medium whereby they can enjoy those activities, either as a participant or spectator, which are consistent with his life-style.

BIBLIOGRAPHY

Avendon, E. M., and Brian Sutton-Smith, *The Study of Games*. New York: John Wiley & Sons, 1971.

Caillois, Roger, *Man, Play and Games*, tr. Meyer Barosh. New York: Free Press, 1964.

Fogelin, Robert, "Sport: The Diversity of the Concept," Unpublished paper delivered at the 13th Annual Meeting of the American Association for the Advancement of Science, Dallas, Texas, Dec. 28, 1968.

Graves, H., "A Philosophy of Sport," *Contemporary Review*, 78, Dec. 1900, 877—893.

Huizinga, Johan, *Homo Ludens—A Study of the Play-Element in Culture*. Boston: Beacon Press, 1955.

Keating, James, "Winning in Sport and Athletics," *Thought*, XXXVIII, 149, Summer 1963, 201—210.

Keating, James, "Sportsmanship as a Moral Category," *Ethics*, LXXV, No. 1, Oct. 1964, 25—35.

Keating, James, "The Heart of the Problem of Amateur Athletics," *The Journal of General Education*, 16, No. 4, Jan. 1965.

Keating, James, "Athletics and the Pursuit of Excellence," *Education*, 85, No. 7, March 1965, 428—431.

Lewis, Guy M., "The Ladies Walked and Walked," *Sports Illustrated*, 27, Dec. 18, 1967, R-3-4.

Loy, John W., "The Nature of Sport: A Definitional Effort," *Quest*, X, May 1968, 1—15.

Schiller, von Friedrich, *Essays, Aesthetical and Philosophical*. London: George Bell & Sons, 1875.

Schmitz, Kenneth, "Sport and Play: Suspension of the Ordinary," Unpublished paper presented at the 13th Annual Meeting of the American Association for the Advancement of Science, Dallas, Texas, Dec. 28, 1968.

Sutton-Smith, Brian, "Games-Play-Daydreams," *Quest*, X, Spring Issue, May, 1968, 47—58.

Weiss, Paul, *Sport: A Philosophic Inquiry*. Carbondale, Ill.: Southern Ill. University Press, 1969.

5/Sport: How?

Among the various topics we are considering in this book, the subject of the "how" of sport is the one that bears the closest relationship to educational philosophy. In fact, a strong case can be made for the idea that educational philosophy revolves primarily around the question of "how." It could be argued that the philosophy of education is a subject of means and ends for the educative process and that the means are always subordinate to the ends or goals to be reached. However, the end results or goals for education are about as diversified as there are people, so we can claim that issues in educational philosophy tend to be largely those involving the process.

One of the most perplexing problems in identifying sport with educational philosophy is that sport is very definitely one of those activities in life which transcends the boundaries of the school. In many respects sport is a much more significant factor outside the school than it is within the framework of formal education. On the other hand, a point can also be made for the proposition that education is an exceedingly broad concept which should not be shackled by a traditional philosophy. Thus, it is possible that the "how" of sport falls within the framework of educational philosophy whether or not it is organized and conducted within the established structure of the school.

Educational philosophy has long been plagued with the difficulty of distinguishing between what is and what ought to be. This difficulty has been manifested in several ways. Frequently, the subject is covered in such a manner that one would be led to believe there is no substantial difference between the status quo and the philosopher's utopia. This seems to be particularly true of those who have followed the "normative" approach to educational philosophy. They set forth their principles as though these were always the guidelines for action. Then, there is the kind of educational philosophizing that never seems to move beyond the current situation. Adherents of this approach seem quite content to accept the practical state of affairs as it exists. Even though discussions ensue under the banner of philosophy, one might wonder whether it is really philosophy or an exploration of practical problems. There is still a third form of educational philosophy which appears to ignore the practical and the actual situations altogether. Although it is the least evident today, the propagators of this form are inclined to be purely speculative in their approach.

Somehow or other it seems reasonable to suggest that would-be philosophers of education should at least attempt to openly consider and distinguish between the status quo on the one hand and value judgments, regarding what ought to be, on the other. With this in mind, we will begin by looking at the way in which sport is organized and/or conducted in the United States today.

However, before assessing the status quo of the "how" of sport, one other inherent problem in educational philosophy should be brought to attention. The problem is basically one involving differences of opinion concerning the usefulness and/or value of the "isms." Again, extremes can be noted. Some educational philosophers, such as John Brubacher,[1] have employed the "isms" as their primary frame of reference. Others, exemplified by Harry Broudy,[2] are advocates of a "grass roots" and inductive approach. They prefer to begin by considering educational problems wherever they are found, without relating these problems to diverse schools of thought.

Our personal opinion is that there is room and justification for both modes of educational philosophy. The "isms" have merit, be it limited, because they offer a launching point for examining specific problems and individual differences. On the other hand, sometimes it is necessary to take a "grass roots" look at the educational scene in order to avoid the stultifying effect which can be evident when everything is viewed from the perspective of established schools of thought. Therefore, when we reach the stage of considering how sport should be conducted, we will begin by suggesting procedures which would be consistent with the tenets of two contrasting philosophies of education—essentialism and progressivism. From there, we should be prepared to offer certain eclectic possibilities for conducting sport, based on an analysis of practical problems which are evident in sport media today.

HOW IS SPORT ORGANIZED AND ADMINISTERED?

IN THE SCHOOLS

Perhaps the first thing that is apparent in looking at the organization of sport in the United States is the noticeable difference within the schools as compared to that found outside the school context. However, even within the school

---

[1]John S. Brubacher, *Modern Philosophies of Education* (New York: McGraw Hill Book Co., 1962).
[2]Harry S. Broudy, *Building a Philosophy of Education* (Englewood Cliffs, New Jersey: Prentice-Hall, Inc., 1961).

structure there are vast differences in comparing elementary with secondary schools and either of these with colleges. Likewise, the public school setup is not exactly the same as that found in the private schools. We will begin with certain generalizations that apply to the organization and administration of sport in the schools.

Customarily, sport in the schools is organized and administered under the banner which we call physical education. The historical basis for this was discussed in the second chapter. During the 20th-century, physical education has come to connote programs in sport, dance, and other forms of physical activity in the schools.

Among the various sport programs within physical education, the most concrete example of sport per se is the intramural sport program. In making this generalization we are adhering to the distinction between sport and athletics as established in the previous chapter. In other words, we will not consider athletics as part of the sport organization within the schools.

The intramural sport program is usually distinguished from the instructional program in physical education. The latter involves what students and laymen more popularly called "gym" classes. However, the entire picture is complicated by the fact there may be instruction through the medium of the intramural sport program. Likewise, the teaching of sport skills is ordinarily part of the instructional program in physical education, and, sometimes, physical education classes even include sport competition. So, the distinction between physical education classes and the intramural sport program in the schools tends to be rather arbitrary and is fraught with all sorts of organizational problems.

In considering educational levels, we can draw another generalization. The organization of intramural sport programs, as such, have been and continue to be particularly characteristic of colleges and universities. To a certain extent, this may be attributed to the size of the institution: one will more likely find a separate intramural sport structure in a large university. Intramural sports are offered at the high-school and junior-high levels, but they are often overshadowed by "gym" classes and the athletic program. An organized program of intramural sport at the elementary-school level is indeed rare.

The matter of personnel has possibly been the most significant factor in determining the organization and administration of sport in the schools. Among the personnel who are involved with either promoting or teaching sport in the schools, relatively few could really be called sport specialists. Generally speaking, they are either coaches and/or physical educators. The only marked exceptions are those people who are intramural sport directors at the college or university level. A few of these can also be found in junior and senior high schools, but, more commonly, the director of intramural sports in the public schools is first and foremost an athletic coach. Thus, sport is likely to be a secondary consideration for him.

In general, elementary-school physical educators also do not have what could be called a sport orientation. Particularly today, they are advocates of "movement education," or similar programs which take the focus away from sports and concentrate on the development of movement fundamentals and exploration through the medium of basic movements. Many of the women physical educators also prefer the movement education approach at the secondary and college levels while their male counterparts are absorbed in their athletic interests. This leaves college intramural sport directors and a few people who are interested in sport studies or the theory of sport as really the only ones who could be called sport specialists.

Thus, we are faced with the paradoxical situation that on the one hand sport is called the focal point of physical education and on the other hand sport actually is an area of tertiary involvement for most physical educators; they are first and foremost interested in and absorbed with athletics, movement education, exercise science, or some other program under the broad scope of physical education.

OUTSIDE THE SCHOOLS

When one looks outside the context of school programs per se, two factors are immediately evident concerning the organization of sport. First of all, the organization of sport tends to be quite different. Secondly, sport has really flourished to a greater extent outside the school setting.

Naturally, there is great variance in the way that sport is organized and administered. Sport organizations outside the school run the gamut from YMCA groups to the ski resort to the swim club to the little league organization to the city recreation program. Many more forms could be cited; these are but examples to show the variety. However, in spite of the variance, certain generalizations can again be drawn.

In making the comparison with school programs there is not the same kind of distinction among play, teaching, and competitive functions. Earlier we noted that the intramural sport program in the schools is usually separated from the instructional program in physical education. Thus, intramural sport is viewed primarily as a medium for play and competition whereas the "gym" class is a place where students work and learn. An example may serve to show the difference when we observe sport outside the narrower educational setting.

When one joins a swim club, he or she may expect to find that the teaching, competitive, and play functions are all organized and conducted under the same auspices. Basically, this means that the same personnel are involved in teaching, supervising the recreational swim periods, and organizing and conducting the competition. Likewise, these functions are centralized under one person. Set times are established for the various functions of the swim club, but there is no arbitrary division of programs. Essentially, the same kind of operation can be noted at a ski resort. People come to the resort and chose from any one of several functions which are centrally organized. The majority may choose to merely pay the tow fees which will enable them to utilize the facilities for their own forms of recreational skiing. However, instruction is also available for those who need and desire this service. Competition may also be organized for advanced skiers. But throughout the entire operation the homogenity of the program is much more evident.

As a second generalization, it can be noted that there is a tendency to more and more organize sport outside the school. Of course, based on certain characteristics set forth in the previous chapter, it could be argued that sport is not sport until it is organized. In other words, the organization represents a major part of the transition from play to sport. However, we are talking largely about a difference in degree. Within the broad spectrum of sport, the focus is increasingly on organization.

In spite of the inclination toward increasing the organizational aspects of sport in this culture, we find that sport flourishes in an unparalleled manner. We say "in spite of" because one might expect that the opposite should be true. Sport seems to everyday lose some of its play characteristics. If it is natural for people to desire play, logic would tell us that they would attempt to make their sport more playlike. But for some reason, this does not seem to be the case.

The father who is wrapped up in organization through his work seems to delight and take satisfaction in the organizational framework of his son's baseball activities. To him, little-league baseball is the epitome for his son at that time and place. In fact, the father will proceed to insure that that particular sport becomes as organized as possible. Apparently, the "organizational man" is quite content to perpetuate and accelerate those organizational structures which permeate his whole life. Similarly, the mother contributes to the organizational promotion by arranging for car pools, selling candy to buy uniforms, and applauding the entire structure as a spectator. Could it be that Americans actually prefer sport to play? Or are they merely caught up in a cultural trend from which the given individual cannot extricate himself?

HOW IS SPORT TAUGHT AND/OR LEARNED?

THE RELATIVE SPECIFICITY OF SPORT SKILLS

The above question has purposefully been worded in a rather awkward manner because the entire subject of the relationship between teaching and learning is just that complicated. We can observe how people teach. We cannot really observe *how* students learn even though we supposedly can test what they have learned. If we actually knew how students learn, then we could proceed to redirect the teaching to bring about the desired results. Since we do not, we will confine our status quo assessment to a summary of the limited research findings that are available with regard to the acquisition of sport skills. At the same time, we can also summarize the situation as to how sport is currently being taught.

What is learning? This is a question that remains unanswered in terms of a succinct statement because psychologists and educators are pretty well in agreement that the answer is largely a philosophical one. A definition of learning is very much dependent on one's conception of human nature, particularly the basis for man's motivation. However, there is some agreement that no matter how learning is defined or described it is an adaptation in behavior. In the case of skill acquisition, as one form of learning, this adaptation may have negative as well as positive effects. In other words, in the initial stages of learning a skill, the student may acquire certain habits which will later prove detrimental or have a negative effect in attempting to master the skill. This brings us to the important subject of transfer of learning which is inextricably related to learning generally and particularly to skill acquisition because of the possibility of both positive and negative effects.

Simply stated, transfer of learning is applying in one situation that which has been learned in another. Thus, in its broadest meaning, transfer of learning is synonymous with learning. Most teaching situations are based on the premise that some form of transfer will take place. However, particularly in the learning of skills, the possibility of negative transfer always looms as a distinct possibility. The baseball player may experience initial difficulty when he takes up the game of golf because he attempts to properly hit the golf ball with his baseball swing. The truth of the matter is that we still lack sufficient evidence concerning positive and/or negative transfer effects between what appear to be similar activities such as tennis and badminton, baseball and golf, and basketball and volleyball. Speculation would suggest that there may be temporary interference in moving from one activity to the other, but it could not really be called negative transfer. Knapp described what appears to be negative transfer as follows: "This means that it temporarily impedes the new learning but still enables the skill to be acquired in a shorter time than would have been possible without the previous training."[3]

One of the most controversial subjects in the teaching of sport skills has been that involving the relative merits of whole vs. parts methods of instruction. In fact, even the research findings, be they limited, also appear to be somewhat contradictory. Among those who have summarized the results of research in this area there seems to be consensus that there is no preferable method as such; choice of the method is dependent on such variables as the nature of the activity, interests and capabilities of the instructor and students, level of instruction, and intent to teach for transfer. Knapp concluded: "There is evidence in favor of various methods and no one method seems conclusively the best for every skill. In fact even for one particular skill, the best method is often dependent to a certain extent on the individual learner."[4]

---

[3]B. Knapp, *Skill in Sport.* (London: Routledge and Kegan Paul, 1963), p. 105.

[4]*Ibid.*, p. 60.

There is a preference for the whole method when the skill to be performed is not too complex. Oxendine cites this as among the conditions which might influence the decision to proceed with the whole method. However, he, too, adds the caution that it is not completely an either-or situation:

The whole method seems best when the amount of learning does not exceed what the learner can comprehend. This method is also better when learners are older, brighter, more highly motivated, and have a background in the task. The whole technique is also favored in the late stages of the learning process and when practices are distributed. When the opposite conditions exist, then part methods seem best. A combination of the two methods is sometimes most successful.[5]

In relationship to the specific topic under consideration, namely transfer of sport skills, it would appear that the whole method is preferred, when feasible. Exposure to the whole provides the student with a "gestalt" understanding which is essential if transfer is to take place among sport skills.

On the other hand, the limited research available definitely seems to indicate that most sport skills tend to be highly specific. Singer summarizes the situation as follows:

It is doubtful if there is such a thing as a general motor ability but rather motor abilities. Motor abilities themselves are usually correlated but only slightly, e.g., the ability to balance does not mean an ability to react quickly or an ability to demonstrate great strength.

Motor ability tests would appear to have their best value in diagnosing extremes, either the highly or poorly coordinated individuals. Beyond this function, these tests have questionable value.

The research that favors task specificity over a general motor factor would also serve to question the belief that there is such an individual as an "all-round athlete." The all-round athlete is an exception not a rule, and success in a few activities is no indication of similar status in other activities.[6]

Thus, there appears to be sound basis for the fact that for the most part the skills of a particular sport are taught as an entity in themselves, whether the whole method, part method, or a combination is used. The one major exception in a teaching approach is found among those who are advocates of the concept of human movement fundamentals.

THE CONCEPT OF HUMAN MOVEMENT FUNDAMENTALS

During the past 20 years there have been frequent references within physical education to such concepts as human movement fundamentals, basic move-

---

[5]Joseph B. Oxendine, *Psychology of Motor Learning.* Copyright © 1968 by Meredith Corporation. Reprinted by permission of Appleton-Century-Crofts, Educational Division, Meredith Corporation.

[6]Robert N. Singer, *Motor Learning and Human Performance.* (New York: The Macmillan Company, 1968), pp. 328–329.

ment, movement education, fundamental activities, body dynamics, basic activities, body mechanics, fundamental motor patterns, and particularly in England, educational gymnastics. Although there are shades of differences among these concepts, for all practical purposes they are virtually the same. In terms of an approach, the focus is on teaching people how to move rather than teaching the skills of a particular sport.

Risking the possibility of over-generalization, we can say with some truth that the teaching approach we are designating as human movement fundamentals has had primary appeal to two groups: women physical educators and elementary-school physical-education specialists. There, of course, could be some correlation here as well because historically the women have been more involved in teaching physical education at the elementary-school level. Only within recent years has the male elementary school physical-education specialist emerged. It would appear that the promoters of this concept have a firm belief in the possibilities of transfer; that is, they would begin by teaching the basic movement patterns with the expectation that these can be positively transferred in acquiring specific sport skills.

There is also a distinctly gestalt flavor in the language of those who have popularized the concept of human-movement fundamentals:

The generality of movement calls for a generality of understanding that cannot be gained through the limited experience of learning a specific method for performing a few specific activities, but rather through experiences which, even though they may be limited, lead to an understanding of the factors involved in movement and in the various methods for approaching the solving of motor problems.[7]

In a similar vein Eleanor Metheny has urged that movement must be first and foremost learned outside the context of sport. She stressed the learning of movement patterns as a basis for sport skills as well as other physical skills. Movement must be learned and understood as movement. This is contrasted with the approach that focuses on the specifics of movement within a particular sport.

... we must teach basic principles of how to use muscles, levers, and joints to accomplish work with the minimum expenditure of energy. We can illustrate these principles through lifting, reaching, pushing, pulling, stooping, carrying, controlling the abdominal muscles in standing and sitting and using alternate muscles, in maintained positions. But our teaching must not stop with showing them how to do these things. We must teach them why.[8]

The basic premise among all the human-movement theorists is that people must be taught how to move. Once learned, the movements can be refined and

---

[7]Marion Broer, *Efficiency of Human Movement.* (Philadelphia: W. B. Saunders Co., 1966), p. vii, viii, Reprinted by permission of W. B. Saunders Co.

[8]Eleanor Metheny, "Are Sports Enough?" *Journal of Health, Physical Education, and Recreation,* Vol. 14, No. 5, (1943), p. 251.

applied to sport skills, dance, physical work, and any other activities wherein human movement is found. Metheny's last statement is also noteworthy because proponents of the human movement concept tend to be very enthusiastic about the need to teach the "why." It is further manifestation of their conviction that a more concerted effort must be made to directly teach for transfer. Thus, it may not be accidental that human movement has also emerged as the favorite umbrella concept for those who are attempting to develop disciplinelike subfields in exercise science and sport theory. They, too, are primarily concerned with the "why"; the hope is that they may be able to offer certain answers to the "why," which in turn can be used by those who teach human-movement fundamentals.

How is the concept of human-movement fundamentals employed in terms of what is actually taught? First of all, there is stress on mechanical principles which govern all movements, determining the potentialities and limitations of the human body. Secondly, students are taught how to perform the basic movements in light of these principles. Some of the basic movements are walking, running, jumping, pushing, pulling, lifting, throwing, and striking. The entire approach is based on the assumption that a movement is a movement. That is, a throw is a throw and a jump is a jump. There is a recognition that a basic movement, such as throwing, may be refined and/or modified to accomplish specific purposes such as passing a football, pitching a baseball, or shooting a basketball. However, the teacher of human-movement fundamentals constantly strives to remind the student that the same, basic principles of throwing always apply. The student is expected to acquire the insights which will enable him to positively transfer the principles of throwing to the execution of a specific throw in a particular sport.[9]

TRIAL AND ERROR OR PROGRESSIVE APPROXIMATION

Frequent references are made to so-called "trial-and-error" learning. Superficially, a couple of thoughts come immediately to mind. One is that people learn in a rather hit-and-miss fashion. Another is that learning is largely a result of self-teaching. Neither of these thoughts do full justice to trial-and-error learning when it is more broadly conceived. In this case the concept may have been handicapped by the semantics involved.

Singer attributes the trial-and-error theory to Thorndike and infers that there may be limitations when compared to more recent theories:

Of interest to physical educators is Thorndike's belief that learning takes place through trial and error. In other words, the learner when faced with a problem does not sud-

---

[9]For a more complete discussion of the ideas of those who have promoted the concept of human movement fundamentals the reader is referred to an unpublished master's thesis completed by Virginia Lee Studer at the University of Illinois in 1966. The thesis is entitled "The Historical Development of Human Movement Fundamentals for College Women in the United States."

denly perceive the solution but rather gradually, through random behavior, learns the correct response. . . . With repeated responses, a problem is solved because of a diminishing of incorrect responses and a fixation of the correct response.

Physical educators might consider the importance of reinforcement as well as acknowledge that practice alone does not make perfect; and, in addition, consider the readiness of the individual to learn. Physical educators might also observe whether their classes contain situations that are trial and error by nature. Are the learners being taught? Are there too many trials and too many errors before success is achieved? It will be interesting for the reader to note Skinner's thinking on this matter of learning and how he would "shape" behavior.[10]

These suggestions imply that sport is frequently taught on a trial-and-error basis. However, there is some question as to whether this is the most effective means of learning a sport skill. Those who would come to the defense of some form of trial-and-error learning might profit from reshaping the concept to what Murphy calls "progressive approximation":

One of the most often repeated statements in the area of skill acquisition is "practice makes perfect." The experienced teacher, however, knows that this is not true, that motor learning is not merely a process of repetition until a habit is formed. Instead, it is more of a process of constant change and variation. Tries are made, errors noticed, and other tries made. This is often called "trial-and-error" learning, but perhaps this is an inaccurate description of the process, for the learner in succeeding trials does not purposely repeat errors of earlier trials. If he did there would be no improvement. Instead, he makes variations in later trials so that they are more nearly correct than earlier ones.

In tennis, for example, the learner may note that the racket was held too loosely or that the racket face was tilted back too much. When he repeats the action he corrects the mistake; he changes a part here or there, noting whether or not the change makes any difference in the end result. A series of such modified repetitions made under the watchful eye of the instructor constitutes effective practice. For this reason, the process of skill acquisition might more accurately be termed "progressive approximation," wherein the learner progressively approximates the correct form or action, after each trial that did not produce the desired result.[11]

Based on Murphy's description, it would seem that sport skills are frequently taught by the progressive-approximation method. Coaches, in particular, use this method in a variety of ways. Generally speaking, the acknowledgment of the specificity of sport skills goes hand in hand with the use of progressive approximation as a teaching method.

---

[10]Singer, *op. cit.*, pp. 271–272.

[11]Chet Murphy, "Principles of Learning with Implications for Teaching Tennis," *Journal of Health, Physical Education, and Recreation*, Feb., 1962. Found in Slusher and Lockhart's *Anthology of Contemporary Readings* (Dubuque, Iowa: Wm. C. Brown Co., 1966), p. 304.

LAWS OF LEARNING AS APPLIED TO SPORT

Thorndike was also the proponent of various learning principles which became known as laws of learning. Four of these laws are readiness, primacy, exercise, and effect. Application of each can be observed in the teaching of sport skills.

The law of readiness refers basically to motivation. Learning is facilitated when the student is motivated. In fact, sometimes no learning may take place without motivation. For this reason we may find coaches and other teachers of sport skills telling their students that a game will be played later during the class or practice session. The hope is that the idea of playing a game will motivate the students to apply themselves in preparation for the game.

Learning takes place more rapidly when the correct way is learned first. This is the essence of the law of primacy. Of course, this is based on the assumption that there is the correct way and that it is known by the instructor. Our observation has been that most coaches and instructors of sport are unconsciously impressed with this law. They will invariably teach a correct way and often state or imply that it is *the* correct way. This is obviously an area where the knowlege of scientific findings is important.

Among the various teaching/learning situations one would be hard-pressed to find a more vivid example of application of the law of exercise than that found in sport-skill instruction. This law states in effect that learning is facilitated by purposeful repetition. In sport-skill instruction, practice or drill is the name of the game. Even the concept of progressive approximation, as discussed earlier, is inextricably related to the law of exercise.

The law of effect seems to refer to the retention of learning. When the learning experience is a satisfying one, there is a greater probability that true learning may occur. We say true learning because to listen is not to learn and, in the case of skills, to do is not to learn. Murphy also comments very appropriately on this point.

Tennis teachers must remember that a skill can be considered to be learned only when it can be called out without a great deal of conscious attention being directed to it. One or two successful performances do not mean an act has been learned.[12]

When skill learning is viewed as Murphy describes it, the law of effect looms as very important. The close relationship to the law of exercise is also readily apparent. If one has to repeat a skill many times in order to actually learn it, he will be much more motivated to do so if his initial experiences with the skill have been satisfying.

Thus far in this chapter we have stayed away from controversy for the most part. The intent was to describe the status quo insofar as it can be determined in the organizing, administering, and teaching of sport. Now, the focus shifts to dif-

---

[12] *Ibid.*, p. 305.

ferences of interpretation regarding what ought to be. The polarities of essentialism and progressivism offer a frame of reference for exploring contrasting and,
sometimes, conflicting ideas.[13]

ESSENTIALISTIC IDEAS FOR THE CONDUCT OF SPORT

Essentialism is not a philosophy per se; it is an educational philosophy. As is true
of all isms, some person or group had to coin it at a particular time or over a
course of years. In the case of essentialism, credit for the term as such is given to
Demiashkevich.[14] Among his contemporaries who were part of this school of
thought he lists William C. Bagley, Thomas H. Briggs, Herman H. Horne, I. L.
Kandel, Paul Monroe, James E. Russell, Frank E. Spaulding, and George D.
Strayer. In Demiashkevich's own words, he and his colleagues "insisted upon
the duty of educators to develop in the young fundamental attitudes, appreciations, skills, and information, the value of which has stood the test of the history
of civilization and which therefore can be regarded as constant, unchanging
fundamentals in the education of man, citizen and world inhabitant."

With this description in mind, the reader will readily note that essentialism
is not just something of the past. Many educators and laymen still adhere to the
tenets of essentialism even though they are probably not avowed essentialists.
In fact, they may not even know that essentialism is an educational philosophy
and could care less. But that is beside the point. The important matter is that they
have a certain temper or disposition toward the process of education which they
share with others. The school of thought could just as well be called something
other than what it is. The name itself is relatively insignificant even though it
just so happens that essentialism is fairly descriptive in this case.

What, then, are some of the other educational propositions which make up
this school of thought which has been designated as essentialism? As a most
basic premise, the essentialists firmly believe that the school should be an arm
of society. In other words, the school should not attempt to change or steer
society but is there to carry out and reflect the broader societal dictates. This,
in itself, places a prescription on the curriculum and the methods employed. We
might add that a corollary to this thought is usually manifested in a suggestion
that society was better in the past then it is now, and all the institutions of society
should move to a restoration of the past.

As a group, essentialists are very enthusiastic about educational objectives.
They may not agree among themselves as to what the objectives should be or the

---

[13]For a more detailed discussion of essentialism and progressivism as educational philosophies
and their implications for physical education, the reader is referred to E. F. Zeigler and H. J.
VanderZwaag, *Physical Education: Progressivism or Essentialism?* (Champaign, Ill.: Stipes Publishing
Co., 1968).

[14] M. J. Demiashkevich, *An Introduction to the Philosophy of Education* (New York: American Book
Co., 1935).

relative priority among those established, but they always think in terms of certain objectives to be reached. Their objectives transcend individuals, and, as might be expected, tend to have a permanence which are not markedly influenced by the times at hand. Basically, they are interested in that which has been tried and supposedly found to be true. Objectives are largely thought of in terms of knowledge and skill to be acquired and attitudes to be shaped. In many cases the objectives also extend beyond an individual teacher's interests or desires; the teacher is expected to adapt to the objectives of the system. Departure from these objectives may well be evaluated as a shortcoming on the part of the teacher.

A curriculum grows out of the objectives or a lack of them. Among essentialists, the former is the case. Objectives predetermine the curriculum. Consequently, it is not surprising to find that essentialists are strong supporters of such curricular matters as required courses, core curricula, course prerequisites, and a definite sequence of courses. Departures from the curriculum are viewed with alarm and/or suspicion. Recognition of individual differences is lost amidst the effort to insure that all who graduate have the stamp of quality as determined by set standards of the past. Generally speaking, essentialists are on the lookout for "gut" courses, "snap" courses, and "soft" teachers. Schools of education have become favorite targets for essentialists because these schools have frequently employed progressivistic professors who are spokesmen for the other polarity.

Essentialists also place a halo around tests, particularly certain kinds of tests. This is to be expected of those who have fixed objectives and a prescribed curriculum. To put it simply, the tests are needed to determine whether the objectives have been reached. A test is viewed as the ultimate in keeping the pressure on the students. However, there is also a priority among tests. With certain essentialists, multiple-choice examinations are the only thing because they test depth and range of knowledge. Other essentialists, more humanistic types, glorify the essay exams because they are comprehensive and require reasoning ability.

Methodology may well be the area which most clearly distinguishes the essentialist. Ironically, they are not at all enthusiastic about the teaching of methods courses for prospective teachers because these courses are considered to lack content. But methods are not to be taken lightly. Some methods are definitely much better than others. Essentialists run a "tight ship," be it through administration or teaching. They frown upon those who appear to be relaxed, flexible, and pliable in their teaching methods. Customarily, the lecture has been assigned a halo alongside tests for the presentation of knowledge-type subject matter. There is nothing which surpasses a carefully prepared and systematically presented lecture; for the student it is supposed to represent the burning point of attention.

Administrative policies of the essentialist reflect very much the same kind of temper which is evident in his methodology. He is a firm believer in a line-staff pattern of control. There is a definite inclination toward an authoritative form of government. An essentialist looks at committee work with suspicion. We once heard an essentialistic administrator describe committees as "the pooling of ignorance." This is obviously an extreme point of view, but after all essentialism is an extreme position; even moderate essentialists feel somewhat that way in spite of the fact that they might couch their feelings in more diplomatic terms. Probably the number-one objection to committee work is that it is a slow and tortuous process.

An essentialist would place the burden of responsibility on the administrator. In short, the administrator must be willing to take a stand on various issues which arise. If he is not, he does not belong in administration and should be replaced by someone who will do so. Furthermore, he must be willing and capable of following-up his thoughts with action. Those working under this administrator may not always agree with him but they follow with the understanding that even the democratic process will not produce results which are fully acceptable to every individual.

Based on this brief description of the essentialistic constellation of beliefs, the reader should now realize that essentialism is not merely a matter of fiction. Most of us have daily contact with essentialists in some form or another, be they extreme or more moderate. We should also add that many kinds of eclecticism can be observed. For example, a given individual could be very essentialistic with respect to his ideas on the curriculum. Yet, he could prefer a more progressivistic administrative process. The question then becomes one of whether or not he is inconsistent. He may or may not be, depending on the extent to which he has thought through his position.

With this sort of background on essentialism, we now turn to the principal matter at hand, namely sport. In light of what we know about essentialism as a constellation of beliefs, how would a pure essentialist conduct a program of sport?

Sport is sport, and education is education! Whenever the two are mixed, certain problems are likely to occur. Education through sport almost amounts to what could be called a misnomer. The purpose of education is to develop the intellect. The purpose in sport is to have fun, pleasure, or enjoyment. Education is rigorous; it requires hard work. When sport is introduced into education, it may well water down the educative process because of the playful nature of sport. Sometimes one can hear reference to an individual as being a person who works hard and plays hard. According to the essentialist, that's the way it should be.

This essentialistic frame of reference should immediately tell us something about how sport should be organized. Preferably, sport is organized outside the context of the schools. When sport is offered under the auspices of the schools, it should definitely be on an extracurricular basis. The essentialist does not shun the concept of extracurricular activities. In fact, it is particularly meaningful and attractive to him. At one time it was customary to speak of extracurricular activities in the schools. But progressivism has made an impact in this respect. Today it is popular to refer to the co-curriculum and the extended curriculum. This is not a mere matter of semantics; progressivists feel that anything offered as part of the total school program should indeed be considered curricular. The reason the essentialist would restore extracurricular activities is that this does not confuse the educational business with recreational pursuits.

Another way of describing the intent is to say that the essentialist would eliminate the physical education or gym class as it is customarily known. The connotation behind physical education is that it is part of education. If sport is to be supported by the schools, intramural sport should be the thing. With this in mind it is not merely accidental that most of the private schools in the United States feature an intramural sport program in lieu of physical education classes. These schools by and large are steeped in the more traditional, essentialistic ideas. The inroads of progressivism are distinctly more evident in the public schools.

One of the reasons why the essentialist would allow room for the inclusion of sport in the schools on an extracurricular basis is that sport fulfills certain needs with regard to surplus energy and worthy use of leisure time. This is probably kind of a "gut" reaction on the part of the essentialist, but something tells him that it may be better for the student to participate in sport rather than some other activities when he is not studying. Thus, it seems desirable and maybe even necessary to organize sport after the classroom hours of the school. If left to his own choosing, without the enticement of an intramural sport program, the student may not participate in some other sport program which is available in the community at large.

There is no apparent reason why sport should be organized differently within the schools than it is without. In either case, sport is not first and foremost educational or curricular; there may be educational benefits, but they tend to be incidental or peripheral. Sport can be taught, but the teaching is of a skill nature, similar to that done by a teacher of trades. A trade school is one thing; an educational institution is something else.

When sport is taught, the essentialist also has some firm ideas as to how the teaching should proceed. To begin with, the laws of primacy and exercise have special meaning for him. In a sense, the essentialist's life is filled with an acceptance, promulgation, and enforcement of correct ways. Value judgments are not foreign to him; they are his life's blood. Sport is no exception. The essentialists believe in teaching the correct way first. For example, in the realm of athletics, as an extension of sport, coaches spend hours teaching what they consider to be the correct way.

An essentialist likes drill because it connotes discipline, order, and rigor. In the learning of sport skills, practice or drill is the name of the game. Many essentialists even go so far as to suggest that the drill and discipline to which the individual is indoctrinated in sport can be transferred to other situations in life.

The sharp distinction between sport and athletics also has special signifi-cance for the proponents of essentialism. It is consistent with their overall objec-tion to integrating activities, mixing apples with oranges. Just as education is education and sport is sport, so, too, athletics is athletics. We mention this here because drill, or application of the law of exercise, should be much more evident in athletics than in sport. Thus, it is not really as proper to say that the essentialist would indoctrinate through drill in sport as to note that the indoctrination is to occur in athletics, as an extension of sport.

Overall, the conclusion would be reached that sport should be conducted as a recreational activity. Those who organize the program and those who teach in the program are not educators in the true meaning of that term. They may be administrators; they may be teachers of sport skills; they could be both. Like-wise, coaches should be coaches. They are not educators, and they are not rec-reational leaders. For these reasons the concept of physical education is one of the most unfortunate to have been established in these areas of interest.

Even though directors of sport and teachers of sport skills are not really educators, they are involved with instruction, when required, similar to the way in which any tradesman may be an instructor. Instruction can be part of any recreational activity insofar as it does not detract from the essence of the activity. In sport it may be necessary to teach a few fundamentals to get the individual started. However, when instruction becomes the focus, the activity is no longer sport.

PROGRESSIVISTIC IDEAS FOR THE CONDUCT OF SPORT

From one standpoint it is not necessary to say anything about progressivism at this point. One could take the position of essentialism and move one hundred and eighty degrees either to the right or the left. However, if we were to follow this tack, we might be guilty of oversimplification and overlook certain points which help to shed light on the progressivistic frame of reference.

In contrast with essentialism, we have to begin by saying that progressivism is a much-abused concept. For many people, to be progressivistic is like being next to God. The situation is very much akin to the connotation of being liberal. People are more inclined to consider themselves as being progressivistic and liberal rather than essentialistic and conservative. However, many would-be progressivists or liberals are neither.

We would also have to say that the term progressivism was not coined by an individual or a group in quite the same way that essentialism came into par-lance. Yet, the educational philosophy of progressivism is probably better known, even though misunderstood. The impact of progressivism is largely attributed to the influence of John Dewey. He was the one who verbalized and even put into practice, through his Chicago laboratory school, many of the ideas which have become the hallmarks of progressivistic educators.

Progressivists are primarily concerned about the here and now and the possibilities for making progress in the future. They do not revere the past. What has occurred may have personal or intellectual interest for them, but they do not wish to use this as their guideline for the present or future. Their basic premise is that there is always room for improvement; change is absolutely necessary.

If society is to be changed for the better, education must do it. Therefore, the school is not an arm of society. The school is the primary institution for bringing about social change. Consequently, the school and its students should not be walled off from society. An education istitution must be made more a part of the real world. Progressivists would tear down the ivory castle and the ivy walls of the educational setting and place the students on the front of social action. In the 1970s we are really experiencing for the first time the full impact of progressivism on American college campuses. Many college students today are more interested in the larger issues in the world around them than they are in textbooks and the traditional courses. For the progressivist, this represents progress. He at last is seeing some of the progressivistic theory in action.

A progressivist begins by rejecting the idea that there even is such a thing as educational objectives; only people have objectives, not a process such as education. Objectives are an individual matter. They grow out of the interests and needs of the individual. Furthermore, there is nothing permanent or enduring about objectives. They may and probably should change from time to time.

This sort of thinking leads to the conclusion that curricular requirements are pure nonsense. They are designed to push all students through the same knothole and shape them all in the identical mold. To require students to take certain courses in a fundamental violation of the recognition of individual differences. A curriculum should be characterized by a dynamic quality. It should be flexibe, diversified, and rooted in the present. Students should play an important role in developing the curriculum. After all, they are the only ones who actually know their interest. Needs should not be superimposed.

Relatively little learning is retained regardless what the conditions are. As a result the most profitable thing we can do as educators is to offer courses which have meaning for the practical problems which are encountered on a day-by-day basis. This is another reason why the curriculum should not be prescribed and laid out in advance. A "good" curriculum will be characterized by latitude that enables teachers and students to keep abreast of everyday problems.

Similar to the curriculum, the methodology of the progressivist is also characterized by flexibility and diversity. There is no clear-cut pattern that all teachers or even teachers in a given subject-matter area should follow. The primary determinant for selection of a method or methods should not be the subject. First of all, methodology will be based on the interests of the students. Secondly, the interests and capabilities of the teacher will be taken into consideration. Methodology is important, but its importance grows out of an understanding of the principles of human behavior.

Administration is nothing more than a facilitating process. Probably the most desirable administration is that which administrates the least. In other words, administration is not the focus. Progressivists tend to be basically suspicious of administrators because they represent the establishment. Generally speaking, the establishment desires to preserve the status quo and is resistive to change.

All who are involved with teaching or learning should share in decision-making. To use the cliché, two heads are always better than one. Even though the democratic process is somewhat cumbersome, it is far more desirable than any other system of government because it at least offers a medium for the expression of ideas. Therefore, committees are a necessity. Communication is a two-way process. To transmit an idea is one thing; to react to an idea and interact with others is something different and far more desirable. In the long run those involved will be far happier and more productive when they have at least had the opportunity to express their opinion. Committee work offers that opportunity.

Progressivists might be considered as utopians. They have an unbounded faith in human nature. They are prone to reject the idea that life is compartmentalized in any way. The focus should always be on the individual, his rights, his freedom, and, most of all, his liberalization. What does that sort of temper imply as far as the conduct of sport is concerned?

A progressivist does not make a distinction between curricular and extracurricular activities. Education is as broad as life itself. Consequently, a curriculum should also be as broad as life itself. Conceivably, there is room for anything in the curriculum, provided it has interest to the individual and contributes to his liberalization. For many people, sport can be that kind of activity. Sport should not be considered as an addendum to the school program. Learning experiences through sport may be just as meaningful as those resulting from what have traditionally been considered the academic subjects.

There should be no sharp distinction between sport and athletics because athletics, as we know it today, should not exist. A progressivist is not opposed to excellence, but he is not as enthusiastic about pushing the pursuit of excellence as is his philosophical counterpart. Due to individual differences, some people will naturally be more proficient than others in sport. However, the excellence should occur in a natural manner without the pressure of external influences. A highly structured program of athletics is designed to "cream off the top" at the expense of the masses. Sport for all tends to suffer when the emphasis is placed on an athletic program.

The progressivists also refute the idea that a sharp contrast should be made between a teacher of theory and a teacher of skills. Such a distinction smacks of an intellectual bias, grounded in an exclusive interest in subject matter, which overlooks that which should be the focus in education—the individual. Ironically, a true progressivist would be just as opposed to the concept of physical education but for altogether different reasons than the essentialist. Physical education implies some sort of mind-body dichotomy which also takes attention away from interest in the individual student as an integrated being. Consequently, a teacher of sport skills is much more than just that. He contributes to the total education of the individual through sport. Rather than be called a physical educator, he could more properly be called a teacher of sport, regardless of any theoretical vs. practical differentiations.

Teaching for transfer has special meaning for the progressivist because he is first and foremost interested in seeing to it that education does not consist of a series of esoteric activities. The entire process of education should be one of transfer of learning. Nevertheless, he is violently opposed to certain interpretations as to how transfer takes place, particularly the formal discipline theory. This theory suggests that some subject matter has priority due to its disciplinary nature. Sometimes sport and athletics has been defended by essentialists as being unique in building character or developing manly characteristics. This, the progressivist approaches with skepticism.

In a somewhat different vein, the progressivist is also not wildly enthusiastic about the identical-elements theory. It smacks too much of an exclusive subject-matter emphasis, narrowly conceived. Furthermore, it seems altogether too impersonal. Instead, transfer should be interpreted from a more gestalt frame of reference. After a sufficient exposure to sport, people acquire an appreciation of sport which includes an understanding of skills integrated with attitudes toward sport which may be transferred to other situations in life. Sport, itself, should not be administered and taught as an esoteric emphasis. This is one of the reasons why sport should be an integral part of a school curriculum and not an addendum to the curriculum.

Another paradox emerges when one considers that the progressivist of today is no more enamored with "gym" classes than is the essentialist. However, again, the reasons for his objections stem from an altogether different basis. As a progressivist looks at the typical "gym" class in American schools, he notes the following characteristics. Classes are scheduled at definite times of the day and for set periods. Considerable attention is devoted to such matters as taking attendance, being in the proper uniform, and maintaining order. The entire enterprise is characterized by structure. A certain amount of time must be devoted to instruction, even if it is forced.

In place of the systematized gym class the progressivist would substitute a modular form of sport instruction for those who desire and need it. Teachers could be available during certain periods, and students would register for instruction on an elective basis. Similarly, "free play" and competitive periods are available. However, in all cases, scheduling is characterized by diversity and flexibility. For instance, there would be no objection to taking the students to the golf course for a morning. In fact, a "mini" course might even be scheduled wherein students would spend a week on the golf course, receiving instruction, practicing, and competing.

Thus, we see that in the progressivist's conception sport may at the same time be both a recreational activity and an educational experience. The orientation is always on the individual. What is mostly educational for one may be primarily recreational for another. Teachers should not get caught in the either-or trap. They should be flexible enough to recognize that two individuals participating side-by-side in a sporting activity may differ from one another considerably both in terms of motives and the nature of the values to be derived from the activity.

Sport is not a panacea either for recreation or education. People may choose to recreate through sport and they may benefit from it in various ways, some of which are quite undefinable. Others may elect to be partially educated through sport, and they may derive any one or several of a combination of educational benefits. On the other hand, recreation and education may well be a simultaneous enterprise for certain individuals. Life is not a series of neat compartments, mutually exclusive from each other. Sport ought to be organized, administered, and taught with these considerations in mind.

ECLECTIC POSSIBILITIES FOR CONDUCTING SPORT

One of the potential problems regarding any presentation of the "isms" is that the reader or listener may be led to believe that his ideas should fit into one camp or another. Life is not quite that simple. All people are not either Republicans or Democrats, liberals or conservatives, idealists or realists, essentialists or progressivists. We suspect that a continuum is again very much in effect.

Progressivism $\longleftrightarrow$ Essentialism

The majority of people probably have an educational philosophy which is located on the continuum, somewhere between the two extremes. Their positions may also change a bit from time to time, although hopefully they are not vascillating in their approach.

Those who do not adhere to any one of two extreme positions could be called eclectics. There have been suggestions that eclecticism is philosophically indefensible, but that may not be true, depending on one's interpretation of eclecticism. Purposefully taking the middle road would indicate a lack of philosophical commitment. If that is what is meant by eclecticism, we could not go along with it. However, if one thinks through his own position, wherever that might place him on the continuum, this can be defended and is what we call eclecticism.

With progressivism and essentialism as a frame of reference but not as prescriptions, we will take the liberty of expressing our personal ideas as to how sport should be conducted. The reader will undoubtedly note that some of these thoughts seem very essentialistic; others have a progressivistic tinge. No effort has been made to locate our position on the continuum because it appears quite incidental.

Sport should be organized, administered, and taught first and foremost as sport, a form of recreation. That is, the enterprise of sport should not be confused with either athletics or education. On the other hand, these areas are not mutually exclusive either. Athletics is an extension of sport. Therefore, certain sporting activities may tend to be more athleticlike than others; that is, competition is more important in them. There is nothing inherently wrong with this. It should be taken into account when sport is structured.

Similarly, among the various sporting activities, there are those which would appear to have more to offer in terms of educational benefits. That, too, is entirely justifiable and should be promoted rather than overlooked or purposefully ignored. For example, some sports are more complex than others due to the strategy, skill, or any combination thereof. When they require relatively more thought, the educational potential is increased.

If sport is a form of recreation, there seems to be no logical reason why it should be conducted differently within the school than it is outside the school setting. Physical education is an ill-conceived concept and probably has done more to hinder the development of sport in the schools than it has to advance it. "Gym" classes tend to be too structured and artificial; for certain reasons they do not really enhance natural interests in sport. For the most part the program of sport in the schools should consist of opportunities to practice sport skills and organized competition. Instruction would be available when needed and requested. The concept of teaching through progressive approximation should be utilized at every opportunity.

The only place we could defend required participation in sport would be at the elementary-school level. A critic might respond to this suggestion by stating that this reveals inconsistency in light of the previous statement to equate the conduct of sport within and without the school structure. There may well be a bit of inconsistency on this point. However, the elementary setting really is one of providing an opportunity in lieu of a requirement. If they are not in school, boys and girls participate in various form of play and/or sport on a daily basis. When they move to the school setting, a five-day program in sport will not actually be viewed as a requirement. Rather, it aids the transition from the play world to the school world.

Furthermore, the elementary level is not really the place for choices and electives. It *is* the place for breadth and exposure to a variety of experiences. Similarly, art and music are and should be required. A five-day program in sport is recommended due to the natural desire and need of the child to participate in active physical recreation whether or not he is in school. Again, instruction would be available as required. It is reasonable to suggest that almost all boys and girls could benefit from some sport-skill instruction at this level. The concept of progressive approximation should prove particularly meaningful and should be employed at every opportunity. As indicated earlier in this book, we do not share the enthusiasm of certain others for utilization of the concept of human-movement fundamentals or movement education.

From the junior-high level on, sport participation should not be required. For those readers in doubt at this point, there would not be required physical education at any level under our conception. Basically, the programs from junior high school through college would be what are commonly known as intramural sport, with instruction available when needed and requested. In other words, we are not advocating a sport program of any type during the normal school day—the time set aside for curricular pursuits.

We think that during the school day students should be involved only with those pursuits which are of an academic nature. This would, of course, include time for library work and other forms of study in addition to classroom study. Then a period of time, say 3:30 to 5:30 p.m., would be set aside for recreational pursuits. These include not only sport but music, drama, crafts, and other activities. Participation in all these activities would be voluntary, not required. Similarly, an athletic program would be available after school for those who are capable and desirous of pursuing excellence in this area. The objection could be raised that we are not very practical in suggesting that an athletic program and a sport program could be conducted during the same period of time because of conflicts in utilization of facilities. We recognize this practical limitation and can only suggest that the two programs be conducted simultaneously within the limits of the physical arrangements. Under many conditions it might be necessary to conduct either the sport program or the athletic program before school in the morning, during the lunch hour, or in the evenings. After all, many boys will voluntarily participate in little league baseball, pee wee hockey, Boy Scouts, and other recreational activities during the early evening hours. Is there any reason why they would not return to the school for a sport program, offered under the auspices of the school?

As indicated earlier, sport-skill instruction would be available for those boys and girls who need and desire it. Students would register for instruction in an area of their choice. The instruction need not be for a set period of time; this would depend on the progress of the individual student. We suspect that the reaction to this kind of an arrangement would be far more positive than one derived from a "gym" class where the student is often bored by listening to a presentation of basic skills which he has already acquired.

This writer cannot help but reflect at this point on certain observations which we made while visiting student teachers a few years ago. The situation was in one of our large cities, and basically this was what we saw. During a given period of time, such as six weeks, the city-wide limit in public-school physical education was volleyball. At the elementary school they were playing volleyball. The same thing could be witnessed in the junior high and high schools. What is worse, we strongly suspect that the same students were exposed to this experience each year from elementary through high school. Basic skills were repeated year after year. Is it small wonder that physical education has not achieved as much acceptance as had been hoped for at one time?

We see no need to change the basic structure of the sport program from junior high to high school to college. The activities may well be different; the principles of operation are the same. In each case the focus is on sport as a form of recreation. Instruction should be available as needed and requested. One would expect that there should be less need for instruction at the college level, but there will always be need for some instruction for certain students, particularly in selected activities.

We can think of no more glaring error in a sport program than to offer instruction just for the sake of offering instruction. That statement probably requires further clarification. In physical-education classes teachers are often assigned to teach a variety of sport skills. Often this includes skills in which they have relatively little proficiency and/or knowledge. They do the job the best they can, but they are handicapped by a system which forces an artificial situation. As an example, if a qualified golf instructor is not available, it would be better not to offer golf than to force a system of offering certain activities just to have them available. To do the opposite is a direct violation of the law of primacy. Possibly, even more significantly, it is difficult to imagine that the concept of progressive approximation can be utilized to its fullest extent when a relatively unqualified instructor is supposedly guiding the learning. We believe firmly in progressive approximation as a means for teaching and learning sport skills. Primarily for this reason we cannot condone any system which calls for teachers to attempt to teach a sport skill, regardless of background and capabilities.

The above is another reason why there is an urgent need to make certain aspects of the conduct of sport in the schools more like that found outside the schools. An elaboration of the example in the previous paragraph may again reveal what we have in mind. If one were to go to a golf course and sign up for lessons, he would certainly expect that the instruction would be given by a golf "pro" who was qualified to perform the task. The customer pays his money with the expectation that there will be positive results. There is no apparent reason why the situation should be any different within the school. Sport-skill instructors are employed by the school through taxes, tuition, fees, or any combination thereof. Even though the process is more indirect, the customer, in this case the student, expects results. It is rather unlikely that results will be forthcoming when a tennis coach, who took up the game of golf two years ago and plays occasionally, is assigned a golf section as part of his overall teaching responsibilities in physical education.

Evidence shows that sport skills tend to be quite specific; that is, there is relatively little positive transfer from one skill to another, particularly when the identical elements between the two are minimal. This does not mean that one should overlook those possibilities which do exist to teach for positive transfer. It does mean that sport administrators should be more realistic when assigning teachers to instruct in various sport skills. Chances are that the specificity of ability in sport may apply just as well to the teachers as to the students.

BIBLIOGRAPHY

Broer, Marion, *Efficiency of Human Movement.* Philadelphia: W. B. Saunders Co., 1960.

Broudy, Harry S., *Building a Philosophy of Education.* Englewood Cliffs, N. J.: Prentice-Hall, Inc., 1961.

Brubacher, John S., *Modern Philosophies of Education.* New York: McGraw Hill Book Co., 1962.

Demiashkevich, M. J., *An Introduction to the Philosophy of Education.* New York: American Book Company, 1935.

Knapp, Barbara, *Skill in Sport.* London: Routledge and Kegan Paul, 1963.

Metheny, Eleanor, "Are Sports Enough?" *Journal of Health, Physical Education, and Recreation,* XIV, No. 5, 1943.

Murphy, Chet, "Principles of Learning with Implications for Teaching Tennis," *Journal of Health, Physical Education, and Recreation.* February, 1962.

Oxendine, Joseph B., *Psychology of Motor Learning.* New York: Appleton-Century-Crofts, 1968.

Singer, Robert N., *Motor Learning and Human Performance.* New York: The Macmillan Company, 1968.

Studer, Virginia L., "The Historical Development of Human Movement Fundamentals for College Women in the United States." Unpublished master's thesis, University of Illinois, 1966.

Zeigler, Earle F., and Harold J. VanderZwaag, *Physical Education: Progressivism or Essentialism?* Champaign, Ill.: Stipes Publishing Co., 1968.

6/Why Is The Individual Attracted To Sport?

We now turn to those matters which are at the heart of any inquiry related to the philosophy of sport. These are the points of speculation and analysis involving the "why" of sport. As indicated in the preface, all the other questions have in a sense been preliminary to the consideration at hand. "Why" is the question which provokes curiosity; it leads to speculation and hopefully, to a concerted effort to arrive at some answers.

Unfortunately, to date we really have relatively few answers to the "why" of sport. The social science of sport is virgin territory. However, as stated earlier in this book, there are evidences that we may be embarking on a new era in which there will be scholarly study of sport. Should this occur, the question "why" will take on a new dimension, involving less speculation. In the interim we will have to restrict ourselves to noting those elements of speculation on which there has been some concensus. Likewise, the territory is still open to engage in a little speculation of our own.

In this chapter we begin by analyzing seven hypotheses which have been set forth as to why the individual is attracted by sport. There is nothing magic about the number seven. Others have obviously been postulated. We have rather arbitrarily selected those which strike us as having a fair amount of popular support. The eighth hypothesis, that sport is a stimulating form of recreation, is not novel. It too has been suggested in various forms. We save it for the last because it happens to be the one to which we can most subscribe at this time. The truth of the matter is that some kind of case can be made for all eight.

CULTURAL DEMAND

The individual is attracted to sport because of certain cultural demands placed on him. From one standpoint this is the simplest explanation. However, it tends to beg the question. A deeper question always remains: why does a culture place these demands on an individual? Part of the latter question is the topic of the next chapter, but even that does not suffice because a group is also part of a larger cultural setting. In other words, a curiosity always remains as to why the collective culture is as it is. A culture is a combination of individuals and groups with certain mores, practices, and values which the members share in common. So, one would be led to believe that the cultural-demand hypothesis can only be explained by searching for deeper reasons why the individual and the group are attracted by sport.

Nevertheless, the cultural-demand postulate is one of the favorites among the public and even those who have given some thought to sport. It may well be a particularly satisfying approach for those who would really prefer to avoid the question "why" and describe the "what." Implicitly, there is a suggestion that a description and an analysis of the situation sets forth the reasons which explain why it is so.

Adherents of the cultural-demand theory are most inclined to delineate those factors which may explain why the culture as a whole is absorbed with sport. The assumption is the majority of individuals are thus attracted because, after all, they comprise the culture. Our cultural frame of reference here is America, so we will examine those factors which have been set forth in an effort to explain America's sporting craze.

Much has been made of the relationship between sport and religion. A strong case may be made for the idea that the two can be positively correlated, but the history of the relationship has been more on the negative side. When we speak of religion in this context we are referring to it as a social institution or, in other words, the organized church.

Until the 20th century, religion or, more specifically, the organized church, was one of the dominant institutions in this culture. The doctrines of Thomas Aquinas and John Calvin were particularly influential in shaping the popular thought in America. Sport, as a result of its genesis in and association with play, was hindered in its development. Particularly Calvinism, with its emphasis on the moral values of work and denunciation of pleasurable activities as sinful, served as a detriment to the development of sport as another social institution.

Since 1900 there has been a gradual, but nevertheless noticeable, shift away from the puritan tradition as a dominant cultural influence. Cozens and Stumpf state it directly and succinctly: "It is a certainty, that, since 1900, Americans have been busy ridding themselves of the Puritan heritage of associating pleasure with sin."[1] In other words, in the 20th century Americans have actually been seeking play in its various forms, including sport. To play or to participate in sport has become more than acceptable; it has become a standard of conduct for many Americans.

---

[1]F. W. Cozens and F. S. Stumpf, *Sports and American Life.* (Chicago: University of Chicago Press, 1953), p. 8.

As Americans became less spiritual in their concerns, they also began to look at the physical side of man in a different sort of way. Prior to 1900 most people still clung to some kind of notion involving a mind-body. Some still do, but the development in the other direction has been noticeable. The body is no longer relegated to an inferior position of contrast with the mind as it was formerly. Because sport demands physical prowess as one of its most distinguishing characteristics, it is quite natural that sport should emerge as a significant form of play in an age where the physical side of man has achieved fuller acceptance.

Possibly the most significant factor in the rise of sport has been industrialization with all its accompanying social changes, such as urbanization. John Betts is one who particularly stresses this factor in accounting for the sudden rise in sport interests at the turn of the last century. "Industrialization and urbanization were more fundamentally responsible for the changes and developments of sport during the next generation than any other cause."[2] Betts cites a growing leisure class, higher standard of living, and better transportation facilities as among the subfactors which caused sport to advance hand in hand with industrialization and urbanization. A tertiary effect can also be noted. The industrial revolution made life considerably more sedentary for some who turned to sport as a recreational activity which fulfilled their need for physical activity.

Increased technology also resulted in the production of new and increased amounts of equipment. This factor should not be overlooked, because sport almost always utilizes equipment in some form. Many sports require an extensive outlay of equipment. Amidst their materialistic concerns, Americans have also been enthusiastic about the various kinds of sport equipment. In fact, the equipment may often be the initial attraction to sport. The sport equipment may be viewed as more than just a means of participating in sport. Similar to the automobile, the kind of sport equipment (including the clothing) may become a symbol of prosperity. Thus, it becomes important to not only ski, but also to own a certain make of skis.

These are among the factors which may account for the current absorption with sport in this culture. However, they fail to give an accurate account of individual motives because they rest on the assumption that an individual is solely a product of the culture in which he lives. Human factors tend to be minimized amidst broader, more impersonal factors.

Arnold Beisser is one who definitely seems to be in support of the cultural-demand theory to explain the individual's attraction to sport. The only problem with his thesis is that he may have refuted his own arguments by failing to distinguish between sport and athletics.

---

[2]John Betts, "The Technological Revolution and the Rise of Sports," in *Sport, Culture, and Society*, eds. John Loy and Gerald Kenyon. (New York: The Macmillan Co., 1969), p. 146.

How different the situation is in sports! The adult world not only looks with favor on the role of athlete, but deliberately fosters it. American youth is explicitly prepared for the athlete's role in exquisitely accurate miniaturizations of the professional team. Little League baseball and Pop Warner football are almost exact duplications of major professional sports. The uniform, the publicity, the arduous practice, the complex plays, and, most of all, the pressure of adult expectation, make the role of professional athlete not only a future possibility, but a present reality. . . .

Moreover, this role is thrust upon boys at ever younger ages. A football-shaped rattle for infants is now available to get them started right. Before children can read they wear replicas of sports uniforms. Once they can walk, training begins in earness.[3]

In other words, Beisser sees the American culture as forcing boys to athletic participation. He may be entirely correct in this assumption because of the highly structured nature of athletics. Organization breeds organization; the organization man seeks to also organize his son's activities through the medium of athletics.

But this argument can scarcely be used to explain why millions of Americans seek active participation in sport either in addition to or in place of athletic interests. In fact the American stress on athletics almost works at cross purposes with sport involvement because when the American is actively participating in sport, he is not part of the army of spectators. The individual who seeks sport may be working against the main stream. What, then, attracts the sport enthusiast? Perhaps it is the desire to be part of a group?

SOCIAL THEORY

Much has been made of the so-called social theory in an effort to explain the individual's attraction to sport. We say "so-called" theory because technically a proposition cannot be called a theory until there is some factual basis for it. We doubt if there is such a factual basis in this case.

In simple terms this pseudotheory suggests that an individual seeks sport due to his natural desire to be with others, to be part of a group. The most obvious limitation of this hypothesis is that there are numerous groups, other than sport groups, through which the individual may attain social identification. Any uniqueness with regard to sport groups would probably have to reside in the fact that they tend to be active and quite visible.

Of course, the frequently encountered problem of cause-effect relationship is also germane here. The problem hinges around the following question: does a man participate in sport because of his social nature or does he become more

---

[3] Arnold Beisser, *The Madness in Sports.* Copyright © 1967, by Meredith Publishing Company. Reprinted by permission of Appleton-Century-Crofts, Educational Division, Meredith Corporation.

social as a result of his involvement with sport? This is akin to the "chicken and egg" controversy. As is typical of many either-or questions, the answer may well be both or neither. An individual may be attracted to sport because of social needs and desires. On the other hand, he may become more socially conscious as a result of his participation in sport. But, in either case, it would appear that claims for the uniqueness of sport should be treated with extreme caution.

Paul Weiss is one who rejects the social theory as an answer to the question at hand, but once again the reader will recognize that his failure to distinguish between sport and athletics leaves one in doubt as to the validity of his conclusion:

Let it be granted, though, that play is an agency for maximizing participation in group activities. This is not yet to make evident why young men interest themselves in athletics. What may be true of the play of children is not necessarily true of the sport which interests those a dozen or so years older. The sport of men and the play of children, subsequent discussion will, I hope, make evident, are distinct from one another in structure. They have different aims and produce different results. But even if they were rather similar, or closely linked, the social theory would not help us much in learning why some men participate in sport. Though all children seem to want to play, not all want to turn themselves into athletes; though all men seem to enjoy watching athletic events, not all want to participate in them. The theory fails, too, to explain why some men interest themselves in individually pursued activities, such as golf, diving, surfing, shooting, ice skating, dressage, or weight lifting, unless we exaggerate the truth that even individual sports have a public and social dimension.

There are athletes who are individualistically minded. Though they compete against records set by others, or against a nature which challenges them all, though they are socially trained and normally act in terms of imagined competitors, and though they judge themselves or are in fact judged by others in public, common terms, they do not always take themselves to be part of some joint enterprise. If athletics is a means of making men social, it is a means which operates against the conscious and sometimes the express intent of some men who spend a good part of their days in athletic activities.

It is usually not too difficult to complete as part of some team. If all that was sought was an opportunity to be with others to unite with them, this could be done straight away by working with them then and there. One would have no need to subject oneself to a long and arduous discipline. The social theory does not explain why a man should willingly undergo long and grueling training, often by himself, at a pace and under conditions set by himself alone.[4]

If Weiss is exclusively talking about athletics, we are in full agreement with his assumptions and conclusion. However, he fails to leave the door open for a middle ground between play and athletics. He begins by recognizing that children may indeed be attracted to play for social reasons. There seems to be no

---

[4]Paul Weiss, *Sport: A Philosophic Inquiry.* (Carbondale, Ill.: Southern Illinois University Press, 1969), pp. 24—25.

argument on that point. Yet, is it valid to suggest that play is exclusively the province of children? We will grant that children find it easier to play and probably exhibit a more natural form of play, but sport, too, has its genesis in play; when sport is sport, certain playlike characteristics are evident. Furthermore, there is no apparent reason why sport is excluded from children or why adults may not engage in varieties of play other than sport.

When Weiss makes the leap from play to athletics he gets caught up in problems of over-generalization. It certainly is true that all children do not wish to become athletes, and all men do not have a desire to participate in athletics. I suppose it could also be said with some degree of assuredness that all children and men do not share the wish to participate in sport. Many do have this desire, but some prefer other varieties of play. Play is the universal want, not sport or athletics. Nevertheless, the probability is considerably greater that children and adults would prefer participation in sport rather than athletics, due to the nature of the latter. We do not feel that Paul Weiss does full justice to the social theory of sport.

It is true that the social theory fails to explain why certain men interest themselves in individually pursued activities, whether they be in the form of sport or athletics. However, some of the examples cited by Weiss may not be the best. For instance, he mentions golf as one. Golf may be considered an individual activity because one can play golf by himself. On the other hand, there is very definitely a social dimension with regard to golf that surpasses even that found among many of the team sports. We would speculate that most people who play golf do so for one or more social reasons. Among his examples, weight lifting may be one of the better, But, even then, a social basis can be found in the form of a weight-lifting club. Be that as it may, the overall point is well taken that some sporting activities tend to be more social than others.

The very nature of sport is such that the participant does not subject himself to long and grueling training; if he does, he has taken a step along the continuum from sport toward athletics. Sport is for fun, enjoyment, pleasure, diversion. Many people find enjoyment in being part of a group, be it a sport group or some other. Therefore, the social theory of sport cannot be entirely disregarded. It merely has to be approached with certain limitations in mind because sport is one of but several means for socialization.

One of the characteristics of sport which may place it in a somewhat different light in terms of attractiveness is competition. Many groups other than sport groups get involved with competition, be it overt or subtle, but the competitive dimension of sport is most visible. When people enter the sporting enterprise, they immediately recognize that they will be competing in some form or another. In the case of team sports, they are faced with a blend of competitive-cooperative elements.

The competitive element of sport may serve as an attraction, a deterrent, or both, in terms of socializing influence. It all depends on the individual. Some people find competition to be socially stimulating; others feel that competition works at cross-purposes to their social desires. Shaw[5] found that a competitive situation will generally produce the reaction of being more interesting and stimulating for the members involved. This is particularly true when two or more members of a team have been successful in competing against opponents. Thus, sport offers a certain degree of attractiveness through the expectation that there may be a social bond in excelling over others.

There has also been speculation and limited research with regard to the idea that mutual respect may be gained through competition; this would include respect of both partners and opponents. For example, Wilson et al.[6] found that the mere interaction of individuals in a competitive situation tended to enhance mutual respect. However, even here the cause-effect relationship poses a problem which may never be uncovered through research. It is most difficult to say whether individuals may be socially attracted to sport because of the anticipation of gaining mutual respect through competition or whether sport tends to be satisfying due to the mutual respect gained through competition. Again, we suspect that either, neither, or both may be the case.

So, the would-be social theory of sport should not be merely cast aside. Undoubtedly, it has been exaggerated by certain people and overlooked by others. It may be a partial explanation as to why some people are attracted by sport. However, sociability usually implies a fair degree of cooperativeness. There are those who would argue that man seeks out sport due to his natural aggressive instinct.

OUTLET FOR AGGRESSION

There is no denying the fact that people may exhibit aggression through sport. In some cases the aggression is overt and obvious. More frequently, the aggression is disguised amidst subtle overtones. But it is still somewhat tenuous to postulate that an individual is attracted to sport because it offers a socially acceptable medium to display or work off his aggression.

Possibly the most serious limitation of a blanket acceptance of the aggression hypothesis for sport is that sport would seem to lose its essential nature when aggression dominates the situation. The athlete is expected to be aggressive; the sportsman is expected to show more generosity. Certainly, there may be room for a degree of aggression in sport, but it is doubtful that sport is the most suitable medium for those who are trying to work out their aggression.

Then, too, there is the problem of differences among either sporting or athletic activities in terms of the potential for aggression. The contact sports— football, wrestling, hockey come immediately to mind. An aggressive football

[5] M. E. Shaw, "Some Motivational Factors in Cooperation and Competition," *Journal of Personality*, 27, 1958, 155–169.

[6] Wilson, Warner, and Miller, "Shifts in Evaluation of Participants Following Inter-Group Competition," *Journal of Abnormal and Sociological Psychology*, 63, 1961, 428–431.

player is not only sanctioned but also praised; aggression is the name of the game. However, an aggressive golfer cannot and should not be aggressive in the same way. If he starts to overpower the ball, it may actually work to his disadvantage. A tennis player may exhibit aggression by slamming an overhead shot at his opponent, but, generally, he is more concerned about keeping the ball as far away from his opponent as possible. Numerous other examples could be cited, but, for the most part, they would be very obvious. Overall, the major point is that one cannot take a single dimension of aggression and apply it equally to all sports. If aggression was *the* driving force in drawing individuals toward sport, it would be reasonable to expect that most popular sports would always be those which offered the greatest potential for aggression.

Paul Weiss also rejects the aggression treatise for athletics but for a different reason.

It is by no means evident that there is a native, primary, aggressive drive. No evidence has been provided for supposing that aggressiveness is more basic or more universal than self-maintenance, kindness, generosity, or sociability. There are men to whom passivity seems more natural or more civilized than aggression. They would rather submit than fight. . . .

Many sports require considerable cooperation on the part of all. All demand dedication and sacrifice. Every one of them offers a test of a man's capacity to judge and to control himself. Unless we insist on viewing its opposites as manifestations of itself, we cannot treat aggression as a primary drive, underlying all others. Though it may be possible to consider diving, weight lifting, marathon running, and mountain climbing as offering outlets for aggression, they, and other sports, can even more readily be treated as occasions for the release of excess energy, for attracting attention, or—what I have already suggested is the proper answer—for exhibiting and testing how excellent one can be by putting all his energies at the service of his body.[7]

Weiss is undoubtedly correct in his assumption that there is a lack of evidence which indicates that all men are naturally aggressive. However, by the same token, it could be questioned whether all men have the desire to pursue excellence. At any rate, sport is not a primary medium for either aggression or excellence. Athletics reveals the pursuit of excellence, and some athletic activities also display aggression. If *all* men are by nature aggressive, then one would have to conclude that *all* men desire to make their sporting activities more athleticlike. Such does not seem to be the case.

Part of the problem in assessing the merit of the aggression hypothesis hinges around a definition of aggression. Webster defines aggression as "a first or unprovoked attack, or act of hostility; also, the practice of attack or encroachment." Thus, it would appear that, technically speaking, aggression need not involve hostility. The person who is aggressive takes the initiative and the

---

[7]Weiss, *op. cit.*, pp. 33–34.

offensive. Often this will manifest itself in hostility, but hostility is not a necessary condition. In other words, aggression may come very close to Weiss' pursuit of excellence.

A positive relationship can also be noted between aggression and level of aspiration. Cratty devotes an entire chapter to aspiration level while pointing out that related concepts have a bearing: "Other terms are related to aspiration level and denote concepts which interact or at times are identical with aspiration level, e.g., self-confidence, ascendance, competition, and dominance."[8] Although he does not mention aggression per se, it could easily be argued that aggression is not far removed from the desire for ascendance and dominance. When one takes the initiative in going on the attack, it would appear that he most frequently does so in an effort to ascend or dominate.

According to Cratty, among the variables which influence aspiration level are past experience, nature of the task, maturity, parental standards, social factors, and personality traits. Studies conducted certainly indicate that aspiration level varies considerably from one individual to another. There is also some question as to whether we can properly refer to an overall or general level of aspiration for an individual. Aspiration may be specific to the task; that is, a given individual may have an intense desire to ascend with regard to one activity but remain relatively passive in pursuing another task. Cratty cites contrasting results in studies which have been conducted on this subject. Trow[9] and Gould[10] found that "aspiration level and confidence are specific to the kind of task under consideration." Based on their studies, Frank[11] and Ryan[12] lean more to the "general quality" thesis for level of aspiration.

If level of aspiration is as much of a variable as it appears to be, there is every reason to suspect that aggression is just as much if not more of a variable. Therefore, we find it rather difficult to accept the idea that either aggression or the pursuit of excellence is a universal quality. Certain individuals may be attracted to athletics because they are aggressive and/or desire to pursue excellence through that medium. These same individuals may choose to engage in sport for altogether different reasons. If sport is indeed characterized by generosity and pleasure, it could have special appeal for those individuals who aspire highly and find a need to be aggressive in other activities of life. In other words, sport is truly recreation for them because it frees them from the pressure of aggression and pursuing excellence.

---

[8] Bryant Cratty, *Social Dimensions of Physical Activity* © 1967, p. 19. Reprinted by permission of Prentice-Hall, Inc., Englewood Cliffs, New Jersey.

[9] William C. Trow, "The Psychology of Confidence," Archives of *Psychology*, 1923, 67.

[10] Rosalind Gould, "Some Sociological Determinants of Goal Striving," *Journal of School Psychology* (New York: Macmillan Co., 1941), 13, 461–473.

[11] J. D. Frank, "Recent Studies of the Level of Aspiration," *Psychological Bulletin*, 1941, 38, 218–226.

[12] Dean Ryan, "Competitive Performance in Relation to Achievement Motivation and Anxiety." Paper presented to the National Convention of the American Association of Health, Physical Education and Recreation, Minneapolis, Minnesota, 1963.

What is there about sport which might even hint that it is associated with aggressive characteristics in man? Even though we do not go along with the argument, as noted above, two possibilities for association might be found. One stems from the fact that sport is competitive. It could be argued that to compete is to compete. Room is not allowed for shades or degrees of competition. Sport is attractive because it offers competition. Aggression is broadly interpreted; competition is one of several varieties of aggression. As a result, the man who seeks sport is really manifesting his aggressive instinct. Even the skier who is not engaged in competition with others is aggressive because he is competing against the physical elements. The slope, snow, wind, cold, and skis present a challenge to him—a difficulty to be overcome. He takes the initiative in attacking the situation.

The fact that sport demands the demonstration of physical prowess offers another possibility for association with aggression. Even though aggression need not appear primarily in a physical form, most people are inclined to first of all think of the physical when aggression is considered. Physical manifestations of aggression are the most readily apparent; they are the most concrete and dramatic. As a result, the aggressive basketball player will draw attention sooner than the aggressive bridge player.

It has also been suggested that people sublimate their aggressions by becoming physically active. Sport offers a modicum for both physical activity and pleasure. If people were not physically active in sport, they might choose other, less desirable means to release their aggressions. This comes close to the surplus-energy theory which has also been postulated as the raison d'etre for sport participation.

SURPLUS ENERGY

Once again we begin by noting that the so-called surplus-energy theory cannot technically be called a theory because of the deficiency in scientific evidence. However, for purposes of brevity and simplicity we will continue to refer to it as a theory in our discussion here with the hope that the reader will not be misled by this casual usage of the term.

In the third chapter we briefly referred to this theory as the basis for the promotion of sport by parents and educators. A fairly popular idea is that sport is an excellent medium for youth to "let off steam." Within this context sport is viewed as a safety value for the release of pent-up emotions. Thus, it is felt that the individual is attracted to sport, be it an unconscious attraction, because sport offers the sort of physical/emotional release which is satisfying to the individual.

This sort of thinking not only draws promotional support from parents and educators, but is also reflected in the reactions of adults who participate in sport. I have frequently heard businessmen and professors extol the effects of a noontime handball game, not because they won or lost, but because of the feeling of relaxation it gave them after a morning of physical inactivity and strained emotions. They may not actually be aware of what it really was that attracted them to the handball match, but their "gut" response has some kind of relationship to the surplus-energy theory.

Credit for postulation of the surplus-energy idea as such is usually given to the German philosopher, Friedrick Schiller, who described play as being "the aimless expenditure of exuberant energy."[13] In light of current thinking about play, his definition would hardly be complete. Play may be quite passive and not involve physical activity. His description would be more appropriate for sport, if the adjective "aimless" was deleted. The organizational nature of sport makes it something other than aimless.

The name of Herbert Spencer has also been associated with the surplus-energy theory of play. Although he saw play arising from an instinctive urge involving a complex of factors, he did specify that the make-up of the nervous system in animals is such that there is a need for activity when the nerve centers are rested. It is interesting to note that in another statement he may also have lent support to the aggression theory: "The love of conquest, so dominant in all creatures because it is so correlative of success in the struggle for existence, gets gratification from a victory in chess in the absence of ruder victories."[14]

Thus we see that when more broadly interpreted, the surplus-energy idea may not be restricted to the mere release of physical energy but may also refer to an emotional concomitant, which is more of a gestalt idea. Sport, specifically, and play, more generally, may be a means of revitalization after long hours of work.

Once more we note that Paul Weiss' rejection of the surplus-energy theory as an explanation for an individual's attraction to sport does not really hold up under criticism because he is only referring to athletics, as an extension of sport.

Young men could be said to welcome training, practice, and competition because these provide them with opportunities to master the way their energies are expressed ... They must, it seems, live through tensions and crises before they can be at peace with themselves. The struggles they go through quiet their violence and structure their expressions to bring them into a vital relationship with their fellows. . . .

This account fits all athletes somewhat, and some of them quite well. Certainly in the beginning, and often throughout their careers, all are involved in the controlled expenditure of excess energy. They are usually restless; if they do not work off their energy in well-organized ways, they remain unfocused. When they become tired, more often than not they stop and rest awhile. If they feel they have passed their peak, they shift the center of their interests and allow sport to occupy them only in spare time. But not all

---

[13] J. C. Friedrick von Schiller, *Essays, Aesthetical and Philosophical.* (London: Bell & Sons, 1875), p. 112.

[14] Herbert Spencer, *The Principles of Psychology.* (New York: O. Appleton & Co., 1873), p. 631.

athletes answer to this description. Many of them continue to prepare and act, well beyond the point where they have energy to spare. Sometimes they urge themselves beyond the limit of fatigue. They call on unknown reserves to make use of energy which could have been deployed in other areas, or which need not have been tapped at all. More important, athletes, by and large, are men who obligate themselves to strive to realize a difficult goal. References to their surplus energy do not tell us how or why they make these severe demands on themselves.[15]

There is no denying the fact that the athlete goes well beyond the point of participating in order to find a release for his pent-up energy. His challenge is more frequently one of finding enough energy to carry him through a grueling match or a long season. This situation is so obvious that it scarcely needs to be mentioned. The surplus-energy theory was not postulated for work; athletics is work; it should not be confused with play.

However, as noted earlier, the surplus-energy theory would appear to be more applicable to sport than to play due to the physical prowess characteristic of sport. Even with regard to sport, certain limitations of the surplus-energy theory may be revealed. We can begin by noting the vast differences among the sports in terms of physical energy required or expended. For example, the range from swimming to archery is great. Similarly, how can handball be compared with bowling as to physical-energy demands?

If one wishes to extend the surplus-energy idea to a more gestalt realm, involving emotional or nervous-energy constituents, there are still problems in making the applicability to sport. This interpretation would hold that sport offers a medium for release of tension.

We will take golf as our example here to point out some of the problems encountered when one attempts to generalize with regard to this issue. Anyone who has played golf recognizes that the game requires much in the way of a blend between concentration and relaxation. The individual who plays golf with surplus energy (of the tension variety) finds that he is immediately frustrated because he can neither concentrate nor relax. As a result there is relatively little satisfaction, and it is not recreation. Now, of course, we recognize that all individuals will not react in the same manner. There will be those who can immediately leave the problems and tensions of everyday life and enter the golf endeavor with relaxation and concentration on the game of golf. For them, golf may offer a release from surplus energy. However, in general, it would still be tenuous to say that individuals are attracted to golf due to surplus-energy demands.

To summarize this analysis of the surplus-energy theory we would conclude that it does have some applicability in that sport may be a medium whereby certain individuals find a release from surplus energy and/or tension. There may be those sport participants who are consciously aware of this possibility

---

[15]Paul Weiss, *Sport: A Philosophic Inquiry.* (Carbondale, Ill.: Southern Illinois University Press, 1969), pp. 22—23.

and who seek out sport participation accordingly. By and large, we would speculate that the surplus-energy idea only enters partially in their motivation. There is something more gestalt, to be discussed at the conclusion of this chapter, which prompts them to seek out sport.

Somewhat akin to the surplus-energy theory is the suggestion that people participate in sport because of supposed physical values which may accrue to the individual. Physical educators have often used this suggestion to encourage participation in their programs. We will examine some of these proposed physical values in detail through our discussion in Chapter 8. But let us briefly look at the subject here from the standpoint of physical values as a motivating device.

SUPPOSED PHYSICAL VALUES

From time to time, an extensive propaganda program has been waged with regard to sport and physical fitness. Unfortunately, the latter concept has never been clearly interpreted or understood, even though we do have quite a bit of information on certain physical values which may result from physical activity. By and large the layman does not take the time to examine the particulars. Any interest which he has in sport from a physical standpoint tends to be of a more gestalt nature. Those who are intent on promoting sport have capitalized on this blanket acceptance of the physical by the layman. Sport has often been proposed as a cure for all ills, spiritual and emotional as well as physical.

Any tendency to be attracted to sport because of supposed physical values is entirely natural in light of the fact the demonstration of physical prowess is one of the characteristics of sport. The reasoning would proceed that since sport is physical, participation in sport should have beneficial physical effects.

We do not reject the physical value hypothesis as, once again, a partial explanation as to why sport is attractive. It might be a reason, for instance, that explains why one may prefer tennis to chess. However, this thesis can be found deficient when other items are factored into the total analysis.

First of all, even though people have a gestalt, physical conception of sport, they do recognize that certain sports are distinctly more physical than others. There is greater expenditure of physical energy in swimming than in bowling, playing handball than golfing, wrestling than in archery, etc. If the physical was the primary attraction, we would certainly expect that the sportsman would first and foremost gravitate toward those sports which offer the greatest physical demands. Such hardly seems to be the case when we note the vast number of people who bowl, play golf, and participate in other sports which may be challenging but require less in the way of physical output. At times, the attraction seems to be away from those activities which are more physically demanding.

Secondly, if one is interested in obtaining purely physical values through exercise, there are more efficient ways of doing it than through sports, even though the more vigorous are selected. As a case in point, jogging will be the most rewarding from a physical perspective within a given amount of time available. Weight training will be similarly productive. Therefore, those who choose sport over jogging or weight training must be motivated by something other than possible physical values.

Another factor which casts some doubt on the physical value motivation toward sport is that sport has flourished during times in which physical fitness has not been in popularity. This was exemplified in the 1920s and 1930s when the emphasis shifted from education of the physical to education through the physical. As we noted earlier in this book, the concept of education through the physical contributes to sport promotion. A strong case could be made for the idea that within physical education sport emphases often work at cross-purposes with physical fitness emphases and vice versa. We have frequently heard physical fitness exponents suggest that we must take more of the sport out of our programs and concentrate on those activities which have more to offer in terms of potential physical benefits. If these physical fitness adherents have any sort of effect on public opinion, it is difficult to imagine that the physical dimension attracts individuals to sport.

Thomas K. Cureton is one of those who dramatically and forcefully present and apply the point of view that the business of physical fitness should not be confused with sport:

Competitive football, basketball, track and field, baseball, wrestling, tennis, fencing, swimming, and gymnastics developed in the colleges as "athletic association" sports; and the high schools and junior high schools in imitation adopted them in a similar pattern; elementary schools adopted the elements of such games as physical education. These sports are usually administered apart from required physical education (1885 to the present) and are also taught in required physical education classes. It seems certain that physical education relinquished too much of its basic developmental and conditioning work for fitness in the urge to "play." In fact, "Throw out the ball" too frequently supplanted systematic progressive physical training.[16]

Ironically, Cureton's monograph is a report of research in the Sports-Fitness School at the University of Illinois. However, his report clearly shows that sport instruction must be placed in perspective; it should not become the focus at the expense of eliminating vigorous physical activity. Cureton and others in the physical fitness camp are not against sport. They view sport as being essentially recreational. By and large sport is sport, and physical fitness is a result of physical training.

---

[16]T. K. Cureton, *Improving the Physical Fitness of Youth.* Monographs of the Society for Research in Child Development, 95, 29:4, 1964, p. 6. Reprinted by permission of the Society for Research in Child Development, Inc.

Particularly since 1955 the voices of the physical fitness promoters have come through loud and clear. Americans have become more physical fitness conscious than ever before. At the same time, as noted earlier, sport has also flourished in an unprecedented manner. But the physical fitness and sport developments have been more parallel than overlapping or linked together.

In recent years, jogging has become very popular with adults in the United States. For instance, the popularity has been sufficient to make it the featured topic in the *New York Magazine* section.[17] Unfortunately, the title of the article is a misnomer. Jogging is "in," but it is not a sport. It would appear that any interest which Americans have in vigorous physical activity is not primarily motivated by an interest in sport. Again, Cureton comes to mind because the publicity associated with him has at the same time promoted jogging interests and toned down the association of sport with physical values.

Fitness directors repeat this axiom: You get fit to play games. You don't play games to get fit. But most games played with rackets contribute to fitness, including tennis, squash, badminton, lacrosse (handball, too). Sports of little value include baseball, bowling and golf—which Cureton calls "a good way to spoil a healthful walk."[18]

On the other hand, the individual's attraction to sport due to supposed physical values cannot be completely disregarded. Some people are undoubtedly convinced in their own minds that sport has physical value, regardless of what the evidence may show. A few years ago I played golf with a friend from college days who since has been involved as an administrator in the business world. He faces the typical problem of many businessmen, namely, having too much time for eating and not enough for exercise. During our round of golf he commented very openly and without hesitation that he really enjoyed the activity because it was exactly what he needed—exercise. We did not pursue the point because it might have prevented him from enjoying the actual benefits, those of a more gestalt, recreational nature. But whenever one hears a "gut" response of this type he cannot help but think that the elements of attraction are not always commensurate with the facts at hand concerning the values of any given activity.

In a similar vein, it is also fairly common to hear people suggest that they prefer to get their exercise through sport. The basic idea behind this line of thinking is that exercise per se is drudgery. There is no denying the fact it is work. So, when one participates in sport, he can have the best of two worlds. If he can have fun and receive physical benefits at the same time, this is hard to beat. I would have to be the first to admit that I am one who basically falls into this pattern. I will jog when I cannot find someone or do not have the time to play handball, squash, or tennis. Now this is done with the full realization that

---

[17]Hal Higdon, "Jogging is an In Sport," The *New York Times Magazine*, Section 6, April 14, 1968, 36—49, 52.

[18]Curtis Mitchell, "Run For Your Life," *The Healthy Life*, Time-Life Books Special Report (New York: Time Incorporated, 1966), pp. 35—41.

the physical values may very well not be the same. There seems to be little doubt that in a given period of time it is difficult to match jogging if one is only interested in possible physical gains. On the other hand, the rewards from an activity such as handball may be more satisfying even though the exercise component is not as evident in comparison to exercise per se.

Overall, this leads us to the conclusion that people generally are attracted to sport as a result of something more than just supposed physical values. For some, the physical dimension of sport may be the attraction. For others, the physical element may be incidental. Still others may hope to accrue physical benefits while recreating. But, if a given individual is searching for what might be called purely physical values, he will probably recognize that sport is not his most expeditious means.

GENERAL INCOMPETENCE

If sport is considered to be one of several forms of recreation (which appears to be a legitimate assumption), the argument could be raised that sport is attractive to those who do not have the ability to recreate through other means. In other words, if someone lacks an appreciation of art, music, fine literature, or other more "cultural" pursuits, he turns to sport as an area which offers something for everyone. Sport, then, becomes a recreational haven for those who are generally incompetent by comparison with the societal elite.

The reader will recognize that there are people who hold to this line of thinking. Naturally, it tends to be a viewpoint which is held by those who are not particularly interested in sport. A kind of snob effect prevails. On the other hand, their so-called prejudicial outlook may have some validity. There is no denying the fact that sport does seem to be for everyone, whether this is by choice or default of the masses.

A first limitation which one encounters in assessing the general incompetence hypothesis is that there is quite a difference between talking about sport and participating in sport. We suspect that any bias which the sophisticates have against the "sports nuts" stems from a feeling that a large mass of men are only capable of talking about two subjects—sport and sex, not necessarily in that order. They note, for instance, the vast numbers of American males who confine their reading to a glance at the front page of the local newspaper and a memorization of the details found on the sports page. Thus, based on distinctions made earlier, the talk is distinctly more about athletics than sport. In other words, reading, talking about, and watching athletics (particularly on TV) becomes the favorite recreation for the masses, particularly the males.

What do the facts show? Are Americans attracted to sport, as participants, or to athletics, as spectators, because they are relatively unenlightened or lack sufficient competence to pursue other forms of recreation? Do we have any facts? Unfortunately, because sport theory is still virgin territory, we do not have as many facts as one would desire. But a few studies are available which relate to the question at hand.

One of these is a study by Stone.[19] His conclusions are based on 566 interviews. Among his concerns were interpretations of the meaning of sport, the saliency of sports, favorite sports, sex differences in conversing about sport, socio-economic differences as they relate to sport conversation, and the relationship between sport conversations and situational contexts. Let us list some of the conclusions in his own words. We can then proceed to determine which of these conclusions may have bearing on the general incompetence hypothesis.

Now to begin with, all I did was ask these people what activities they thought of when they heard the word "sport." Over 2,600 activities were mentioned, so that each person on the average mentioned between four and five activities. There is a status relationship or socio-economic relationship between the number of activities that were reported or mentioned by these people. In general, the higher the status the greater the number of activities mentioned. This, I think, should be taken with a grain of salt because it may indicate merely a difference in verbalization among the strata and I may be reporting that rather than the fact that sport has a greater saliency for upper status people than for lower status people. But the consistency between the middle and the lower socio-economic strata suggests that this may only be partially true, since there is no great difference between the middle strata and the lower strata . . . there are only 6 people of the 562 who answered the question who could not come up with any activities relating to sport, so certainly this underscores Dr. Lüschen's observations to the effect that sport has a profound saliency in our entire society.[20]

A question arises as to the relationship between one's ability to articulate his conception of sport and his interest in sport. Generally speaking, I suppose we would expect the relationship to be a positive one. Stone seems to infer that it is when he concludes "that sport has a profound saliency in our entire society."

If one assumes a positive relationship between conception of sport and interest in sport, he then faces a second question of the relationship between general competence and socio-economic status. Our understanding is that competence refers to level of ability and does not imply a lack of potential. If that is true, generally higher competence can be expected among those in the higher socio-economic classes due to their advantages in educational opportunity. This, in turn, would lead us to conclude that there is relatively little, if any at all, in the way of a negative relationship between higher level of competence and sport interests. In fact, if anything, the opposite might be inferred from Stone's study.

---

[19] Gregory P. Stone, "Some Meanings of American Sport: An Extended View," *Sociology of Sport*, ed. Gerald Kenyon (Chicago: The Athletic Institute, 1969), pp. 5–16. Reprinted by permission of The Atheletic Institute.

[20] *Ibid.*, p. 6.

With regard to his initial question, he also drew a conclusion as to which category of sport received priority: "Spectator sports received the most frequent mention—football, baseball, and basketball; and that the mentioning of participant sports is somewhat less. In short it seems that in the public mind, sport is still primarily a spectator or a spectatorial affair, a spectacle, if you like."[21] Basically, what he calls spectator sports is what we refer to as athletics. Once again, the basic confusion manifests itself. It is most difficult to determine the degree of an individual's interest in sport or his reasons for being attracted thereto, if sport and athletics are thrown into the same barrel for reaction or discussion purposes.

I then asked people "what is your favorite sport?" Now, here we get into less difficulty in terms of saliencies and you can see that in terms of favorites, the people are about evenly divided between the selection of a spectator sport and a participant sport. The one point I think I'd like to make in terms of Table 3, is that we tend to think of spectatorship as being somehow low status or lower class in character. So that we tend to look at spectatorship as being lower class. Now you will see a slight tendency—I don't think it's enough really to warrant a great deal of emphasis—for participation as a favorite sport to be somewhat greater in the lower strata than in the middle strata, which I think is rather interesting.[22]

His reference to the popular association of spectatorship with the lower class is akin to our earlier discussion of the idea that there is a general association of talk about athletics with those who are less educated. Stone fails to point out that his Table 3 does show 64.4 percent of the upper socio-economic strata favoring participant sport or, in other words, sport in the true sense of the term. This serves to cast further doubt on the hypothesis that the individual is attracted to sport due to general incompetence. On the other side of the coin, as he indicates, his data comparing the middle strata with the lower strata show a slight tendency to the contrary. In general, the data are such that a valid inference cannot really be drawn.

Table 5 shows that in the first place it is a man's world; that the conversation about sports is quite frequent for men. About two-thirds of them say that they talk about sports frequently or very frequently, compared to somewhat more than a third of the women. Women, by the way, resent this, although I don't have time to go into it, but some of them are avid sports fans and they have a difficult time in finding anybody to talk about sport because the men refuse to discuss it with them.[23]

First of all, there is a problem here in arriving at any sort of opinion as to whether conversation about sports reflects an attraction to sport as a participant. Certainly, athletics lend themselves more to conversation because they are

---

[21] *Ibid.*, p. 7.
[22] *Ibid.*, p. 9.
[23] *Ibid.*, pp. 11–12.

geared to that end—to draw spectators, promote conversation, and thus draw more spectators. Secondly, if women tend to talk less frequently about sport, even though they might wish to, this lends more support to the cultural demand idea. The men in a male-dominated culture would prefer it that way. Thus, again we note that an individual's attraction to sport may well relate to a cultural demand, whether the attraction is to participate in sport or talk about it. What dictates the cultural demand? That is still the unanswered question.

I would then point out that the prime situations then for the discussion of sports in the lower strata aside from neighbors, are at work. This is a very important activity at the work scene and in public places such as bars, taverns, and the like. For the upper stratum it is in the family, with friends, on parties and on the sports scene itself. One of the consequences of this is that sport involvement may operate to increase family cohesion in the upper stratum. Although differences are not reported here, this may well be because membership in associations dealing with sport or peripheral to sport, like country clubs and so forth, are often family memberships in those strata.[24]

Again, it would appear that all classes are attracted to sport, regardless of educational advantages or overall level of competence. In short, sport seems to cut across intellectual and social/economic barriers. Members of the lower stratum may be more inclined to discuss their sport interests at the work scene just as a partial measure to relieve themselves of some of the boredom of routine tasks. In essence, they are seeking a diversion through talk about sport. Members of the upper class may be somewhat more inclined to talk about sport in connection with their participation in sport. Overall, there is nothing in Stone's study which would imply that an individual is attracted to sport because he lacks competence in other recreational pursuits. Possibly the opposite is true; could it be that the individual is attracted to sport because of his desire to pursue excellence?

PURSUIT OF EXCELLENCE

We will discuss this hypothesis only briefly, because the truth of the matter is there is doubt as to how much can be said about it. As we noted earlier, Paul Weiss more or less devotes an entire book to the subject. But he is actually writing about athletics, so it is quite understandable that he saw fit to discuss excellence in depth. As an extension of sport, athletics really is the pursuit of excellence.

What of sport? Can excellence in any way be associated with activities that are a modicum for diversion and pleasure? The answer probably hinges around a conception of the excellant man. Who is he? What conditions must be met in order to be excellent? Because Weiss has given much thought to the nature of excellence, we will begin by noting a few of his observations.

---

[24]*Ibid.*, p. 16.

Excellence excites and awes. It pleases and it challenges. We are often delighted by splendid specimens whether they be flowers, beasts, or men. A superb performance interests us even more because it reveals to us the magnitude of what then can be done. Illustrating perfection, it gives us a measure for whatever else we do. . . .

These excellent men are exceptions. Large enough for all of us to see, they are too large for most of us to imitate except at some remove. It is easier for most men to reach, not an excellence which requires them to first attain some perfection privately and then to impose it on a public body or world, but an excellence which results from a mastery of the body or of the things in the world. . . . But young men find it easier to master their bodies than to be truly noble, monumental, pious, or wise. We have here one reason why they readily occupy themselves with sport.[25]

If a case is to be made for the association of excellence with the central question of this chapter, at least two conditions must be met. To begin with there must be a willingness to accept Weiss' premise that all human beings have the desire to either pursue excellence or to identify with the excellence of others. As is true of all theoretical, speculative propositions, this is a point which could be endlessly debated. However, his reasoning makes sense to us, so we are willing to accept the pursuit of excellence and/or identification with it as one of a few, fairly universal qualities of man.

Then, the matter becomes: what of excellence and sport? Weiss' case for excellence and athletics is clear. The relationship to sport cannot be so easily arrived at, but two possibilities emerge. The first of these involves an identification with the performance of the athlete, other than being a spectator. Weiss alludes to this when he states that "they are too large for most of us to imitate except at some remove." Thus it could be argued that the young boy participates in the sport of football through his desire to identify with the excellence of his hero—the professional football player. This explanation holds up quite well until one realizes that a boy may also choose a sport in which there is no visible athletic model to imitate. In short, it may be an explanation as to why certain boys are attracted to sport. This attempt to reconcile sport with excellence becomes even more tenuous in the adult world where ideal models tend to lose some of their significance.

The second possibility is more abstract, although it may have greater potential if excellence is to be actually associated with sport rather than athletics. It stems from the thought that the truly excellent man is a complete man who lives his life in harmony, basically the Platonic conception of the ideal. The goal in life is viewed as that of trying to maintain a balance between extremes. If a man is exclusively devoted to his work or even worse, his specialized interest, he becomes too one-sided. He fails to appreciate the full meaning of life. It might even be said that "he cannot see the forest because of the trees."

---

[25]Weiss, *op. cit.*, pp. 3—4.

In this conception, sport is viewed as a means to liberate man from provincial thinking and narrowness of purpose. Man's attraction to sport stems from an unconscious recognition that he needs it to round out his life. We would probably be willing to accept this hypothesis if it were to be said of play rather than sport. Schiller's idea that "a man is not a man unless he plays" makes sense. For all practical purposes it could also be said of recreation because play and recreation seem to be essentially the same. But to say that a man is not a man unless he participates in sport is somewhat more questionable. We prefer to take a more cautious tack by suggesting that sport is one of the favorite forms of play or recreation because it is stimulating.

STIMULATING FORM OF RECREATION

I mentioned at the outset that among the eight hypotheses which are analyzed in this chapter, this is the one to which we can most subscribe, at least at this time. Individuals are attracted to sport because it is a stimulating form of recreation. The reader's initial reaction might be: so what?; you have stated the obvious. Our reply is that the obvious is often overlooked amidst an effort to arrive at deeper reasons. Permit us then to examine claims for sport as a stimulating form of recreation.

What is stimulating? Something is stimulating if it arouses the senses. Stimulating experiences are vivid experiences. When one is stimulated he is motivated to action of some form or another. Stimulating experiences tend to be attractive, particularly when coupled with previous experiences which would indicate that they may also be satisfying. What, then, are some of the characteristics of sport which would set it off as a stimulating form of recreation which attracts individuals?

ACTIVITY

Sport involves activity. Although the nature of this activity varies considerably from one sport to another, by and large people engaged in sport are on the "go." It is not accidental that the originators of the "Pepsi" advertisement presented pictures of youth on the "go" through sport.

Paul Weiss says that "excellence excites and awes." The same can be said of sport; it too excites and awes because it is active. We noted earlier that sport demanded the demonstration of physical prowess as one of its characteristics. This is inextricably related to the concept of activity. Of course, there may also be mental activity, but it is not nearly so readily apparent. Our reference to activity here is of the physical variety. As humans, we are inclined to be particularly awed when we see people move quickly and with agility. More importantly, in terms of our own sport participation, we have a natural desire to move with a purpose in mind. By comparison with other forms of recreation, sport fulfills that desire.

Particularly in this culture, passivity is considered to be a mark of blandness and indifference. We expect people to be active. We refer to the relatively inactive person as being one who lacks color. Therefore, it is not surprising that we are attracted to an active form of recreation, namely sport.

CONCRETENESS

Sport is a very visible sort of recreation. The activity of sport partly accounts for this visibility, but there is more. Sport facilities seem to have an eye-catching quality about them which is a bit difficult to describe. It may be because they seem to be set apart from the natural world; they have their own contingencies of space. There is something intriguing about noting the landscape architecture of a golf course while driving along the highway. Likewise, a swimming pool is a fascinating and luring entity. Bowling alleys, tennis courts, baseball diamonds, football fields, and large houses have similar, it not identical effects. They are there for all people to readily see. Not everyone is attracted by sport facilities. In fact, inadequate facilities may "turn people off." But sport facilities tend to be impressive, and they are readily discernible.

There is also a certain concreteness with respect to sport equipment. For instance, this is evidenced early in life when the young child is attracted by balls of various kinds. At that point, the ball may be no more attractive than any other toy, but, as the child gets older, sport equipment gradually replaces the toys as concrete objects that lure participation. Much the same thing is evident in the adult world. The young man is awed as he walks through the sporting-goods store and sees shining skis, colorful golf bags, and the fine leather in the assortment of footballs, basketball, and baseballs. Then too, the attractiveness of sport clothing should not be overlooked. Skiing again is a vivid example. It would be difficult to say how many people are attracted to skiing as a result of elaborate displays of ski sweaters, parkas, pants, etc., but certainly, along with other factors, these must have appeal.

CHALLENGE

Sport tends to be challenging. Naturally, some sports are more challenging than others, but, overall, sport ranks as one of the more challenging recreational pursuits. What makes an activity challenging? A challenge occurs when a difficulty or obstacle is not easily overcome. People need challenges in life in order to maintain their interest. Some people find a challenge in their work. Others do not; for them sport participation may offer even greater potential.

The skills of a sport are not easily mastered. If one could bowl a "200" game after having bowled only a few times, it is doubtful whether bowling would be attractive. It is the challenge of the sport activity that keeps people coming back for more.

Similar examples of challenges can be found in forms of games and recreation other than sport. For example, bridge tends to be very challenging by comparison with other card games. We have frequently heard people say that this is what they enjoy about bridge. But, overall, sport stacks up very well when one begins to evaluate recreational activities in light of the challenge they offer. It is the challenge which makes possible the diversion because it causes people to be utterly absorbed with what they are doing. If sports were not challenging, the participants might still be thinking about their everyday work activities.

COMPETITION

Competition is related to but not the same as a challenge. To compete is to contend in rivalry or emulousness. Very frequently challenges result in competition. Likewise, competition usually offers a challenge. But neither of these conditions is entirely dependent on the others.

One of the attractive features of sport is that it offers both competition and a challenge. Again, the competitive dimension of sport may vary a great deal and usually does, but competition, in some form or another, is part and parcel of sport. Not all individuals have the same desire to compete. Furthermore, many individuals may choose to compete only outside of sport. Yet, the urge for competition is universal enough to assist in making sport attractive. The competitive element in sport is extremely visible. It is there for all to see; there is nothing hidden or submersive about sport competition. This, too, helps to make sport appealing.

SUMMARY

Overall, if we examine the possible reasons why the individual is attracted to sport, we emerge with a gestalt effect. There is no simple answer. The individual himself is the important variable. He is probably attracted due to a complex of factors. Furthermore, at any given time in his life, a particular factor may be more significant than others. Later the "weighting" of these factors may change. But we do feel that, in general, sport is attractive among the forms of recreation because sport offers activity, concreteness, a challenge, and competition.

BIBLIOGRAPHY

Beisser, Arnold, *The Madness in Sports*. New York: Appleton-Century-Crofts, 1967.

Betts, John, "The Technological Revolution and the Rise of Sports," *Sport, Culture, and Society*, eds. John Loy and Gerald Kenyon. New York: The Macmillan Co., 1969.

Cozens, F. W., and F. S. Stumpf, *Sports and American Life*. Chicago: University of Chicago Press, 1953.

Cratty, Bryant, *Social Dimensions of Physical Activity*. Englewood Cliffs, New Jersey: Prentice-Hall, Inc., 1967.

Cureton, T. K., *Improving the Physical Fitness of Youth*. Monographs of the Society for Research in Child Development, 95, 29:4, 1964.

Frank, J. D., "Recent Studies of the Level of Aspiration," *Psychological Bulletin*, 38, 1941.

Gould, Rosalind, "Some Sociological Determinants of Goal Striving," *Journal of Social Psychology*. New York: Macmillan Co., 13, 1941.

Higdon, Hal, "Jogging Is an In Sport," The New York *Times Magazine*, Section 6, April 14, 1968.

Mitchell, Curtis, "Run For Your Life," *The Healthy Life*, Time-Life Books Special Report. New York: Time Incorporated, 1966.

Ryan, Dean, "Competitive Performance in Relation to Achievement Motivation and Anxiety," Paper presented to the National Convention of the American Association of Health, Physical Education and Recreation, Minneapolis, Minnesota, 1963.

Schiller, Friedrich, *Essays, Aesthetical and Philosophical*. London: Bell & Sons, 1875.

Shaw, M. E., "Some Motivational Factors in Cooperation and Competition," *Journal of Personality*, 27, 1958.

Spencer, Herbert, *The Principles of Psychology*. New York: O. Appleton & Co., 1873.

Stone, Gregory P., "Some Meanings of American Sport: An Extended View," *Sociology of Sport*, ed. Gerald Kenyon. Chicago: The Athletic Institute, 1969.

Trow, William C., "The Psychology of Confidence," Archives of *Psychology*, 1923.

Weiss, Paul, *Sport: A Philosophic Inquiry*. Carbondale, Ill.: Southern Illinois University Press, 1969.

Wilson, Warner, and Miller, "Shifts in Evaluation of Participants Following Inter-Group Competition," *Journal of Abnormal and Sociological Psychology*, 63, 1961.

7/Why Does the Group
   Promote Sport?

In the third chapter we noted that various groups are involved with the promotion of sport. This fact again leads us to ask the question: why? As is true of many questions, particularly those involving "why," there is no simple answer to the question of this chapter.

At least one answer is strikingly obvious. Some groups promote sport in order to make money. This is even more true of athletic groups, but the fact should not be overlooked that sport may also be promoted for purely financial reasons. As an example, we are thinking of a group of entrepreneurs who build the facilities and form a swim club for that purpose.

Other pragmatic reasons for sport promotion can also be found without too much difficulty. A group of parents or educators may encourage and/or provide for sport participation by youth to provide for what they consider worthy use of leisure time; that is, they hope the sport participation will keep the youth out of mischief. Physical educators may promote sport to enhance their professional status. Coaches may promote sport to provide lead-up interest and activity for their athletic endeavors. However, none of these more obvious and superficial answers is our concern in this chapter. We wish to focus on the question as to why any group might desire to promote participation in sport among its members in order to contribute to the solidarity of its members. An answer may be found in the nature of groups. What is it that distinguishes one group from another?

THE SIGNIFICANCE OF SUBTLE GROUP DIMENSIONS

A group of people may be nothing more than an assemblage of two or more individuals. However, almost everyone recognizes that groups are frequently much more than just that. This is particularly true when groups are organized. An organized group is usually formed with a certain purpose or purposes in

123

mind. As groups are formed or developed, they acquire certain characteristics or dimensions. Some of these characteristics are very obvious such as the size, sex, age, level, and overall purpose of the group. Other group dimensions are what the sociologist calls "subtle"; they are not easily recognizable, but in the long run they may be the most significant.

The group dimensions to which we are referring have been labeled as density, permeability, stability, naturalness, and internal cohesion.[1] Often, the members of the group are not consciously aware of these dimensions as such. They may recognize certain strengths and/or limitations of their group, but they fail to analyze those social processes which undergird their relationships.

This does not negate the fact that the success of a group, in terms of achieving its goal or goals, is very much dependent on these dimensions. Of course, internal cohesion is the ultimate. The name itself implies that a group with internal cohesion is likely to be more successful. But, although internal cohesion may be a gestalt factor, it is not an entity unto itself. Density, impermeability, stability, and naturalness may all contribute to internal cohesion.

Group density refers to the degree to which a group is primary or secondary. A primary group is one in which the members have a relatively large number of face-to-face relationships. The potential is there for the members to interact with each other. Generally speaking, a secondary group is a large group. However, size is not always the primary determinant. Sometimes, fairly large groups tend to be quite primary. By the same token, small groups do not always have the number of face-to-face relationships which they might desire. The significance of group density lies in the fact that by and large a primary group is more successful in reaching its goals. For instance, we have frequently heard members of academic departments deplore the situation within their department. More often than not, when the situation is analyzed, problems may be attributed to a lack of communication among the members. This can be found in both large and small departments. Rapport has not been established due to failure on the part of the constituents to interact with others.

As used in this context, permeability is related to accessibility and entrance. The idea of exclusiveness pervades the reciprocal of permeability, namely impermeability. When admittance to a group is relatively free of restrictions of any kind, it is said to be permeable. The possible restrictions are found in all kinds of forms, ranging from money to age to intelligence to level of physical ability. Sometimes, a combination of restrictions is in effect. Those groups which are somehow or another impermeable tend to have more homogeneity. The net result is that the activities of the group are facilitated, and, all other factors being equal, the group is likely to be more successful In doing what it set out to do.

---

[1] For a discussion of these dimensions in relation to physical education, the reader is referred to K. W. Bookwalter and H. J. VanderZwaag, *Foundations and Principles of Physical Education* (Philadelphia: W. B. Saunders Co., 1969), pp. 166—185.

Stability, as used here, has nothing directly to do with emotions. Sociologically speaking, stability refers to the permanence and continuing or enduring make-up of a group. A stable group is one which remains more or less intact over an extended period of time. Within instable groups there is either considerable flux, with people coming and going, or the entire group is of a short-term nature. The significance of the stability dimension should also be quite apparent. One can generally expect that a more stable group will have greater success in reaching its goals. Of course, exceptions can always be found. The cliché that "familiarity breeds contempt" is sometimes evident. But the odds still favor the idea that group accomplishment goes hand in hand with the duration of association of its members.

A natural group is one that is formed more or less of its own accord. External factors do not dictate the existence of the group. The opposite of a natural group is a forced group. The latter lacks spontaneity and often is deficient in motivation. Unfortunately, in a society with many social pressures, groups often tend to be somewhat forced. People are faced with a compulsion to belong to one or more groups. On the other hand, the satisfaction of belonging to a natural group is something for which most people strive. In a complex social order it is not easy to find and identify with a natural group. The entire concept of social conformity works against naturalness. Needless to say, a natural group has much going for it in terms of internal cohesion. It is reasonable to assume that a natural group is more likely to be polarized, and the members will be inclined to identify with each other as a result of this polarization.

Internal cohesion, as a desirable group dimension, does not exist in isolation. Not only naturalness but also the other subtle dimensions contribute to internal cohesion. Generally speaking, those groups which are primary, relatively impermeable, and stable are more likely to achieve internal cohesion. Of course, it could also be argued that internal cohesion is not necessarily desirable. But that is beside the point for purposes of discussion here. We are merely suggesting that a group may desire to promote sport participation among its members in order to assist in achieving internal cohesion among the group. Their success will be very much dependent on the relationship between sport and the other subtle dimensions.

GROUP DENSITY AND SPORT

It is not accidental that when a group of people are planning for a picnic, one of the first thoughts which comes to their minds is to make provision for the playing of softball, volleyball, or similar sporting activities. The direct idea of attempting to make their group more primary may not even occur to them, but they do recognize that these activities tend to serve as "mixers." In other words, sport offers an excellent medium for people to interact. One of the interesting things about sport is that there are several modes of interaction. The physical prowess and strategy involved account for many of these modes. Forms of inter-action vary from sport to sport, but potential for considerable interaction is found in almost all sports, even those which are considered to be individual in nature.

Parents and educators also recognize the potential of sport in enabling youth to identify with a primary group. The need to have friends seems to be a universal need. Sport participation does not guarantee the forming of friend-ships, but it offers distinct possibilities. It is difficult for one to acquire friendships unless he has primary group associations. In this culture, sport groups are very visible, primary groups. Therefore, parents and educators seize the opportunity to encourage primary group associations through participation in sport.

Cratty's summary of applicable sociological research also tends to support the hypothesis that sport offers a medium for acquiring friends:

In general the investigations support the common hypothesis that ability in physical activities contributes positively to social acceptance. Hardy, for example, surveyed the extent to which measures of strength and physical ability were related to students' ratings of "least popular," "average," and "most popular." Based upon measures gained from over 400 subjects, it was found that the best-liked pupils were markedly superior to the other pupils in tests of physical achievement, with 70 percent of them scoring above the mean of the total group. . . . Tyron likewise found in a survey of 100 boys age 12 that a reputation for being "good at active games" was associated with a reputa-tion for being a "leader" and "friendly."

Tyron's findings demonstrated, however, that by age 15 the behavior syndrome associ-ating skill at active games with outgoing sociality while present was not as high as it had been at age 12. Of most importance in Tyron's investigation was the finding that girls at ages 12 and 15 possessing ability at "active games" gained little prestige and were at times looked upon with disfavor. By the age of 15 it seemed that girls who were classified good at games benefited from it in terms of prestige only if they were not successful in heterosexual relations.

Kane in a recent study utilizing 412 boys whose average age was fourteen years found that extroversion was substantially and positively related to physical skill, strength, and size and that sociometric status was also positively related to physical ability.[2]

The fact that the hypothesis does not hold up as well with regard to girls merely points to the cultural expectation factor which was discussed earlier. Parents may be more inclined to seek other means, such as Girl Scouts, band, orchestra, and 4-H clubs, in order to make available primary group relation-ships.

Assuming, then, that sport groups tend to be primary and offer numerous opportunities for face-to-face relationships, the question then becomes one

---

[2]Bryant Cratty, *Social Dimensions of Physical Activity*, © 1967, pp. 14–15. Reprinted by permission of Prentice-Hall, Englewood Cliffs, New Jersey.

of attempting to determine the quality of these relationships. The potential for group interaction through sport appears to be found in what Ulrich calls the "patterns of social processes."

The five basic social processes can be identified as *competition, conflict, cooperation, accommodation,* and *assimilation.* Each of these is related to the others, and most social situations involve several of the processes and very seldom just one. The basic concept of sports and games seeks to utilize the entire continuum of social interaction and never just one aspect of it. Thus, sports and games do involve competition, but they also involve cooperation. Even conflict must have a cooperative base of two interacting groups who agree to have conflict. A game situation has often been compared to life itself, and the desire to participate in such an artificially constructed contrivance has been related to the desire to play the game of life within known boundaries, with known roles, known rules, and known penalities. Sport offers the individual the opportunity to test himself against unknown odds through social processes to see if he measures up to expectation or is found wanting. The responsibility of sports to the socialization process and to understanding of the ways that process works is fundamental to an understanding of life itself.[3]

Although we suspect that Ulrich places a rather strong value judgment on the possibilities for transfer from sport situations to circumstances in life generally, she does point to those specifics which might cause a group to promote sport in order to enhance the density of the group. Let us analyze each of these interacting patterns in the order presented by Ulrich.

We noted earlier in this book that competition is one of the essential characteristics of sport. When people enter the area of sport, they fully expect to compete. To what extent a group may promote sport to facilitate competition among its members or with another group is entirely another matter. A universal demand or need for competition is not that clear-cut. It all depends on one's conception of competition. Ulrich's description of competition clearly places it within the realm of sport because she views competition as something which is desirable and which can be controlled. People compete to achieve the same goal. This obviously causes interaction and shows the close relationship between group density and the potential for internal cohesion.

One of the interesting features about sport competition is that it is so overt and recognizable. It is conscious and there for all to see. Sometimes people are inclined to hide their competitive instincts and drives. But when they participate in sport, their competitive nature is usually revealed. Sport, as contrasted with athletics, does not penalize those who are less competitive. In essence, sport offers a range for those who desire to compete in any one of several forms and degrees. When sport is recognized as sport, it does not place a negative value judgment on those who cannot compete as well and those who chose to compete in a milder manner.

---

[3]Celeste Ulrich, *The Social Matrix of Physical Education,* © 1968, p. 76. Reprinted by permission of Prentice-Hall, Inc., Englewood Cliffs, New Jersey.

Conflict emerges as an extension of competition. It might be said that competition is to sport as conflict is to athletics. However, that would be a slight exaggeration of the truth. The continuum effect between sport and athletics is also applicable here. Just as there is a continuum extending from sport to athletics, so, too, competition and conflict can be placed on a continuum. Conflict is an extreme form of competition in which the contestants have the urge and frequently proceed beyond the rules of conduct which have been established for the conduct of the activity. As one moves from sport toward athletics, the possibility also increases that he will move from competition to conflict. The situation is schematically represented by two parallel, related continua:

Thus, it would appear that a group might promote sport for its members in order to provide for interaction through competition. If and when the competition changes to conflict, the design for the group has not been met. At that point the group may also choose to alter its purposes, but at any rate it can no longer be considered as a group engaged in sport. Competition within the group and with members of another group can contribute to internal cohesion. Conflict within the group is obviously contrary to the concept of internal cohesion; on the other hand, conflict with another group may serve the same purpose as competition with another group.

Among the social processes listed by Ulrich, the two pillars in terms of their applicability to sport are competition and cooperation. However, cooperation is so inextricably related to internal cohesion that it requires no elaboration at this point. It might simply be said that cooperation is a process which is a necessary condition of the goal or end, internal cohesion.

Ulrich states that "accommodation may be thought of as antagonistic cooperation."[4] This suggests that accommodation is a blend between cooperation and conflict. Sport is replete with examples of accommodation. To begin with, participants accommodate themselves to the rules, even though these rules may be foreign to their habits or tastes. The individual player also accommodates himself to the style of play of his partner(s) and/or opponent(s). Similarly, the sportsman is forced to accommodate himself to the environmental conditions under which he participates. The skier must accommodate to the conditions of the slope and the weather generally. A baseball player must assess the conditions of the playing field. The golfer is forced to adjust his game to meet the exigencies presented by a "new" golf course. In many outdoor sports, the wind becomes an important accommodation factor in and of itself. Nevertheless, the most important accommodation component is usually

---

[4] *Ibid.*, p. 85.

found in the relationship to another human being, be he a team member or an opponent. Here the accommodation primarily involves a reaction to emotions and attitudes, which, in the long run, are much more critical than any accommodations to knowledge and skill.

Lastly, Ulrich discusses assimilation as a social process, without direct reference to assimilation among sport groups. "When different groups are merged into a homogeneous unit, we can assume that assimilation has taken place."[5] It seems that assimilation is the only one of the social processes which requires interaction with another group. Assimilation might be viewed as being accommodation among groups. The concept of accommodation could well involve one of the more subtle reasons why a group might choose to promote sport participation among its members. Numerous groups will organize sport teams to assimilate with other groups.

The entire realm of intramural sport in the schools is a vivid example of assimilation. A fraternity enters its basketball team in the fraternity league in order to assimilate with other fraternity groups. The same thing applies when a residence hall unit enters the division of residence-hall sport competition. Faculty wives in a university organize a bowling league wherein various groups assimilate. Workers, representing various departments in a factory, engage as teams in a twilight golf league. Boys from different sections of a town organize their football teams to compete against other teams similarly organized. We could go on and on with these examples, but, needless to say, assimilation is one of the key processes in sport.

Now, all this leads to the matter of attempting to determine to what extent a group may arrange for sport participation in an effort to enhance its primary characteristics. It seems fairly safe to say that whatever is done in this regard is mostly of an unconscious nature. A group may well have some sort of gestalt feeling of desiring to have the members interact through sport, but, for the most part, they do not give that much attention to the modes for interaction.

But, in spite of this relative lack of overt, specific reasons, it may be hypothesized that sport groups are appealing in part because of their primary nature.

Of course, one could also take the approach that group processes cannot really be isolated from individual motives. This line of reasoning would suggest that the real answers as to why a group promotes sport are to be found in the cumulative effect of individuals' motives, as discussed in the previous chapter. There is some merit to this suggestion. However, it is entirely predicated on the assumption that people participate only in those activities which have intrinsic interest to them. Such an assumption fails to account for social pressures. Not everyone yields to these pressures, but many people are influenced in their activities by the promotional efforts of their group.

---

[5] *Ibid.*, p. 86.

What happens is that the leaders of a group seek means to get the members more involved. These considerations become particularly important in a large group where constant effort must be made to maximize the primary characteristics of the group. An excellent example of such a need is found in the large state university. For the most part the thousands of undergraduates in this kind of institution experience relatively little identity with the university at large and with their fellow students. Thus, it becomes essential for administrators to promote smaller, subgroupings within the larger structure. In general, people have a need for some form of primary group association.

Today the problem is more acute than ever before for several reasons. Universities have been growing at an extremely rapid rate. Certain types of primary group relationships are not as popular as they were at one time. For instance, in general there is less enthusiasm for fraternities and sororities than there has been in the past. Skyscraper dormitories have been built on many campuses. These structures add further to the impersonality of the large universities. Students get the feeling that they are living in a hotel room. More recently, the movement is away from this kind of dormitory living to apartments scattered around the university town and neighboring towns. Students are marrying at an earlier age. Today, the married undergraduate is fairly common. The net result of all this is that university administrators are searching for means to bring the student body together in primary group relationships. Particularly, these administrators attempt to promote those means which do not conflict with the purpose of the university. Sport falls into that category. Sport participation may not be among the central purposes of a university, but, at least, such participation is not designed to detract from the overall mission.

The above example is one of but many which could be cited wherein the leaders of a large group will provide for and encourage sport participation among its members. Whenever this is done it apparently proceeds from a two-fold recognition. First of all, members of a large group have a basic need to identify and interact with part of the constituency through association with smaller and primary subgroups. Secondly, sport is one of several media which will assist in meeting this need. This line of reasoning makes no particular claim for the uniqueness of sport as a catalyst in forming primary group relationships. There indeed could be something unique about sport in this regard. But, at this point, that still remains a subject which has to be explored scientifically.

IMPERMEABILITY AMONG SPORT GROUPS

The slogan "sports for all" is frequently uttered. This states very directly that sport is really very permeable; the boundaries leading into sport are easily crossed. There is an inherent assumption here that almost everyone can participate in sport if they so desire. From one standpoint, there is nothing wrong with the slogan and assumption. Certainly, by contrast with athletics, sport is quite permeable. However, more careful analysis will likely reveal that sport is not as permeable as it first appears.

Most people have the opportunity to participate in one or more sports. To that extent, sport could be called permeable. However, any given group proceeds to develop its own restrictions for participating in the sporting activities of that group. The answer as to how this is done may be found by looking at those factors which tend to make sport somehow or another exclusive.

Among these factors are money, sex, age, level of ability, previous experience, availability, and cultural expectations. Not all these factors are equally applicable to every sport, but one or more in combination usually accounts for the way in which a particular sport group is somewhat exclusive. A few comments on each of these factors in relationship to sport groups may help to reveal that sport can indeed be and often is quite impermeable.

The financial cost of participating to such sports as golf, bowling, skiing, sailing, and horseback-riding is generally rather high. Other sports could also be included in this category, but these are among the better-known sports wherein the financial limitation of participation is commonly recognized. There is, of course, variance even among these activities, such as the comparison of bowling with skiing. Then, too, sometimes these activities are made available to those who would not normally have the money to participate. This might occur through the offerings of public education. But, by and large, when those listed are compared with other sports, the financial limitations are evident.

Within any one of these sports, financial boundaries are set to establish and maintain the exclusiveness of a group. Thus we find that participation in golf, ranges from those who can afford to join the most exclusive golf club to those who pay a high greens fee to play at a semiprivate club to those who stand in line at 6 A.M. to gain admission to one of the municipal golf courses in a large city. The interesting feature about this situation is that each one of these subgroups of golfers has its own degree of exclusiveness. In other words, even though the municipal-park golfer cannot afford to join the neighboring country club, he can afford to at least play golf, which is not true of everybody. When he and his buddies are playing golf, they may even temporarily suspend themselves from the everyday world by imagining that they are part of the elite group of people in this world who are known as golfers, regardless of where they play. We can observe that any group of people can actually promote their own kind and degree of impermeability through the medium of golf. Similar efforts to make one's group financially exclusive can be noted in the other sporting activities listed above.

Sex is also used as a basis for making one's sport group more impermeable than it would otherwise be. We noted earlier in this book that there are vast differences in the extent and kind of sport participation for women as compared with that for men. Certain males capitalize on this cultural pattern to make their sport group partially impermeable. The "boys" get together in a game of touch football or softball to reenact the rites of masculinity. This is a throwback to earlier days when they were truly boys and they saw to it that no "foolish girls" were permitted to play in their sporting games.

On the other side of the coin, we see that females also take measures to insure that the boundaries of their sport group are preserved. The establishment of departments of physical education for women has at least in part been directed to that end. When Mabel Lee stated that the women of the physical education profession were "determined to keep them free of all taint of professionalism and commercialization—to keep them quite informal, entirely sane, and absolutely wholesome,"[6] she was speaking for some if not all physical educators. Even though she was referring to athletics, in essence she was stating that the desire was to preserve their sport as sport.

Women will also use sport to enhance the impermeability of their group in much the same way as men. The ladies bowling league is more than just a night for recreation. Through bowling the ladies reinforce their identity as a group. Even though they will likely have no objection to co-recreational bowling, they also desire to have other associations in a group comprised only of women. Bowling or some other sport can be used to accomplish this purpose in much the same way that bridge fulfills this need.

Needless to say, age is one of the most significant factors in making a particular sport group impermeable. Sport may be for all ages, but a specific group proceeds to establish the age boundaries for entry into their sporting activities. Age differentiations are, of course, most evident in the childhood and adolescent stages, but they do not stop there. Even the "golden agers" sponsor their own sports which are restricted to the members of their organization.

The attempt to make the sport group impermeable by virtue of age is probably most dramatized at the junior-high-school level. There it is very common to hear boys refer to their 7th-grade group or 8th-grade group that participates in sport competition which they have organized on their own. We are not referring to teams organized according to grade by school officials. In other words, these junior-high-school students are very conscious of age differentials, and they will promote sport competition within their age and grade-level group to reinforce the boundaries of their group.

Level of ability is an interesting and complex factor in relationship to degree of permeability among sport groups. Theoretically, one would suspect that level of ability should not be a precluding factor whatsoever in gaining admission to a sport group. It certainly isn't by comparison with athletics, wherein level of ability is far and away the number one factor in making athletics a very impermeable activity on the relative scale of enterprises. However, as is true of

---

[6]Mabel Lee, "The Care For and Against Intercollegiate Athletics for Women and the Situation Since 1923," *The Research Quarterly of the American Physical Education Association*, Vol. 2 (May, 1931), p. 127.

many of these possible precluding factors, sport groups proceed to develop their own breed of impermeability based on level of ability.

In spite of the fact that sport is conceivably for everyone, the participants find that they obtain considerably more pleasure from their participation when they are grouped according to level of ability. Consequently, even though it may not be a forced situation, as in athletics, a kind of natural selection process takes place. When a group is organized with sport as its raison d'etre, there is generally no great problem in this regard. Participants with approximately the same level of ability are likely to ban together and remain together as a sporting group. The possible problems occur when any group, preformed for some other reason, decides to engage in sport. They frequently find that the homogenity of their group does not extend to sport activities.

A group of bridge players who have been associated together in a bridge group for some time may suddenly decide that they should all play tennis as a group. However, the correlation between their proficiency as bridge players and their ability to play tennis is purely accidental. The result could be that the decision to play tennis might actually work at cross-purposes with the intent of keeping the group together or adding to the enjoyment received from the social processes of the group. As a result, among all the exclusive factors under consideration here, it appears that level of ability may be the most problematical if one is viewing it from the standpoint of why a preformed group initiates the decision to promote sport among its members.

Level of ability is not entirely dictated by but is very much related to previous experience. Thus, the analysis of previous experience as one of the impermeable factors among sport groups is not too different from that noted with regard to level of ability.

Previous experience is perhaps the most critical factor when several individuals get together and decide to form a sport group. Usually what happens is that those members who have had some experience in a particular sport ban together and arrange for continuing participation as a group. As an example, let's say that several new faculty members come to a school or university in the same year. One or more of these faculty members who happen to be golfers with a fair degree of ability will seek out other newcomers who share this interest and ability. The group is formed somewhat ad hoc, but it is nevertheless formed with previous experience as a criterion. Needless to say, previous golf experience becomes a factor of impermeability.

As with level of ability, the leaders of an established group (other than an established sport group) have to give serious consideration to the matter of previous experience before they proceed to promote sport participation among the members. In a large group there will likely be no great problem because they may be able to divide the members into subgroups according to previous experience. However, the cohesiveness of a small group could be impaired if the members lack any degree of homogenity with respect to a background in sport.

The availability of facilities is very definitely a precluding factor in terms of an individual being able to participate in certain sports. A classic example here involves activites such as handball and squash. Undoubtedly, many more adult males would be playing squash today if the facilities were more readily available to them. But these facilities are not nearly as abundant as those for golf, tennis, swimming, and other sporting activities. Those available are primarily found in colleges and universities, YMCA's, and private clubs. The net effect of this is that an activity such as squash becomes even more attractive among those people to whom it is accessible. A group leader, be he an intramural sport, YMCA, or club director, is able to capitalize on this particular factor of impermeability to promote participation in squash. In fact, he does not really have to promote. If his facilities, in turn, are limited, which is often the case, he is faced with the uncomfortable situation of trying to accommodate all those who desire to play. But, be that as it may, the relative exclusiveness of the facilities tends to draw together those who are able to play.

Perhaps the most subtle factor of impermeability among sport groups is that involving cultural expectations. This, of course, is one of the major reasons why several sports are relatively impermeable to women. It is also a major reason why boys and men seldom play field hockey in the United States. However, the cultural expectation factor of impermeability extends beyond exclusiveness according to sex. Unfortunately, the cultural expectation component is not easily pinpointed. That is why we referred to it as the most subtle factor.

Essentially what is involved is that certain groups and individuals with certain kinds of life styles are expected to participate in selected sports whereas other individuals are more or less excluded due to subcultural patterns. Money is one of the concrete components of the cultural expectation factor, but there is more than money involved.

Tennis and golf can be used as examples although these examples are not as pure and valid today as they were 20 years ago. Traditionally, golf and tennis have not been viewed as being sports for the working classes. In a similar vein, black people have been somewhat excluded from these activities. Financial resources or the availability of facilities may account for this in large part but not entirely. Fortunately, there has been somewhat of a breakthrough with respect to these two sports in recent years. Factory golf leagues are a case in point. Also, the increased availability of municipal tennis courts has broadened the base of participation. Nevertheless, in spite of any efforts to make golf and tennis sports for all, there is still a lingering social climate which implies that these sports are somehow or another for the elite and not the commoner. Even those working-class people who do have money for recreational sport seem more inclined to bowl than to play golf or tennis.

Whatever exists in the way of social stratification and cultural expectation can be and frequently is used by leaders of a group to promote sport participation among its members. Each social subset has a feeling of pride that goes along with its participation in a sporting activity which is associated with the status of the group.

We see, then, that any one or a combination of exclusive or semi-exclusive factors of sport may be used by the leaders of a group to enhance the processes of interaction within the group. Not all these factors are equally applicable to stimulating group interest. Also, it is important to recognize that for the most part these factors are not part of the conscious thinking of the group leaders.

STABILITY OF A SPORT GROUP

The group that plays together stays together. This is another one of those statements which has been expressed so frequently that it has virtually become a cliché. However, all clichés need not be summarily disregarded just because they are what they are. This may well be one which should be given further thought.

Although again the research evidence is far more limited than one would like to see it be, Lüschen has summarized that which is available. It points to the fact that sport may indeed be a rallying point in keeping a group together:

Piaget and Helanko give insight into the process of socialization through sport and games. Piaget in his study of the game of marbles finds how the child gets more and more involved in this game and its structure and thus learns not only to understand the game, to respond to other members of the play group involved but as well insight and understanding of social norms in responding to the rules and their reciprocity.... His findings that the game of marbles owes its rules to the children themselves is consistent with Helanko's results obtained in boy's gangs that sport as the main gang activity has its origin in the gang and in the specific age-group of 9 to 16. Sport is not only important in its integrative function during the gang-age but also in the period following this stage when young people aggregate and in obtaining sport often lay the ground for sport clubs. The ever growing involvement, the "expansion of socialization" from pairs before the gang-age to aggregates which lead to secondary types of groups with sport as the main activity shows a "rhythm of socialization"....[7]

A stable group is one which remains relatively intact over an extended period of time. Certain members may come and go, but there is a nucleus which preserves the continuity of the group. The kind of evidence cited by Lüschen can certainly be observed in everyday life. We have all known of groups which have retained a thread of continuity over the years, based on a mutual interest and participation in sports. It is not uncommon for the boy's basketball group to appear in later years as a men's bowling team or the group of men who regularly get together on Saturday or Sunday morning for a round of golf.

Two general limitations to this thesis should be noted. First of all, the kind of stability among sport groups as referred to here is more likely to be found in

---

[7]Günther Lüschen, *The Sociology of Sport*. (The Hague Paris: Mouton and Co., 1968), p. 13.

a small town than in a large city. Secondly, the mobility of people today causes this form of group stability to be less evident anywhere than it was 30 years ago. However, neither of these factors negates the importance of stability as a group dimension. In fact, if anything, it causes group leaders to search for additional means, be they through sport or other media, to keep a group together.

It also seems important to note that the use of sport and other media to keep a group intact does not always have a positive valence. Sport can be used to promote the stability of a group but at the same time, and more importantly, to retain the power of the group leader or leaders. Frequent references have been made to William Whyte's study of bowling participation among a neighborhood gang. His study brings out the point that bowling was used by the leaders of the gang to maintain their status as leaders. Whyte states: "Group activities are originated by the men with highest standing in the group, and it is natural for a man to encourage an activity in which he excels and discourage one in which he does not excel."[8]

In other words, one of the possible reasons why the leaders of a group may promote sport participation among its members is to reinforce their position as leaders. We indicated earlier that this might not be viewed positively. On the other hand, it could also have positive effects. This would be especially true if the leaders were indeed leaders rather than people who took control by means of domination. A leader, in the purer meaning of that term, is one who obtains that role through selection by the group. His power is not a self-designated power. It is expected that such a leader will also relinquish his power if and when he no longer has the support of the majority in the group. Under these conditions there would be nothing particularly negative about a leader promoting sport in an effort to hold the group together and at the same time to support or reinforce his position as a leader.

This kind of situation can be observed each day on the numerous playgrounds throughout the country. The leader or leaders of the neighborhood boys' group will arrange for sport participation. Invariably, the leader will suggest those sports in which he excels. Generally speaking, this is not resisted by the other boys in the group. They are inclined to accept this as the modus operandi.

The subject of leadership in relationship to group stability has another possibility and connotation which should not be overlooked. Within a large group, the emergence of one or more cliques is often evident. The one real limitation of a clique is that it often tends to work at cross-purposes to the design and intent of the larger group. In general, cliques do not contribute to the stability of the larger group. More frequently they are a disintegrating factor; they may lead to collapse of the larger group or at least preclude the assemblage from being able to function as a group.

Possibly herein lies one of the most significant factors as to why the leaders of a large group may decide to promote sport. There is a hope that sport will

---

[8]William Foote Whyte, *Street Corner Society*. (Chicago: The University of Chicago Press, 1943), p. 25.

serve as a catalyst in breaking down cliques and at the same contributing to mutual understanding among members of the larger community. For instance, in the school setting intramural sport directors have an excellent opportunity to utilize sport with that purpose in mind.

Even though cliques may work as a deterrent to group stability, they pose a much more serious problem in attempting to attain or retain internal cohesion. Therefore, we will forego further discussion of cliques at this point and make a few final observations when the relationship between sport and internal cohesion is considered.

THE NATURAL GROUP IN SPORT

Supposedly, a natural group is one that is not forced. That is, it does not arise as a result of external pressures, of one form or another. I imagine it would be possible to argue that there is really no such thing as a purely natural group. The very fact that a group is formed indicates some kind of pressure and/or motivation to combine as a group or to join a group. Pressure has a more negative connotation than does motivation. One could be pressured into joining a group against his wishes; on the other hand, pressure can lead to motivation, which is an intrinsic quality.

The existentialist[9] would be inclined to suggest that most groups are somehow or another forced. Groups tend to detract from the individuality and freedom of the would-be autonomous man. Thus, the concept of a natural group does not strike him as being a very realistic idea. But aside from any philosophical differences of interpretation as to what constitutes naturalness, any neutral observer would have to conclude that some groups are more forced than others. The continuum extending from play to sport to athletics is partially a continuum of degrees of naturalness.

Play $\longleftarrow$ ———Sport————$\longrightarrow$ Athletics

Natural group $\longleftarrow$ —————————————$\longrightarrow$ Forced group

The above suggests that a play group is basically a natural group whereas athletics consists of forced groups. This is obviously an oversimplification. Sometimes forced characteristics enter into the play picture. Similarly, not all athletic groups are entirely forced. In general though, the distinction will likely hold.

The position of sport in relationship to naturalness is difficult to assess. It would appear that a sport group is less natural than a play group and less forced than an athletic group. Based on distinctions among play, sport, and athletics, noted earlier, there is general merit in this assumption. However, because sport covers a very wide spectrum of activities, many exceptions can be found.

---

[9]H. J. VanderZwaag, "Sport: Existential or Essential," *Quest*, XII, May, 1969, 47–56.

A further complication stems from the central question of this chapter. The very idea of promotion seems contrary to naturalness. To promote an activity is to contribute to the establishment or development of that activity. A promoter is one who fosters or encourages. On the other hand, it can also be argued that the successful promoter is one who capitalizes on the natural desires and instincts of man. If a case is to be made for relating sport to group naturalness, one would almost have to proceed from the premise that the sport leaders recognize the human need and urge to play. When the leaders of a group desire to enhance the natural characteristics of that group, they may elect to promote sport, particularly if the playful characteristics of sport can be preserved.

Once again the intramural sport program in the schools offers a vivid example of how sport can be used to assist in reaching desirable group characteristics. The reader will note that a value judgment has been inserted here when we stated desirable group characteristics. I feel that naturalness is among the more desirable of the subtle group dimensions. This does not negate the fact that a strong case can also be made for athletics, consisting of forced groups. But the case for athletics must be made along different grounds, other than the suggestion that athletics is first and foremost characterized by naturalness.

Intramural sport is essentially characterized by voluntary participation. This is the number-one factor in explaining why most intramural sport groups are characterized by naturalness. Athletics also consist of voluntary participation, but there is often a social pressure which causes the young man with fine physical capabilities to feel that he must try out for the team. Generally speaking, such pressure is not found in intramural sport. This is one of the reasons why would-be athletics sometimes forego their athletic activities to pursue the sport endeavors of their choice in the manner and extent to which they desire. Intramural sport directors can augment the natural dimension of their enterprise by offering a wide variety of activities for all groups at various times.

A similar situation exists with regard to the recreational sport program within the community. The recreational director who is interested in contributing to the natural quality of the various groups with which he works will make every effort to refrain from promoting certain sports at the expense or exclusion of others. Of course, money and facilities are always the most limiting factors, but our reference is to offering as wide a scope as possible within the financial limitation. We have all lived in communities where the majority of the support and financial resources is directed toward the promotion of baseball, basketball, hockey, or some other single sporting activity. There is nothing inherently wrong with this, but the conditions which lie back of this kind of situation should be recognized for what they are. The director and the community which supports him have a philosophy of athletics which overshadows their philosophy of sport. Also, one would have to conclude that the director and the community are not particularly concerned about promoting the natural dimensions of groups.

The only real problem here is the hypocrisy which often surrounds on organization of the kind referred to above. As an example, I will refer to a hypothetical community in which the focus is on hockey, although any one of several other sports would offer similar examples in other communities. We will assume that the recreational director is a hockey "nut." He is assisted in his promotion of hockey by a vocal and capable group of individuals in the community who share his interest in this one sport. Now, we should add that all this is done with good intentions, and, in fact, much "good" may result. However, whatever good results from such hockey fanaticism should not be confused with a philosophy of sport that includes the promotion of natural groups through sport.

The chain effect of this hockey promotion within our hypothetical community would be something like the following. Leagues are formed with coaches, officials, and sponsorship. Uniforms are issued, and premium equipment becomes an important item. Car pools are formed by parents to get the boys to the hockey rink. Adult work and recreational schedules are interrupted and changed to facilitate the entire operation of the hockey program. Soon, games are scheduled with neighboring towns and even towns from other states, involving all-star teams. New boys move into the community. They may have had other sporting interests elsewhere, but they are soon caught up in the hockey craze. Hockey becomes the principal topic of conversation around the household dining table and even at social functions within the town.

Again, we hasten to add that there is nothing wrong about all these concomitants of the hockey program although the enthusiasm may not be shared by all those who are affected within the community. The problem, if there is one, is related to the superficial philosophy that is often uttered so glibly by those who promote and administer the program.

At the luncheon meetings of civic organizations and other public gatherings one can hear all the standard clichés that have accompanied the entire sport picture over the years. Athletic proponents will tell their audiences that they are offering sport for all. Every boy is given the opportunity to play. Hockey appeals to the natural instincts of the boy. The important thing is that the entire program is directed toward the building of character; winning is not really important. There is something for everyone in this activity.

We could go on with this list of clichés, but the readers have heard these and others so frequently that our point should be clear. The program does not always square with the philosophy which supposedly undergirds it. It would be so much better if the hockey leaders came out and stated that they were developing a program of excellence through hockey.

Why have we devoted so much space to describing an example which seems to be contrary to the idea of the natural group in sport? Our basic intent was to demonstrate that naturalness may be difficult to pinpoint, and it is not always that which is most visible. In our hypothetical community, hockey was extremely visible. The citizenry at large might reasonably conclude that the natural sort of thing for boys to do is to play hockey. They fail to recognize the subtle pressures and promotional schemes which are basic to the emergence of any single activity.

I mention this last point because it offers still another possibility in attempting to answer the question as to why any given group may decide to promote sport. Leaders in sport fully recognize that play is a universal need. People do not have to be forced to play; they will play of their own accord. Furthermore, the popular conception is to lump sport and play into one barrel. Many people may sense that sport is not exactly the same as play, but they also feel that whatever differences there are hardly deserve serious consideration. The same holds for any attempt to distinguish between sport and athletics in the public mind.

As a result, the leaders of any particular group may promote sport on the grounds that participation in one or more sports is the natural sort of thing to do. Sport is associated with play as being purely voluntary in nature. For the most part the masses are not cognizant of the subtle, organization pressures which cause them to seek out sport participation with their peers. There is nothing illegitimate about either the promotional efforts or the basis for being attracted to sport. The question remains as to what extent a sport group is a natural group. But aside from that question, which may be purely academic, there seems to be little doubt that sport may be promoted under the guise that it is a natural activity, calling for voluntary participation.

STRIVING FOR INTERNAL COHESION

Internal cohesion is the ultimate among the subtle group dimensions. It is the most difficult to identify and achieve, but, at the same time, it lies at the very basis of group existence. A group without some degree of internal cohesion is not a group in the truer meaning of that term. Leaders of a group are constantly striving to establish or maintain internal cohesion if they are actually the leaders of the group. On the other hand, superficial or would-be leaders may attempt to divide or split the group because they recognize that they do not really have the active support of the majority.

At least two constituents lie at the root of internal cohesion. First of all, the members of the group have a common goal. They may share more than one goal in common, which is likely to enhance the cohesiveness, but it is most important that there be at least one common denominator that represents something for which they are mutually striving. Secondly, the members of the group should be able to somehow or other identify with one another.

Looking at these two conditions of internal cohesion, we find it easy to see that they are not entirely exclusive of each other. As a matter of fact, they usually exist hand in hand, although exceptional cases can always be found. Having a common goal naturally tends toward mutual identification. By the same token, those who strongly identify with one another are more likely to seek a common goal. The exceptions to this combination are usually to be found in those situations where one of the conditions is so strong that the other cannot detract from the one element of cohesiveness.

One of the interesting features of internal cohesion is that it is very much dependent on and an outgrowth of the other subtle group dimensions. All other factors being somewhat equal, one would expect the following set of conditions to prevail. A primary group is more likely to have internal cohesion than a secondary group. Impermeability enhances internal cohesion. A relatively stable group generally has more internal cohesion than one in which the members come and go with many variations in membership. Something which at least approximates a natural group obviously contributes to internal cohesion.

From the simplest frame of reference, it could then be argued that a group promotes sport merely to add to its internal cohesion. This would be based on the collective assumptions noted earlier in this chapter. Sport offers numerous opportunities for adding to the primary nature of a group. There is an impermeable aspect among sport groups. Sport may contribute to the stability of a group. Although sport groups may not be as natural as one would desire, they are at least more natural than some others, and they may add to internal cohesion by appearing to be more natural than they actually are. In addition there may well be another aspect of cohesiveness in sport which transcends any collective result of the relationship between sport and the other subtle dimensions of groups.

If the leaders of a group are striving to enhance the cohesiveness of the group through sport, they will likely focus on those elements in sport which will draw the members together. Competition is definitely one of those elements:

Shifts in group cohesiveness and in an individual's feelings toward other members of the group have been noted to change after competitive behavior. In general, a competitive situation will usually be reported as more stimulating and interesting to the individuals composing the group. . . . Attraction of individual members toward one another increases, as might be expected, if they have been successful when competing in pairs. Moreover, Wilson, after periodic evaluations of members' "mutual attractiveness" at various phases of the task (involving the retrieving of objects from boxes using wires), found that simply interacting in a competitive situation enhanced members' feelings toward one another. . . .

In general, individuals group together for several reasons, including the satisfaction of individual needs to affiliate and the achievement of group outcomes in terms of productivity. Therefore, to some groups and to some members in a given group, the manifestation of group effort in the form of some performance score is subordinate to the mere fact they are affiliating. . . .

One of the reasons for the apparent high spirit and mutual productivity of college freshman teams with whom the author was at one time affiliated was perhaps partly due to their relatively recent acquaintanceship and their primary focus upon playing the sport at hand. On the other hand, it is a frequently noted problem that teams whose members are also associated socially in some way (e.g., the same fraternity) at times permit social interactions to interfere with the over-all team effort.[10]

---

[10]Cratty, *op. cit.*, pp. 39–40.

We have included several of Cratty's observations on the available research pertaining to cohesiveness in sport because they point to the complexity of the subject. It appears that, in general, competition will assist in attaining cohesiveness. This is due to the close association between interaction and cohesion. Group leaders may then decide to offer sport competition with that purpose in mind.

On the other hand, if the primary goal is to win the game, previous associations or too much emphasis on identifying with other members of the group may actually detract from the primary goal. This, of course, again brings us to the matter of athletics rather than sport.

The sport group is constantly striving to maintain a balance between the common goal of group success on the one hand and the feeling of mutual attractiveness among its members on the other hand. Whenever the sporting activity becomes more athleticlike, the group leaders no longer have internal cohesion as the primary objective.

I have given this much attention to the subject of group promotion of sport to stress the fact that an individual's motives are often quite different from those of the various groups with which he associates. It is one thing to consider the question as to why the individual is attracted by sport. It is another matter to determine why a group promotes sport. We cannot merely assume that group motives are a collection of motives of the individual members.

As we have attempted to describe in this chapter, it appears that group motives are more frequently those of a leader or leaders. The majority of the members may initially be introduced or ushered into the activity due to the group pressure. However, the reason for any given individual's sustained interest or attraction to sport may well be aside from and in addition to the overall purposes of the group.

In succeeding chapters we will also consider the question "why sport" but from a different perspective. Our interest shifts from the subjects of individual and group motivation to an analysis of possible theoretical bases for supporting a sport program. There is no denying the fact that large amounts of the taxpayer's money are spent on sport. Sport facilities are among the more expensive items in the capital outlay budget of a school. In addition, the taxpayer has the burden of financing numerous other sport facilities in the community. Aside from any attraction to the individual or the group when sport is available, the question then really becomes one of trying to determine why it is justifiable to make sport available to the extent which is evident. In other words, if any administrator was starting from scratch, why might he argue for the inclusion of a sport program?

BIBLIOGRAPHY

Bookwalter, K. W., and H. J. VanderZwaag, *Foundations and Principles of Physical Education.* (Philadelphia: W. B. Saunders Co., 1969), pp. 166–185.

Cratty, Bryant, *Social Dimensions of Physical Activity.* (Englewood Cliffs, N. J.: Prentice-Hall, Inc., 1967), pp. 14–15.

Lee, Mabel, "The Case For and Against Intercollegiate Athletics for Women and the Situation Since 1923." *The Research Quarterly of the American Physical Education Association.* Vol. 2 (May, 1931), p. 127.

Lüschen, Günther, *The Sociology of Sport.* (The Hague Paris: Mouton & Co., 1968), p. 13.

Ulrich, Celeste, *The Social Matrix of Physical Education.* (Englewood Cliffs, N.J.: Prentice-Hall, Inc., 1968), p. 76.

VanderZwaag, H. J., "Sport: Existential or Essential." *Quest.* XII, May, 1969, pp. 47–56.

Whyte, William Foote, *Street Corner Society.* (Chicago: The University of Chicago Press, 1943), p. 25.

8/Why Sport?
Physical Values?

Perhaps the most often suggested reason for initiating a sport program, encouraging participation in sport, or defending a sport program is that sport somehow contributes to that which is called physical fitness. This undoubtedly proceeds from the recognition that sport has the demonstration of physical prowess as one of its more distinguishing characteristics. When one is attempting to justify a program, he usually searches for a unique contribution which that program may have to offer. Because sport has a physical dimension, in contrast with other forms of games and recreation, it is not surprising that much attention has been drawn to the possible physical values to be derived from participation in sport.

What is surprising is that there are at least three possible limitations of associationg sport with physical fitness. One of these is the vagueness which surrounds the concept of physical fitness. People talk a great deal about physical fitness, but even the so-called authorities on the subject are in fantastic disagreement as to what characterizes the concept. A second limitation, assuming one accepts the concept of physical fitness, is that sports vary markedly from one another as to their physical demands. The third limitation stems from the hypothesis that sport may not be the most efficient means of attaining physical objectives.

I would prefer to proceed from the premise that sport may offer certain physical values for the participant without reference to physical fitness whatsoever. To make a claim for physical fitness is analogous to thinking only in terms of general intelligence while failing to recognize that intelligence has many variables. It seems that there are at least three physical attributes which may be developed through the medium of sport. These are flexibility, agility, and coordination. Other physical attributes, such as strength and speed, could and probably should be considered, but I will focus on the three mentioned because they seem to cut across and be evident in so many sporting activities. However, before analyzing the concepts of flexibility, agility, and coordination, we should give further attention to the limitations in associating sport with physical fitness.

Since the early 1950s the preachers of physical fitness have been very evident in the United States. Americans have been repeatedly told of their relatively poor state of physical fitness by comparison with Europeans and other people throughout the world. Many efforts have beeen employed to stimulate interest in physical fitness. Much of this is creditable, were it not for the fact that physical fitness is such an ill-conceived concept. Any attempt to develop the physical attributes of people would obviously have to be applauded. The problem occurs when these attributes are disguised and muddied amidst the vague concept of physical fitness.

Some people have suggested that physical fitness is virtually synonymous with total fitness. The inference here seems to be that man must be viewed as an integrated being; his physical functions cannot be isolated from his mental and emotional functions. That idea can scarcely be denied, but it is only further evidence why the concept of physical fitness presents many problems.

Others have taken the approach that physical fitness is meaningful when considered as a composite of several factors. This might be called the components approach. Several components of physical fitness have been listed from time to time by various physical educators. Among the numerous components suggested have been strength, endurance, agility, flexibility, coordination, power, speed, balance, and cardiovascular efficiency. The assumption seems to be that one can begin by identifying certain physical components. These can then be added together, and we have that which is called physical fitness.

Superficially, the above assumption would seem to have merit. But, at least two problems are most apparent. One is that there is marked disagreement in identifying the components. A particular writer may suggest that the components are strength, endurance, and cardiovascular efficiency. Another will state that endurance *is* cardiovascular efficiency. Still another will conclude that the components are more in number, to include such factors as balance, speed, and flexibility. In short, all kinds of combinations can be found among the listings of those people who are supposed to understand physical fitness.

A second problem relates to disagreement regarding the priority among the components. For many people, physical fitness is cardiovascular efficiency. All other components would be incidental or secondary to cardiovascular efficiency. If that is the case, physical fitness might as well be called cardiovascular efficiency, and the obscurity would be eliminated. But, it is never that simple. Someone else suggests that strength is really the dominant factor among the components of physical fitness. Still another relates physical fitness to health, stressing weight control and proper nutrition. So, the discussion continues endlessly while physical fitness is publicized and attracts many adherents who are in disagreement and in doubt about that in which they so firmly believe.

As a concept, physical fitness also presents problems when compared to related concepts such as motor fitness, general motor ability, physical efficiency, and health. If physical fitness is to be equated with total fitness, it might as well be called health; for all practical purposes, health, total fitness, and physical fitness would be one and the same. On the other hand, if physical fitness is but part of health or total fitness, one wonders what the difference is between physical fitness and motor fitness. Some people say that motor fitness is more specific than physical fitness, whereas others reverse the relationship. In a similar vein, physical efficiency has been compared with physical fitness. The former was a popular concept around the time of World War I. As noted earlier, physical fitness has some popularity today. But who is to really say what the difference is between the two concepts?

Physical educators are also sometimes inclined to speak of physical fitness in relationship to general motor ability. However, there is serious question as to whether there even is such a thing as the latter. It would seem to make very little difference if one were to suggest that physical fitness is part of the general motor ability or merely reverse the relationship

Thus, we cannot help but conclude that the concept of physical fitness lacks the concreteness to be considered really meaningful. There has been and continues to be a state of confusion regarding the nature of the concept and the relationship to similar concepts.

ESSENTIALISTIC PREJUDICES WITH REGARD TO PHYSICAL FITNESS

If we are correct in our assumption that the concept of physical fitness is relatively unmeaningful, the question then becomes one of trying to determine the basis for promulgation of such a concept. The answers may be found in the essentialistic stance which is taken by certain educators and laymen.

An essentialist is very concerned about the matter of justification. He proceeds from the basic framework of having a hierarchy of values; in his opinion, some educational programs are definitely much more important than others. Any new or relatively new program is assessed in relationship to this matter of justification. Many physical educators with essentialistic learnings have reacted strongly to this need for justification. They have searched for their unique contribution which might be cited as a justification for what they are doing or would like to do. This has often resulted in the proclamations regarding physical fitness. If one feels this strong need to justify a physical education program, it is logical that he might first turn to the physical values because these represent the one dimension which is not shared by other educators.

Furthermore, it appears that physical fitness has emerged as *the* concept for many of the physical education essentialists because they see it as the parallel to the stress which other essentialists place on intelligence and knowledge. Hunsicker presents the case well for those who hold to this point of view: "Some educators have been reluctant to use tests of physical fitness on the grounds that the test constructors are not in complete agreement on a definition of physical fitness. However, there is as much agreement on the concept of physical fitness as there is regarding the nature of the intelligence"[1]

The tie-in of physical fitness with testing is not accidental. This, too, is entirely consistent with the main stream of essentialistic thought. As a group, the essentialists are firmly convinced that testing is of great importance in the educational process. Measurement of the extent to which objectives have been reached can only be accomplished through testing. Therefore, it is not surprising that several of the attempts to define and circumscribe physical fitness are to be found in the various tests and measurements books which have been written by physical educators. The concept of physical fitness has at least in part been popularized to demonstrate to other educators that physical educators have an objective and an area for testing which are just as legitimate as the stress on intelligence and knowledge.

For these reasons we find that many of the essentialists within the profession of physical education are not as enthusiastic about sport as are their colleagues. Their hesitancy toward sport as part of their program manifests itself in two ways. First of all there is a general skepticism as to how much sport contributes to the development of physical fitness. Essentialists are most inclined to associate sport with play and recreation. By contrast, physical fitness is closely idenified with work. Although there is a recognition that sport may have something to offer in terms of physical fitness outcomes, it is relegated to a lower scale in favor of conditioning programs which are geared toward physical fitness per se. In brief, the physical fitness benefits of sport tend to be more incidental than primary. The result is that an emphasis on sport can detract from the unique contribution of physical education as a legitimate part of the total educational program.

In the second place, even those physical education essentialists who would accord some place to sport proceed with caution in selecting the sports for their programs. Generally speaking, they will emphasize that one important criterion must always be met: the sport must involve large muscle activity of a vigorous nature. They are not content to interpret the physical prowess dimension of sport in a loose manner. For them, the physical prowess in sport should be of a strenuous nature. The effect of this kind of orientation is that sports such as bowling, golf, archery, and horseshoes end up on a lower scale of things. Although they may be recognized as recreational activities of some value, they should not be confused with the business of physical education. The requirement of physical skill is overlooked because the essentialists' criterion demands more than skill. Some sports just do not meet the test of significantly contributing to the primary objective, physical fitness.

As stated or implied earlier, I am unwilling at this point to share this kind of enthusiasm for physical fitness as a concept. As a result, the essentialistic

---

[1]Paul Hunsicker, "Myths about Fitness." *Journal of Health, Physical Education, and Recreation,* XXXI, No. 2 (February 1960), p. 26.

concerns about sport in relationship to physical fitness do not concern me in the same way. On the other hand, I am not prepared to reject the idea that certain physical values may accrue through sport participation. As indicated earlier, the potential physical values which I prefer to consider in relationship to sport are flexibility, agility, and coordination.

THE CONCEPT OF FLEXIBILITY

Simply stated, flexibility refers to the range of motion permitted by the various joints of the body. At least, this is the basic meaning of the concept as we are considering it in this context. Webster defines flexibility as the state of being pliable or tractable, not rigid. Pliancy, suppleness, and mobility are other characteristics associated with flexibility.

There was considerable discussion about flexibility following the publication of the Kraus-Weber test findings in 1954.[2] One of the items in the test battery was what could be called a flexibility item. It was designed to test the extensibility of the back and hamstring muscles by having the subjects touch the floor with their fingertips while keeping their feet together and their knees straight. Controversy ensued when it was found that American children were below par when compared with their European contemporaries, and that the highest percent of American failures (44.3%) were on the flexibility item.

Mathews seems to summarize much of the reaction to this test when he states:

Exactly how much flexibility an individual should possess has not, as yet, been scientifically demonstrated. In the Kraus-Weber floor touch test, which involves the extensibility of the erector spinae, gluteal, hamstring, and gastrocnemius muscles, a passing grade is the ability to touch the floor. The only reported validity for this test is the evidence gained from examination of numerous patients by the medical people who have assisted Kraus.[3]

Perhaps the first statement is the key to the entire matter. Undoubtedly, we do not know how much flexibility an individual should possess. It is reasonable to assume that we may never know this. Furthermore, there is a serious question as to whether the attempt should even be made.

It seems that the focus should shift from the subject of how much flexibility to a recognition that flexibility is important even though the importance varies from individual to individual, situation to situation, and task to task. This we do know, flexibility has long been recognized as being of great importance in

---

[2]Hans Krauz and Ruth Hirschland, "Minimum Muscular Fitness Tests in School Children," *Research Quarterly*, 25:177–188, 1954.

[3]Donald Mathews, *Measurement in Physical Education* (Philadelphia: W. B. Saunders Co., 1968), p. 284. Reprinted by permission of W. B. Saunders Co.

many sports. It is important in two ways. (1) Sport participation requires varying degrees of flexibility in various ways. Many of the "loosening-up" exercises are designed to permit more flexibility in sport participation. But there is no single quality of flexibility which is equally required in all sports. Thus, the golfer may provide for greater flexibility in his swing by a preliminary exercise on the first tee. He holds the club with both hands behind his back while he pivots his body back and forth. Similarly, but with a different element of flexibility in mind, the football punter extends his leg as high as possible several times prior to receiving the pass from center. In both examples, the participant recognizes the importance of flexibility in executing a specific sport skill.

(2) There is also good reason to believe that flexibility is not only a condition of preparation for sport but also a result or effect of sport participation. We know that the extent of flexibility seems to decrease with age. As people get older, they generally have less flexibility. However, we have all also observed people who have been active in one or more sports for many years. In general, these people seem to display greater flexibility than those who have restricted themselves to more passive forms of recreation.

For still another reason, it is virtually impossible to state how much flexibility is desirable. The anatomical/physiological make-up of the individual is an important variable. The sport instructor will frequently encounter students who are too inflexible to perform the necessary skills. The inflexibility may result from short capsular structures around the body joints or muscles which are short and do not yield to stretching. It, of course, could be argued that such an individual does not have enough flexibility. However, it would be more valid to say that he lacks the necessary flexibility for the task at hand.

Within the limits of the individual, flexibility is developed by gradually increasing the amount of force used in elongating the muscle and, at the same time, moving closer to the upper end of the range of flexibility. In most cases, the individual will have a greater range of flexibility than he ordinarily exhibits in everyday activities. The various moves in sport participation frequently force the participant to move closer to the limits of his flexibility. Of course, there is also the possibility that his concentration on the sport will cause him to exceed his limits of flexibility and injury will result. The squash player may forcefully extend his arm, while reaching for a shot, and dislocate his shoulder. Nevertheless, in spite of the risk of injury, many people would not approximate the limits of flexibility in their bodily movements if it were not for their participation in sport. An exercise program per se may be designed to increase the range of flexibility, but such a program often presents psychological barriers which prevent the individual from actually realizing his potential.

Stretching is the term that probably best describes the action which must take place if flexibility is to be enhanced. When the muscular action around the joint is slow and sustained, stretching is most likely to occur. In other words, ballistic stretching should at least be preceded by a more gradual extension of the muscle fibers. For this reason, the warm-up is important. Even though the warm-up may not add to the range of flexibility, it prepares the muscles and ligaments for the ballistic type movements which expand the limits of motion. Coaches and trainers have long recognized that resistance to muscle tearing can be increased by a few preliminary stretching exercises before applying strenuous effort.

Although I am suggesting here that flexibility is one of the physical attributes which may be developed through sport, I would have to be the first to admit that we are more inclined to think of flexibility for sport than sport for flexibility. The following is fairly typical of statements which have been made, pointing out the importance of flexibility in sport:

A swimmer with relatively flexible ankles has the possibilities of more effective force for propulsion on every down-beat of the foot, because in hyperextension of the ankle, the water is driven backward and downward at a more favorable angle. In the use of the shoulders, arms and chest in respiration, suppleness is a great asset because the movements may be made more easily without disturbing the all important aspect of body balance necessary for minimum resistance. Flexibility exercises for swimmers have been made famous by Bob Kiphuth, Yale swimming coach, the trainers of the Japanese Olympic Champions, (1932), and by the followers of the Danish gymnastics.[4]

However, as is true of many considerations of this kind, this is definitely not an either-or proposition. There seems to be a fair amount of consensus on the idea that flexibility is significant as a condition to adequately perform many sport skills. This does not mean that flexibility cannot be enhanced as a result of the sport performance.

One of the reasons for suspecting that sport may contribute to flexibility is that it has been demonstrated that flexibility is highly specific. Earlier in this book we noted that sport skills tend to be very specific. The degree of flexibility may be one of the reasons for this. The flexibility required to swing the golf club in its proper arc is fairly specific to that activity. A proficient golfer may be relatively inflexible in terms of the range of motion permitted by certain joints of his body. But this in no way negates the fact that continued golfing will contribute to the development and/or preservation of a specific kind of flexibility.

Perhaps the strongest support which this author has found for the hypothesis that sport may enhance flexibility is found in the summary statements of Falls *et al.*:

Although there is an abundance of literature dealing with flexibility, a clear definitive statement regarding each of its many facets has not, as yet, been established. This is evidenced by a comprehensive review of the literature on the physiology of flexibility presented by Holland (1968). In addition to the different degrees of flexibility found

---

[4]T. K. Cureton, "Aspects of Flexibility and Its Relationships to Physical Education," *Research Quarterly*, 9 (October, 1938), p. 10.

among different persons, he indicates a consensus that there is a high degree of specificity of flexibility of the various joints of the body. The range of motion determined in one part of the body does not necessarily offer a predictive factor for flexibility in other body segments. Rasch and Burke (1967) also emphasize that flexibility is a specific factor for each joint.

Here again the SAID principle applies. As Holland (1968) reports, specific patterns of flexibility result from participation in physical activity that is specialized. With changes in range of motion coming about "naturally" by specialized forms of activity, it becomes evident that increased flexibility can be gained by adaptations to specifically imposed demands.[5]

Earlier in their book, the authors have described the "said principle" in this manner:

As Steggards (1960) most aptly put it, "I am fit to do things that you cannot do because of the type of physical activities I have forced my nervous system to adjust to." The body responds rather specifically to demands placed on it. This is a unifying principle that applies to any of the characteristics that comprise physical fitness. The concept is called the SAID principle. The word has been coined from the first letter in the phrase: "Specific Adaptations to Imposed Demands" (Wallis and Logan 1964). This principle provides a general guide to the design of an exercise program.[6]

This description seems very similar to the concept of specificity of motor skills. Just as individuals learn motor skills in a highly specific manner, so, too, flexibility is specific to the activity. There is good reason to believe that certain kinds of flexibility are developed and preserved by continued participation in sport. As noted with regard to many of the generalities with regard to sport, there is naturally a great variance from one sport to another. But, at least the claim for relating sport to flexibility is not a vague notion.

THE CONCEPT OF AGILITY

One hears frequent reference to the concept of agility. Coaches and spectators are most inclined to refer to the athlete who is quick and agile. Particularly in some sports, such as basketball, agility is recognized as a significant aspect of good performance. There seems to be little doubt that agility is considered to be a desirable physical attribute for a variety of reasons. Unfortunately, the attempts to measure agility have been relatively futile. There seems to be a gestalt aspect of agility which defies precise definition and therefore precludes the possibility of objective assesssment.

---

[5]H. B. Falls, E. L. Wallis, and G. A. Logan, *Foundations of Conditioning*, (New York: Academic Press, 1970), p. 50. Reprinted by permission.
[6]*Ibid.*, p. 43.

As an example of this measurement problem we might compare the so-called agility items on two well-known test batteries. The AAHPER Youth Fitness Test has a purported agility measure which is a 40-yard shuttle run. The subject is required to retrieve two objects at the end of a 10-yard course which is covered twice up and back. By contrast, the New York State Physical Fitness Test has an agility item which is called the "sidestep."

The subject starts from a center line and sidesteps alternately left then right between two lines 8 feet apart. The right foot must touch the floor beyond the right-hand line, and the left foot must touch the floor to the left of the left-hand line. The head and body must not be turned, and the feet cannot cross. The score is the number of "touches" made in 10 seconds.[7]

Surely, these two test items cannot be purported to measure the same thing. Yet, who is to say that both are not test of agility? It seems more appropriate to suggest that agility manifests itself in several ways; there are various aspects of agility.

The tennis player displays agility when he moves from side to side and up and back to retrieve shots hit all over the court. A basketball player relies very heavily on his agility as he dribbles around his opponents while driving in for a lay-up shot. Agility is most evident in soccer as a player positions and moves the ball with his feet. The wrestler must be agile as he moves about the mat to avoid a takedown by his opponent and at the same time to maneuver himself into a favorable position. Numerous examples could be cited for other sports, but these should suffice to reinforce two points. First of all, agility is an important attribute in many sports. Secondly, agility is highly specific to the activity. That is, the agile wrestler may not be an agile basketball player.

When one begins to examine the various manifestations of agility, at least four constituents can most frequently be noted. These are speed, accuracy, change of body-part position, and change of whole-body direction. Perhaps most frequently the combination of speed and change of whole-body direction is involved. However, agile movement is also accurate, in contrast with inefficient or wasted movement. Likewise, change of the body-part position may accompany the gross movement of the body. Thus, the tennis player shifts, his racquet from one side of the body to the other as he moves across the court. There seems to be a positive relationship between agility and flexibility. At least, one could hypothesize that flexibility aids or contributes to agility.

Although agility has not been one of the favorite topics among the researchers who are concerned with physical attributes, there is some evidence to support the claim that agility is related to success in many sports skills.[8] Those who

---

[7]Carlton R. Meyers and T. Erwin Blesh, *Measurement In Physical Education*, Copyright © 1962, The Ronald Press Company, New York.

[8]D. Beise and V. Peaseley, "The Relation of Reaction Time, Speed and Agility to Certain Sport Skills," *Research Quarterly*, 7 (March, 1936), pp. 110—118, and L. B. Keller, "The Relation of Quickness of Bodily Movement to Success in Athletics," *Research Quarterly*, 13 (May, 1942), pp. 128—133.

have observed coaches at their work cannot help but be impressed by the stress which these practitioners place on agility as they prescribe drills for their players. A common photograph on the sports page of the newspaper in early fall is that of football players running through a course of automobile tires. That is an agility drill if there ever was one. Similarly, the basketball coach may place a row of chairs on the floor and have his charges dribble in and out through the row of chairs instead of dribbling in a straight line. The baseball coach also recognizes the importance of drilling for agility as he hits ground balls to the left and right of the infielders during infield practice.

In light of the examples which have been used, it should now be clear that agility, along with most other physical attributes, does not exist in isolation. I have already mentioned that flexibility may be a contributor to agility. More importantly, agility should be assessed as but one aspect of a much broader and more significant concept, coordination.

THE CONCEPT OF COORDINATION

Paul Weiss has devoted an entire chapter in his book to the concept of speed.[9] We can easily see why he chose to do that because speed is fascinating and exciting. In several athletic activities, speed is also the most critical factor. I prefer to accord a somewhat similar place for the concept of coordination. The main reason for this is that coordination is such an all encompassing concept. Furthermore, coordination is important in every sport; there are sports such as golf, wherein the speed of the participants is not relevant.

Even though the reaction may not be as spontaneous and overt, man is also intrigued when he observes coordinated movement. Smooth, fluid, efficient, and natural are adjectives which are used to describe coordinated movement. Unfortunately, coordination is another one of those concepts which is better observed than described. Coordination is a complex of many factors involving principally the central nervous system.

One of the most intriguing things about coordination is that it is talked about so much, and yet we really know very little about the subject. As a result of his factor analysis technique, Fleishman points out the inherent difficulties in attempting to analyze this concept:

An area of physical proficiency which would appear distinct from strength, speed, flexibility, and the other factors mentioned, and important in its own right, is that of coordination. Yet correlational studies have failed to reveal an ability which could be labeled with confidence as General Coordination. An additional question of interest is whether there are several types of coordination.

---

[9]Paul Weiss, *Sport: A Philosophic Inquiry* (Carbondale, Ill.: Southern Illinois University Press, 1969), pp. 100–113.

... So, it appears that the kind of coordination emphasizing simultaneous use of several limbs in operating equipment is not the same kind of coordination as might be involved in athletic type tasks. In our studies with psychomotor devices the subject is seated or standing in one place and is not required to move his whole body. Perhaps, the critical distinction is that movement of the whole body is not involved in the kinds of tasks which appear on the multi-limb coordination factor.

Gross Body Coordination. Cumbee (1953), Cureton (1947), Hempel and Fleishman (1955), Larson (1941), and Wendler (1938) did identify a factor they called Gross Body Coordination, which did seem to emphasize more gross activity of the whole body (e.g., hurdling and jumping tasks). Perhaps this is the same factor which others have called Agility ...

A general factor often labeled Gross Body Coordination can be expected to appear when a number of complex sports skill tests (e.g., ball catching, soccer kicking), are included in a larger battery (e.g., Cumbee, 1953, 1957; Wendler, 1938). However, this tells us little about the precise nature of this factor or its possible components.[10]

Earlier we noted the relationship between coordination and agility. It would appear that coordination is far more encompassing than agility due to the many facets of coordination as referred to by Fleishman. One possible comparison is that agility relates to speed as coordination is dependent on timing. Yet, the agile person possesses more than speed. He, too, has the necessary timing to make the movement as efficient as possible.

Other physical attributes should also be considered when attempting to gain a better understanding of coordination. Balance is one of these. The common denominator between balance and coordination is to be found in the actions of the proprioceptors, cerebellum, and semicircular canals. They relate to the brain the position of the body in space. Coordination would not be possible without this sense of balance.

Similar relationships can be noted in comparing strength and endurance with coordination. Both strength and endurance may be viewed as precursors to coordination. It is frequently noted that a strong person may not be coordinated. But this does not negate the fact that a certain degree of strength and also endurance (in the case of sustained movement) are necessary conditions for a coordinated effort. In brief it might be said that any discussion of flexibility, agility, balance, strength, endurance, or other physical attibutes merely points out the complexity of coordination.

It is this diverse nature of coordination which offers the greatest challenge to the sport-skill instructor. He may provide numerous kinesthetic cues, but he fully realizes through experience that certain "teaching points" will always escape him in terms of facilitating coordination. For this reason I tend to support the teaching concept of progressive approximation as described earlier in this book.

---

[10]Edwin A. Fleishman, *The Structure and Measurement of Physical Fitness* © 1964, pp. 34—35. Reprinted by permission of Prentice-Hall, Inc., Englewood Cliffs, New Jersey.

Coordination is the harmonious action of the muscles, especially the voluntary ones. Thus, the key to a clearer understanding of coordination must be found through whatever insight we have regarding the functioning of the neuromuscular system. The eyes undoubtedly play an important role in most coordinated movements. Depth perception and peripheral vision are instrumental in complex movements, such as catching a ball on the run. Also, the individual is required to adapt to external forces in order to be coordinated. The outfielder catching a fly ball on the run must have more than good depth perception and peripheral vision. He must be able to make the necessary sensory-motor adjustments caused by external forces such as uneven terrain, the wind, and the impact of the ball hitting the glove.

This brings us once again to the central question which was also applicable to our discussions of flexibility and agility: to what extent can coordination be learned? Or, there is another way of stating what amounts to the same question: to what extent is coordination an innate factor? The most obvious conclusion is that this again is not one of those either-or situations. One would almost have to hypothesize that aspects of coordination are both natural and acquired, with the combination of the two differing markedly from one individual to another. Interestingly, researchers have handled this subject with caution and for the most part skirt the issue whenever possible. Singer is one of the few motor-learning investigators who directly discusses the essence of the problem:

Sometimes the word *coordination* is used interchangeably with *timing, skill,* or *general motor ability.* It has been determined from the research that coordination is important to potential athletic success as well as specific to the task achieved. Whether an individual is born with or develops body coordination, and to what extent, as reflected in certain motor skill achievements, is a moot point to be elaborated on in Chapter 4, under "The All-round Athlete."[11]

In Chapter 4, Singer elaborates as follows:

Genetics determine the limitations an individual faces in motor-skill attainment. Even as heredity determines potential intelligence levels, hair color, and body size, it creates the boundaries of motor development. It should be stressed here that research, especially on intelligence, points to the tremendous influence of the environment and life's experiences on an individual's achievements. As a further point, it should be realized that one has to go a long way before he reaches his maximum potential, whether in intellectual or motor pursuits. Thus it may be seen that although hereditary factors contribute to limit potential proficiency in motor acts, many of these factors can be overcome with the presence of the necessary drive and ambition.[12]

---

[11]Robert Singer, *Motor Learning and Human Performance* (New York: The Macmillan Company, 1968), pp. 62—63.

[12]*Ibid.,* p. 116.

The conclusions reached by Singer are most instrumental in our hypothesis that sport indeed has the potential to enhance or develop the coordination of an individual. Whether an attempt should be made to justify sport programs on that basis is still another matter and one that we will withhold personal comment on until the last chapter of this book. The hypothesis stems from a recognition of the following factors which have been cited. Coordination is specific to the activity; in other words, the coordination required in golf is not the same as that demanded in wrestling. Most people do not reach their natural limits in motor performance. Motivation is a most significant factor in enabling people to approximate their potential. Because sport is an extension of play, we would conclude that sport participation tends to be quite motivating for many individuals. Based on these conditions, there is good reason to believe that improved coordination may well be one of the physical values to be derived from continued and varied participation in sport.

WHY NOT CARDIOVASCULAR EFFICIENCY?

By this time I suspect that many readers are disappointed, if not absolutely disgusted, with the approach taken in this chapter. Here we have been writing about purported physical values while scarcely mentioning the one physical attribute which lies at the root of animal existence. Cardiovascular effiiciency is indeed a *sine qua non*. I will hasten to add that the intent was not to offer the unusual nor to minimize the importance of cardiovascular efficiency. As a matter of fact to even hint that cardiovascular efficiency is not significant would certainly be worse than opposing motherhood.

However, for a couple of reasons we have refrained from relating sport to the physical attribute of cardiovascular efficiency. First of all, as pointed out in Chapter 6, there is serious doubt as to whether participation in sport is the most efficient means of contributing to or developing cardiovascular efficiency. The characteristics of cardiovascular efficiency are generally considered to be low pulse rate, normal blood pressure, elasticity of the blood vessels, chemical balance in the blood, large vital capacity, and low breathing rate. Whether research has been done with regard to one or more of these factors shows that jogging is the most direct and efficient means of exercise to bring about desired changes. Swimming may rank a close second, but, after all, swimming is but one of numerous sports. A case could also be made for a sport such as handball. However, several variables such as the level of competition, equality of competition, and duration of play must be considered. Even then, swimming, handball, squash, and basketball represent but a small segment in the broad realm of sport.

This leads us to our second point of limitation in relating sport to cardiovascular efficiency. Some sports have virtually nothing to offer in terms of developing or even maintaining cardiovascular efficiency. Classic examples in this category are baseball, golf, bowling, horseshoes, archery, and shuffleboard. Baseball is a beautiful example because it is such a popular American sport. In this culture it is considered to be a very masculine activity. There is no doubt that baseball demands much in the way of demonstrating physical prowess. Flexibility, agility, and coordination are very evident when one observes the proficient baseball player. However, aside from the pitcher and catcher, few sportsmen or athletes spend more time standing in one place than do the other participants in a baseball game. This in no way makes baseball less of a sporting or athletic activity. It merely casts a shadow of doubt on some of the claims which may be ascribed to it.

Of course, we would have to admit that there is almost always an inherent problem when one attempts to take any of the physical attributes and positively identify it with all sports. Among the three attributes which have been highlighted in this chapter, agility is the most tenuous in this respect. We would really be forced to stretch our imagination if we saw agility as an important determinant in developing the successful golfer, bowler, archer, or horseshoe pitcher. So, maybe sport could be related to cardiovascular efficiency just as well as it is to agility.

Certainly a more substantial argument can be made for flexibility. The variance in demand is great, but we are a bit hard-pressed to think of a sport which does not require and contribute to flexibility in some way or another, be it minor. But, among all the possible physical attributes, coordination is the name of the game in sport. Sport does more than demonstrate coordination; sport demands coordination. Because coordination is such a varied and elusive concept, as well as being specific to the activity, one cannot help but suggest that the development of coordination is a potential physical value to be derived from active participation in sport. Furthermore, even though there may not be such a thing as general coordination (just as general intelligence must be questioned), the evidence would point to the need for a varied sport exposure in order to enable the individual to at least experience several kinds of problems of coordination.

BIBLIOGRAPHY

Beise, D., and V. Peaseley, "The Relation of Reaction Time, Speed, and Agility to Certain Sport Skills, *Research Quarterly* 7, March, 1936.

Cureton, T. K., "Aspects of Flexibility and Its Relationship to Physical Education," *Research Quarterly* 9, October, 1938.

Falls, H. B., E. L. Wallis, and G. A. Logan, *Foundations of Conditioning.* New York: Academic Press, 1970.

Fleishman, Edwin A., *The Structure and Measurement of Physical Fitness.* Englewood Cliffs, N. J.: Prentice-Hall, Inc., 1964.

Hunsicker, Paul, "Myths about Fitness, "*Journal of Health, Physical Education, and Recreation,* XXXI, No. 2, February, 1960.

Keller, L. B., "The Relation of Quickness of Bodily Movement to Success in Athletics," *Research Quarterly* 13, May 1942.

Kraus, Hans, and Ruth Hirschland, "Minimum Muscular Fitness Tests in School Children," *Research Quarterly* 25, 1954.

Mathews, Donald, *Measurement in Physical Education.* Philadelphia: W. B. Saunders Co., 1963.

Meyers, Cartlon R., and T. Erwin Blesh, *Measurement in Physical Education.* New York: The Ronald Press Co., 1962.

Singer, Robert, *Motor Learning and Human Performance.* New York: The Macmillan Company, 1968.

Weiss, Paul, *Sport: A Philosophic Inquiry.* Carbondale, Ill.: Southern Illinois University Press, 1969.

9/Why Sport?
Cognitive Values?

In the previous chapter we noted that there is a somewhat natural tendency to associate sport with physical values because of the physical prowess dimension which is characteristic of sport. Almost the reverse is true when it comes to associating sport with cognitive values. People still have not completely tossed aside the idea of a mind-body dichotomy. Forelin expressed the popular conception quite well when he stated that "bridge or chess seem somehow too cerebral to count as sports"[1] In other words, sport is not generally identified with cognition. The athlete or even the sportsman is not first and foremost thought of as being a thinking man.

The paradox of this situation is that physical educators have constantly striven to intellectualize their area of interest. They have searched for means which would bring their work more in line with the cognitive pursuits of their educational colleagues. This is, of course, entirely natural when one understands the history of physical education, as outlined in Chapter 2.

Now, if one is concerned about the cognitive aspect and values of sport, the question then becomes one of determining the possibilities which exist. The most immediate possibility resides in the hypothesis that people acquire knowledge through their participation in sport. This resembles the idea which is inherent in the concept of "education through the physical." Of course, there is also a recognition that some of this knowledge may be acquired through means other than being an active participant. For example, a spectator may learn the rules of baseball just as well as the baseball player. However, generally speaking, there is an assumption that one must be actively involved in order to fully understand the facts of the various sports.

The second possibility is much more abstract but in the long run offers far greater potential for associating sport with cognitive pursuits. This is the idea

---

[1]Robert Fogelin, "Sport: The Diversity of the Concept," paper delivered at the 13th Annual Meeting of the American Association for the Advancement of Science, Dallas, Texas, December 28, 1968.

that sport offers a medium for developing a body of knowledge. In other words, the suggestion is that the study of sport could be a disciplinelike field. One of the interesting features of this second possibility is that it is not necessarily used to justify the establishment or promulgation of a sport program. Advocates of this position proceed from the premise that sport exists. The problem is one of attempting to know more about that which exists. It could be that sport has received too much emphasis. Or, maybe sport should be organized and structured along different lines. In other words, the supporters of this sort of knowledge pursuit are not willing to accept the status quo. The question "why" looms uppermost in their minds.

ACQUIRING KNOWLEDGE THROUGH SPORT PARTICIPATION

RULES

Probably the first bit of knowledge to which one is exposed when he embarks on a sporting endeavor is that involving rules. In Chapter 4 we noted that rules predominate in a game. Games of sport are no exception. The would-be player is immediately faced with the need to at least learn the basic rules before he can begin to participate. Children demonstrate this need in a most natural manner when they are introduced to a sport. A teacher may choose to begin by talking about and demonstrating basic skills. However, it will not take long before the child will ask a question about the game. How is it played? What are the rules?

In their simplest form, rules represent one of the more rudimentary forms of knowledge. Rules are essentially that which might be called recall knowledge as opposed to thought-provoking knowledge requiring considerable powers of reasoning. On the other hand, it is not entirely accurate to generalize in this way about rules. Over the period of years, some sports, such as football, have developed a set of rules that are quite complex. In these cases, interpretation of the rules becomes an important factor, and knowledge of the rules can no longer be dismissed as being of a simple recall type.

Knowledge of the rules presents some interesting problems with respect to the ethics of the participants. Superficially, one might suspect that those who know the rules most thoroughly would be most inclined to conduct themselves according to these rules because they are cognizant of the possible penalties involved. From one standpoint that is true. However, very frequently, particularly in athletics, knowledge of the rules leads to an unwritten code of conduct in which the informed have learned what they can do and how they can do it without getting caught. Many an athlete has been motivated to learn the rules as quickly as possible with this sort of objective in mind. It is even fairly customary for coaches to teach the rules from that frame of reference. This recognition that one can circumvent the rules by knowing them thoroughly could lead to a tangential discussion regarding other positive claims which have been made for sport and/or athletics, but I will withhold further comment on that point until the realm of attitudes is considered in the next chapter. Of course, our next topic, etiquette, also has some bearing on this matter.

Suffice it to say at this juncture that the entire matter of knowing the rules in sport and living according to those rules is closely akin to the ethical problems which Frankena discusses regarding rules of life generally:

Since, as we have seen, moral philosophy begins when people find their code of prevailing moral rules unsatisfactory, moral philosophers have always been critical of the notion that our standard must be the rules of the culture we live in. To this notion, they raise a number of objections, though they do not all stress the same ones. One objection is that the actual rules of a society are never very precise, always admit of exceptions, and may come into conflict with one another. For example, the rules forbid lying and killing but do not define these terms very clearly. In fact, the rules even permit or excuse certain kinds of lying (white lies, patriotic lies) and certain kinds of killing (capital punishment, war) but they do not have these exceptions built into them in any careful way. Again, two rules may conflict in a given situation.[2]

Learning the rules, as one form of a cognitive endeavor, is likely to have the most appeal for those educators with essentialistic leanings. They would also be the first to suggest that rules are made to be adhered to, not to be broken. The counterpart to learning the rules of sports can be found in other educational subjects in which the stress is on rote memory. For instance, at one time it was very popular in the teaching of English to require the learning of rules of grammar and procedures for diagramming a sentence.

Sometimes the plea for learning rules and conducting oneself according to those rules has also been extended to a broader claim regarding transfer effects. The assumption is that he who learns and abides by the rules of the game may well be prepared to accept and live by the rules of life. Paul Weiss is one who seems to subscribe, at least in part, to this viewpoint:

Rules are comparatively constant, the acceptance of which enables a man not only to fit into a situation, to escape from it, and to vary with it, but to remain selfsame from situation to situation. Because the athlete is rule-governed he can remain steady while a good deal fluctuates. . . .

And the non-athlete, though he would benefit from a submission to rules which make for easier and more successful behavior, often does as he likes.[3]

ETIQUETTE

Rather frequent reference is made to the so-called rules of etiquette. Actually, that is a misnomer. If the guidelines for etiquette become rules, they no longer fall under the category of etiquette. Rules can be directly learned because they

---

[2]William K. Frankena, *Ethics* © 1963, p. 12. Reprinted by permission of Prentice-Hall, Inc., Englewood Cliffs, New Jersey.

[3]Paul Weiss, *Sport: A Philosophic Inquiry* (Carbondale, Ill.: Southern Illinois University Press, 1969), pp. 82–83.

are specifics which are spelled out in detail. Sometimes etiquette also involves specifics, but there is frequently a gestalt aspect about etiquette which does not lend itself to the mere memorization or recall of particulars.

One of the most characteristic features of etiquette is that it tends to be somewhat contextual. The absolutes of etiquette for a sport are fewer in number and not quite as binding as the rules of that sport. Furthermore, penalties for breaches of etiquette are implied or indirect. When the rules are violated, the consequences are overt and direct.

This contrast between rules and etiquette may sound like a mere technicality or formality which is of little practical concern. The question could be raised: who cares whether a mode of operation in a sport falls under the category of being a rule or a point of etiquette? An answer is that the distinction has merit when possible cognitive values are being assessed.

In many respects, the various points of etiquette are closer to attitudes than they are facts of knowledge. However, etiquette can still be taught in a manner which is not applicable to attitudes. An example may help to illustrate the differences. One can teach the rules of golf; he can also teach certain points of etiquette which are customarily followed in golf; he cannot teach a favorable impression of golf. If he hopes that such a favorable impression will be gained, the best he can do is to present the rules, etiquette, and skills in such a manner that they will have appeal. In other words, attitudes are not a direct matter of cognition.

Etiquette is a matter of cognition but not in the same way that the learning of rules is a cognitive process. The specific situation is extremely important in determining the courtesies which are to be followed. Again, our golf example may help to show the differences between the learning of rules and the learning of etiquette. Golf is a valid example because it is one of those sports in which etiquette is most prominent.

Following are some points of etiquette which are customarily followed in golf, regardless of where it is played. (1) The player who is farthest away from the hole hits or putts first. (2) A player should not drive until the group playing in front of him has at least hit their second shots. (3) One should not walk ahead of his partners or opponents. These are but a small fraction of the broad realm of etiquette in golf, but they are sufficient to demonstrate that the learning of etiquette is not quite that simple. For each one of the three situations cited, there is a gestalt feature which defies prescription such as is found in rules. It is not always the most courteous thing to do or a sound procedure of etiquette to have the player who is farthest away from the hole hit or putt first. For instance, two players drive off the tee. The one hits straight down the fairway with the longest drive. The other hooks to the left, and his ball lands slightly in the rough. He ends up with a difficult second shot which requires some study before hitting. In the meantime, another twosome is waiting to tee off. The courteous thing for all concerned might be to have the player who is in the fairway with the longest drive hit his second shot when he is ready. This is a situation of etiquette which can best be learned through experience in playing golf. As another exception, many golfers find it much more comfortable to "putt out" rather than putting, then waiting before the second putt while a partner or opponent, who is farther away, putts. In fact, the more courteous thing is often to "putt out." Unfortunately, there is no neat rule of thumb. So much depends on who is playing, the conditions of the play, and local customs.

Similar exceptions could be cited with regard to the other points of etiquette listed above as well as many other aspects of etiquette in golf. The essence of it all is that golf etiquette cannot be merely learned by reading a book on the subject. A person who has learned the etiquette has acquired a "feel" for the courtesies of the golf game which extends well beyond the matter of knowing a series of dos and don'ts. For this reason, one of the possible values of learning the etiquette of various sports is that it requires more than cognitive recall; reasoning is involved in being a sportsman who is guided by etiquette.

STRATEGY

Among all the features of sport which offer potential for acquiring knowledge through participation, strategy is probably the most promising. Strategy is even much more significant in athletics, but the strategical elements in sport also should not be taken lightly. One of the factors which causes sport to be an extension of play is that sport involves strategy whereas strategy is often not evident in play.

What is strategy? It is a plan for both the expected and the unexpected. The strategist begins by making provisions for that which he can expect, based on his own experience and/or the experience of others. However, in part this experience teaches him that the unlikely is also to occur. We can remember some of the past and observe much of the present; the future is not as easily predicted. Consequently, those involved with the planning of strategy proceed with the recognition of certain viable alternatives in mind. One can frequently hear the coach reminding his charges before the game that the opponent may follow either plan X or Y. On the other hand, the possibility of plan Z (unknown) always lurks in the background.

Strategy is thus not unlike etiquette. Neither can be entirely prescribed or mapped out in advance. Also, like etiquette, sports vary from one another greatly in terms of the amount of strategy required. The extremes run the gamut from a sport like football to a sport like bowling. This is not to say that there is no strategy in bowling, but those who have attempted to teach the strategy in bowling know what I mean; the subject is soon exhausted. It just so happens that bowling also has relatively simple rules. There could be a positive correlation between the extent of the rules and the strategy involved. Certainly another factor in the quantity of strategy is the length of time that the sport has been in existence. The founders of American football could scarcely have imagined that the game would become as complex as it is today. We can safely say that at one time the strategy of football was also relatively simple.

One of the interesting features about strategy is that people often feel the need to manufacture or come up with strategy when it may not even be required. Both physical educators and laymen can be found guilty of this. In the case of the physical educator he seems to be searching for means and content to make his work more academic. Strategy involves cognition so it must contribute to the academiclike quality. With the layman, such as the businessman coaching the little league baseball team, he is striving to be more like the professional. Surely, he must offer an abundance of strategy if he is to be a coach in the true sense of that term.

Kenneth Schmitz indirectly hits at this point in his discussions of "rationalization of techniques."

The second abuse stems from the rationalization of techniques within a sport when the rationalization is promoted by an exaggerated sense of the value of efficiency. Good performance is important and the best performance is a desirable ideal. A coach has always to deal with a definite group of individual players. He must assess their potential for the game, combining firmness with good judgment and enthusiasm with restraint. ... There is a difference, too, between a rationalization which sacrifices everything to technical competence and a reasonable improvement of techniques of training and performance which lift a sport to new accomplishments. Such a drive is more than likely in our age which tends to over-rationalize all life in the name of technical perfection.[4]

Although Schmitz was not talking about strategy per se or exclusively strategy, his remarks are very appropriate for those who would overdo the business of strategy. Excessive rationalization of techniques is an apt phrase to describe the procedures of those who feel the compulsion to present strategy when it is scarce and should be kept to a minimum.

On the other hand, the cognitive pursuit of studying and planning strategy can indeed be a productive and worthwhile endeavor for those who are engaged in sports where there is an abundance of potential for strategy. Sometimes the enjoyment of a sport is even dependent on an understanding of the many strategical possibilities. It is not entirely unfair for some sport promoters to argue that their sport has much to offer because it provides cognitive stimulation through the need to understand the strategy.

TERMINOLOGY AND JARGON

Terminology is another important feature of the world of sport. Each sport has its own language. In addition, there are certain terms which are fairly common as one moves from one sport to another. There is a close connection between terminology and rules because in many instances the rules for a sport cannot be

---

[4]Kenneth Schmitz, "Sport and Play: Suspension of the Ordinary," paper delivered at the 13th Annual Meeting of the American Association for the Advancement of Science, Dallas, Texas, Dec. 28, 1968.

learned unless one has first of all grasped the terminology. For example, the rules for scoring in tennis would have relatively little meaning unless one knew the meaning of the term "love" as used in that context.

For all practical purposes, jargon is much the same as terminology, but there is a technical difference between the two. Webster offers the following as the first or preferable definition of jargon: "Confused, unintelligible language; gibberish; hence: A language, speech, or dialect regarded as barbarous or out-landish." However, a later definition states that jargon is "the technical or secret vocabulary of a science, art, trade, sect, profession, or other special group; a lingo." The jargon of a sport would fall in that category.

The distinction between terminology and jargon is thus a thin one. Over a period of time, elements of jargon may actually become part of the established terminology. An example from football may show how this occurs. The "safety man" has long been part of the terminology of football as it refers to one of the commonly recognized defensive positions. Several years ago, some of the professional teams began to employ what they called the "safety blitz." At the outset, the "safety blitz" could be called jargon because it was part of the secret vocabulary of football players. However, during the past few years the words "safety blitz" have been heard so frequently through the television broadcasts that they have almost become a household term. "Safety blitz" is now recognized as part of the terminology of football.

The position could be taken that all this really makes no difference. Who cares whether the "safety blitz" is part of the terminology or jargon of football? We would have to agree that in terms of the conduct of football it makes no difference whatsoever. I am only making the distinction here to point out that learning the language of a sport may involve more than merely memorizing the common terminology. Once again, participation is a key factor in the differentiation. The spectator or casual observer can rather easily learn the terminology of a sport. The jargon is more likely to elude him because he is not involved with the intricacies from which the jargon usually emanates. On the other hand, in the case of athletics, sportswriters and sportscasters (misnomers) make every effort to expose the public to as much of the jargon as possible. They fully realize that the jargon has appeal because it originates as part of the secret vocabulary of the athlete. When the spectator is informed of the jargon he has the feeling that he has had privilege to the "inside scoop." Thus, eventually the athletic jargon may no longer be jargon. Sportswriters and sportscasters see it that the jargon becomes part of the generally accepted terminology. In the case of sport, the cognitive value of learning the jargon is usually facilitated by being an active sport participant.

A question could then be raised as to the quality of cognition when one learns the jargon of a sport. It seems safe to say that such knowledge is esoteric at best. For those who are interested in transfer effects, the learning of either terminology or jargon will not rank highly on the scale of cognitive values. If there is transfer value in learning terminology and jargon, it would have to be classified as internal. By that I mean that a knowledge of these may assist one in more fully appreciating the sport in which he participates. Under these conditions the cognitive value of learning terminology and jargon would be subsidiary to whatever other values sport might have.

The situation regarding the possible value of knowing either terminology or jargon may be closely akin to Wittgenstein's remarks concerning the description of a game:

> How should we explain to someone what a game is? I imagine that we should describe *games* to him, and we might add: "This *and similar things* are called *games*." And do we know any more about it ourselves? Is it only other people whom we cannot tell exactly what a game is?—But this is not ignorance. We do not know the boundaries because none have been drawn. To repeat, we draw a boundary—for a special purpose. Does it take that to make the concept usable? Not at all! (Except for that special purpose.) No more than it took the definition: 1 pace = 75 cm to make the measure of length *one pace* usable.[5]

The value, then, of learning the terminology and jargon of a sport is to be found within the context of the sport itself—for that special purpose. The "safety blitz" is a relatively unmeaningful and unusable concept for someone who is not interested in either playing or observing football.

EQUIPMENT

Equipment, in and of itself, represents a strange sort of phenomenon within the realm of sport. From one standpoint equipment is a very mundane subject. On the other hand, equipment is an important item for the sportsman. Offhand, I cannot think of a sport which does not require the use of equipment in some form or another. Furthermore, as observed earlier in this book, many sportsmen are at least partially attracted to sport by the equipment which is involved.

Those who participate in sport soon realize that there are things to be learned regarding equipment. Basically, this includes information concerning the quality and use of equipment. Such information may not be the most profound, but it is essential for satisfactory participation in sport. The use of knowledge of sport equipment seems to very closely parallel that which was mentioned with respect to the value of learning terminology and jargon. That is, the knowledge is esoteric; it is for a special purpose. The skier learns much about the relative merits of various kinds of skis, boots, and bindings. I cannot imagine what other use could be made of such knowledge; but, who is to deny the importance of this for the skier?

Paul Weiss takes a most intriguing position with regard to equipment. It is a position which should not be overlooked. I suspect that he has described something which has been felt and observed by many but has not really been expressed as such.

---

[5]L. Wittgenstein, *Philosophical Investigations* (New York: The Macmillan Company, 1953), para. 69.

But no matter what the sport, the equipment it requires offers a challenge to a man, demanding that he not only accept his body but unite himself with items beyond it.

Like the body, equipment is part of a larger world, where it moves at its own pace, follows its own tendencies, and is subject to laws regardless of what men wish or do. But unlike the body, equipment is initially not within the individual's control. It is instead an integral part of an objective world. There it must first be met and isolated, and then be adjusted to, before it can be made into a continuation of a man.[6]

Man's union with his equipment is mostly a matter of skill acquisition, but while he is learning the skill of properly using the sport equipment he must also acquire certain knowledge of the potential and limitations of the equipment. In essence, his skill is partially dependent on his knowledge. Thus, the golfer learns what the brassie, five-iron, and wedge can and cannot do. If he does not learn this, he may be severely handicapped in his performance even though he has the skill to perform the task as intended.

A distinction should also be made between what might be called preliminary knowledge of equipment and that which is acquired through actual participation. Certain features of equipment can be explained and understood in advance. Unfortunately, many other bits of knowledge can only be gained through experience. The conscientious instructor is cognizant of this when he recommends to the novice that he initially purchase secondhand or less expensive equipment before he invests in first-rate equipment that may not be suitable to his individual needs.

Equipment probably represents one of the more vivid examples of the fact that a mind-body dichotomy does not actually exist. Weiss' suggestion that the athlete forms a union with his equipment assists in understanding this point. Knowledge of the equipment is inextricably related to the skill in using the equipment. When one acquires a union with his sport equipment, he has a knowledge of the equipment which can only be gained through extensive involvement with the skill of the sport. His knowledge is such that he no longer has to think about the equipment per se but, rather, is free to concentrate on those aspects of his performance which transcend the understanding of equipment. The association of the sport performer with his equipment thus might be viewed as a difficulty to be overcome. At the outset, the skis, boots, and bindings pose a problem for the beginning skier because they represent a hurdle in his desire to fully enjoy skiing. The boots seem heavy; the bindings are a nuisance; and the skis appear too long and cumbersome. But as time goes on, the skier becomes less cognizant of these equipment distractions. He has acquired knowledge of the equipment through increased skill in using the equipment. His knowledge may be esoteric, but at least it is knowledge which assists him in more fully appreciating that which he set out to do.

---

[6] Weiss, *op. cit.*, p. 74.

FACILITIES

The customary way of distinguishing between facilities and equipment is to suggest that facilities refer to these relatively nonexpendable items which are more or less part of the permanent installation. In sport, facilities usually means the medium wherein sport takes place, whereas equipment contributes to the conduct of sport within that medium. There is no problem in calling the golf course a facility and designating the golf clubs as equipment. Similarly, an item of equipment, the basketball, is used to play the game on the basketball court, a facility. As is so often true, there are gray-area considerations. For example, I suppose one could engage in debate as to whether a basketball hoop is a facility or equipment item. We are not going to engage in that debate because it is not germane to our purposes here. However, if Weiss is correct in his assumption, it could be pointed out that it might be difficult to obtain a union with the basketball hoop even though many players might wish they could.

Our only reason for discussing facilities as an entity other than equipment is to point out that it is still another facet of sport which offers some potential for acquiring knowledge. In brief there are facts to be learned about facilities which are somewhat different than the knowledge of equipment.

I will again use golf as an example to illustrate the point because it happens to be a sport wherein both knowledge of the equipment and knowledge of the facilities have relatively high significance. Earlier mention was made of the need for the golfer to learn the potential of the various clubs. Perhaps more importantly he must learn the features of golf courses generally and the peculiarities of *a* course, more specifically. He soon learns that golf courses are so designed in general to penalize those who slice the ball. He also learns that on most of the holes it is better to be short than over the green. However, the generalities frequently give way to those specific features which characterize the knowledge of a particular course. The local golfer discovers facts about "his" course which facilitate the performance. Again, experience in the actual play of the course looms as a critical factor because these are often facts which must be obtained firsthand rather than through description by another participant.

In many respects the knowledge of sport facilities tends to be esoteric, very much like the knowledge of terminology and equipment. However, I suppose the argument could be raised that almost all knowledge is esoteric in some way or another. I can think of at least one example where knowledge of golf facilities has been utilized by an individual to develop a very rewarding professional career. An acquaintance of mine is a golf course architect. As a youth his primary interest in life was golf; he wanted to be a golf professional. His parents did not share his enthusiasm for that goal and persuaded him that he should pursue a more cognitive endeavor. Consequently, he attended college and graduated with specialized preparation as a golf course architect. Now, of course, this is a rare case. Not everyone is going to be able or interested in developing cognitive values in this way from his interest and participation in sport. I only mention this situation to point out problems of excessive generalization and categorization. Those who would simply dismiss sport as a noncognitive activity are guilty of overlooking some of the possibilities.

Certain physical educators might be cited as another example of a possible link between sport facilities and cognition. Physical education administrators frequently find themselves in a position where they must plan sport facilities. They usually work closely with architects and other school administrators in the planning. The expectation is that the physical educator has the knowledge of sport which will be combined with the knowledge which others have of facilities generally to produce the desired installation within the available limits. There are even a few physical educators who have more or less become known as facilities specialists. They have concentrated their professional endeavors on attempting to know as much as possible about various kinds of sport facilities. Of course, one element should immediately be recognized about this example as well as the example of the golf course architect. Neither is directly applicable to the subject of attempting to justify participation in sport for cognitive reasons. In the cases cited, cognitive values may well accrue from an interest in and involvement with sport, but they are values for a relative few who are in the business of perpetuating sport as it exists.

INSIGHTS

The participant in a sport also acquires insights into the game which extend beyond the realm of rules, etiquette, strategy, terminology, equipment, and facilities. An insight should not be confused with an attitude although the two are often closely related. The former involves understanding or keen discernment. The latter, to be discussed in the next chapter, is the way one feels about something. A person may have an insight which is not expressed or revealed in his attitude. Likewise, attitudes are often derived from a lack of insight.

Insights resulting from participation in sport fall roughly into two categories. First of all, there are those which are more-or-less shared by all participants who have had fairly extensive experience in a sport. This category might be referred to as the modus operandi. Each sport has its own modus operandi, resulting from that which has been tried and found true. It takes a novice a period of time before he can begin to grasp the significance of the various modes of operation in a sport, but he gradually accumulates this kind of insight through continued exposure. Sometimes one hears the colloquial expression that "a certain amount is bound to rub off on him." That, in essence, is a simple way of stating that the individual will acquire certain insights which result from the modus operandi.

What are some of the kinds of knowledge which comprise the modus operandi in sport generally? Following is a listing of certain possibilities.

1. In organizing formal competition in sport, decisions must be made concerning the most appropriate tournament structure to be employed. Some sports

lend themselves very well to round-robin play. In others, a form of elimination tournament may be more suitable. Seeding is customarily used in some sports; handicapping is popular in others. It is usually not necessary for the participants to make these decisions or to even know the basis for the decisions. Those in charge of planning for and organizing the competition will usually take care of those matters. However, the "rubbing off" principle is very applicable here. Even if they do not particularly concentrate on the matter, regular participants in a sport acquire some knowledge of the competitive structure which is employed.

2. Almost every sport has its safety precautions which should be learned. Sometimes these precautions fall in the category of being safety rules, but that is not always the case. As noted earlier, a rule is binding in that an infraction will result in a penalty. Thus, the provision for penalizing clipping can be considered a safety rule in football. On the other hand, a safety precaution in handball is to avoid looking at the ball while your opponent is directly in the act of hitting it. This is not a rule because the player will not be penalized in the game. The player who has acquired this sort of insight learns to follow the ball just prior to the contact by his opponent. This enables him to gain the necessary position, but at the moment of contact he is looking at the front wall as a safety precaution.

3. Experienced participants in a sport learn to pace themselves. They know when to "turn it on" and when to relax a bit. In a way this is very close to being strategy, but there is a difference. Strategy is planned. Pacing oneself grows out of the dynamics of the situation. The coach can teach strategy. He finds it much more difficult to teach his players to pace themselves. The experienced player learns to pace himself by having been part of the modus operandi in previous games, involving similar circumstances. For example, the seasoned tennis player knows when to "take the net." His overall strategy may be to take the net as often as possible. However, the modus operandi of tennis teaches him that certain situations are most advantageous. One of these would be a shot hit deep in the corner to his opponent's backhand.

Part of the insight for the participant in pacing himself also stems from a study of his opponent. By observing the reactions of the opponent, he learns his relative strengths and weaknesses. Also, when he finds his opponent relaxing or getting tired, he may choose to "'turn it on." The critical reader may suggest at this point that I have departed from my initial premise of discussing the cognitive values of sport, that I am now on the subject of athletics. My reply would be that sport does not infer that the participants do not try to win. Major differences are to be found in the preparation for winning and the premium placed on the victory.

4. A fourth kind of modus operandi knowledge is somewhat more difficult to describe. It involves a knowledge of the skill in a sport. To be able to do something (perform a skill) is one thing; to understand the performance is something else. Every sport has its own kind of reactions to specific actions. The skilled

performer who also has the insight is able to understand the basis for the various reactions. Not all skilled performers acquire this sort of understanding. Some continue to function in a more robot manner. They know how to do it, and they figure theirs is not the position to question why. However, most experienced performers attain a degree of knowledge of this kind over a period of time.

The second category of insights may probably best be described as individual or personal. They largely resemble those described under paragraph 4 above except they are not part of the modus operandi. These are insights which the individual acquires concerning the skills in a sport. The insights may be but are not necessarily shared with others. With regard to performance it is often said that each person has his own style. Much the same thing is true when it comes to certain kinds of insights. Everyone does not analyze a skill in the same way. Also, the relationship between one skill and another may be viewed quite differently. Through his association with a sport, each individual acquires his own kind of meaning from that sport.

Needless to say, in terms of the potential categories for knowledge which have been discussed thus far, the broad realm of insights has the most to offer if one wishes to move beyond esoteric considerations. However, even then, there appear to be definite limits if one were to attempt to justify participation in sport for its cognitive values. In the second chapter we noted that about 1964, some people within the field of physical education began to examine the potential for a body of knowledge to be derived from the study of sport. This takes the focus away from knowledge gained through sport participation. The assumption is that sport exists, no particular effort should be made to either justify or condemn that which exists unless we first of all know more about it.

POTENTIAL FOR THE BODY OF KNOWLEDGE IN SPORT

THE DISCIPLINARY PERSPECTIVE

Franklin Henry

It appears that Franklin Henry may have been the first to directly make the distinction between the profession of physical education and the possibility of developing a body of knowledge from the systematic study of sport and/or exercise:

An academic discipline is an organized body of knowledge collectively embraced in a formal course of learning. The acquisition of such knowledge is assumed to be an adequate and worthy objective as such, without any demonstration or requirement of practical application. The content is theoretical and scholarly as distinguished from technical and professional. . . .

There is indeed a scholarly field of knowledge basic to physical education: It is constituted of certain portions of such diverse fields as anatomy, physics and physiology, cultural anthropology, history and sociology, as well as psychology. The focus of attention is on the study of man as an individual, engaging in the motor performances required by his daily life and in other motor performances yielding aesthetic values or serving as expressions of his physical and competitive nature, accepting challenges of his capability in pitting himself against a hostile environment and participating in the leisure time activities that have become of increasing importance in our culture. However, a person could be by ordinary standards well educated in the traditional fields listed above, and yet be quite ignorant with respect to comprehension and integrated knowledge of the motor behavior and capabilities of man. The areas within these fields that are vital to physical education receive haphazard and peripheral treatment, rather than systematic development, since the focus of attention is directed elsewhere.[7]

Several of the statements by Henry help to point out the difference between the kind of knowledge which may be derived from participation in sport and the study of sport as an organized body of knowledge. The very fact that a discipline is an *organized* body of knowledge represents one major difference. We noted earlier in this chapter that the knowledge obtained from participation in sport tends to be either supportive or incidental. I learn the rules and strategy so that I can play the game. The knowledge seems to be of relatively little significance except to the extent that it is related to the skill in the sport.

The idea that the scholarly or disciplinary study of sport is "an adequate and worthy objective as such, without any demonstration or requirement of practical application" is of even greater import in drawing the distinction. This is in sharp contrast with the idea that the knowledge of sport must have applicability in order to be deserving of considerations. For years, physical educators, with their professional orientation, had proclaimed the latter point of view.

In essence, Henry was setting forth a position which has long been made by educational essentialists. The position is one which establishes a hierarchy of subject matter. Not all endeavors which fall under the banner of education are considered to be academic. An academic pursuit is one in which there is sufficient content to require an in-depth study of the subject matter. Henry's position in this regard is made even clearer by a subsequent statement:

Problems certainly occur in delimiting the field of knowledge outlined above. The development of personal skill in motor performance is without question a worthy objective in itself. But it should not be confused with the academic field of knowledge. Similarly, technical competence in measuring a chemical reaction, or computational skill in mathematics, are not components of the corresponding fields of knowledge. Learning the rules and strategy of sports may well be intellectual, but it is highly doubtful if a course on rules and strategy can be justified as a major component of an academic field of knowledge at the upper division college or university level.[8]

---

[7]Franklin Henry, "Physical Education: An Academic Discipline," *Journal of Health, Physical Education, and Recreation*, XXXV, 7., September 1964, pp. 32–33.

[8]*Ibid.*, p. 33.

One can see that in spite of his very clear position, Henry was also careful in his comments. He did not say that there is no place in education for skill learning. Furthermore, he was even willing to recognize the possibility that there could be certain intellectual gains, such as learning the rules and strategy, by participating in sport. All he was really asking is: let us not confuse that kind of subsidiary knowledge with the study of sport as a potential body of knowledge.

Arthur Daniels

It cannot truthfully be said that Henry's comments fell on fertile ground. On the other hand, he was also not a lone voice in the wilderness. Regardless of the Conant reaction, there had been a gradual awakening on the part of certain physical educators to the idea that they must seek a new focus if they were to be identified with the academic realm. Those who recognized this need were opportunists and those with vision, much the same as Jesse Feiring Williams and Jay B. Nash had been earlier when they advocated the transition from education of the physical to education through the physical. Arthur Daniels was one of those who saw that physical education must seek an additional direction if it was to be claimed as having a scholarly dimension as well as being a practical endeavor:

There is a widespread belief on the part of our academic colleagues and most lay persons that physical educators are primarily practitioners. Our programs in basic instruction and intramural and interschool competitive sports programs, as well as our offerings in physical recreation, provide the basis for this belief. While we have no wish to disavow these worthy utilitarian programs, the fact remains that, compared with other disciplines, there has been a paucity of scholarly effort and research.[9]

It is noted that Daniels' comments extend beyond the matter of questioning the cognitive values to be derived from sport participation. He was also questioning the cognitive pursuits of those who teach sport skills and/or administer programs of sport. In other words, it is entirely possible, if not probable, that cognitive values cannot even be claimed for those who teach and administer sport. That is, they cannot be unless the scholarly focus is identified. The answer was not to be found in the traditional, professional preparation courses in physical education because they, too, were directed toward practical rather than theoretical considerations. Courses in methods, curriculum, administration, supervision, and prevention and care of injuries are worthwhile courses but are not known for their academic content. Daniels suggested that the scholarly potential was to be found in the following areas:

---

[9]Arthur Daniels, "The Potential of Physical Education as an Area of Research and Scholarly Effort," *Journal of Health, Physical Education, and Recreation*, XXXVI, No. 1, January 1965, p. 32.

If we are to gain recognition in the academic world we must follow pathways similar to those traversed by other disciplines in achieving their progress. For us this means a greatly expanded program of scholarly activities in such areas as history of physical education and sport, the social significance of physical education and sport in our culture, motor learning, exercise physiology, biomechanics of human movement, and comparative studies indicating the contribution of physical education and sport to international understanding and cooperation.[10]

Of course, a major problem still presents itself before one can claim that any one or more of the above areas has cognitive or academic value. To put it as simple as possible, there must be something to study. Content courses cannot be offered unless the content has been developed through research and scholarly investigation. I am sure that Henry, Daniels, and others were most aware of that. Sport studies was not instantaneously identified as a scholarly area merely by setting forth the possibilities. Consequently, during the next few years, and even continuing to the present, there was considerable discussion within the profession of physical education as to how to proceed methodologically in developing the content. Gerald Kenyon was one of those who offered a framework.

Gerald Kenyon

Whether or not one agrees with his position, Kenyon's paper, presented before the National College Physical Education Association for Men in 1968, was perhaps the most succinct statement of the challenge facing those physical educators who desired to become more disciplinarylike.

In summary, I have tried to identify some of the logical problems confronting us when we set out to structure a highly complex and imperfectly conceptualized field of study. I have looked just at what characterizes a discipline; concluding that there are three major criteria that need to be met by a field of study before it can be considered a discipline: a particular focus of attention, a unique body of knowledge, and a particular mode of inquiry or methodology. Given these criteria, I tried to show that the fusion of the widespread diversity in contemporary approaches to the study of human movement is difficult to defend. Moreover, I suggested that we not think in terms of a single integrated discipline at all, but rather encourage the development of semi-autonomous, discipline-like subfields, which, because of their common interest in human movement, might be loosely affiliated in a consortium of movement studies. On the premise that the primary purpose of each of these subfields is to contribute to and organize knowledge, it behooves us to consider what we mean by knowledge and as such adopt a particular epistemology. I proposed an empiricist frame of reference on the grounds that such an approach has been the most successful to date in generating knowledge capable of public verification, i.e., the criterion of potential universal agreement, or the "principle of verification," as Ayer would have it. Despite the alleged naturalistic heritage of physical education, I expect many would disagree with my choice and be more eclectic,

---

[10]*Ibid.*

allowing for perhaps intuitional and even mystical bases for new knowledge. If we do adopt an empiricist theory of knowledge, I suggest that we are restricted to human movement sciences, and human movement history, although even the latter may not be on the firmest of ground.[11]

In my opinion one of the more significant features of Kenyon's position was his suggestion that the direction should be toward the "development of semi-autonomous, discipline-like subfields." The subfields which he identified were human movement sciences; including the physical science of human movement, the biology of human movement, the social science of human movement; and human movement history. His idea of subfields which would be affiliated in a consortium has merit. However, as noted earlier in this book, considerable debate can legitimately be waged as to what the consortium should be. A consortium is a fellowship or association, implying mutual interests. Even though human movement has been posed by many as the appropriate umbrella name for such a consortium, it is a bit difficult to imagine where the common denominator is to be found. For example, the distance from the history of sport to either exercise biochemistry or exercise therapy is indeed a great one, whether one is talking about a focus of attention or a mode of inquiry. Thus, we suggested earlier two constellations of consortia, namely exercise science and the theory of sport or sport studies. There may still be certain methodological problems within each one of these groupings, but at least each has its own focus of attention.

This matter of identifying the subfields has also received considerable attention from other sources. One of the most concerted efforts in this regard has been that involved in the "Big Ten Body-of-Knowledge Project."

The Big Ten Body-of-Knowledge Project in Physical Education

This project was an outgrowth of the annual meetings of the Western Conference of Physical Education Directors. These meetings have been held since 1930.[12] In 1964, this group embarked on the "body-of-knowledge project" which has shown steady progress since that time. Six areas of specialization were tentatively identified in 1966:

In August the Committee decided to organize the academic content—at least initially— into six specific areas of specialization as follows: (1) Exercise Physiology; (2) Biomechanics; (3) Motor Learning and Sports Psychology; (4) Sociology of Sport Education; (5) History, Philosophy, and Comparative Physical Education and Sport; and (6) Administrative Theory. There has been considerable debate as to what these areas

---

[11]Gerald Kenyon, "On the Conceptualization of Sub-Disciplines within an Academic Discipline Dealing with Human Movement," *Proceedings*, 71st Annual Meeting, National College Physical Education Association for Men, 1968, p. 44. Reprinted by permission of the NCPEAM.

[12]E. F. Zeigler and K. J. McCristal, "A History of the Big Ten Body-of-Knowledge Project in Physical Education," *Quest* IX, *The Nature of a Discipline*, December 1967, p. 79.

are—or should be. For example, it can well be argued that administrative theory is not basic to our discipline—if it is indeed a discipline or whatever it may be named. Conversely, it can be stated that the managing of organizations within our field is becoming so complex that pure and applied research in this developing social science may be warranted.[13]

I have listed the areas which were initially identified by this group because they point to the fact that the focus of attention for these would-be, disciplinelike, subfields may not be as clear as one would hope. Zeigler and McCristal have pointed to one of the problems, namely administrative theory. For instance, if one wishes to begin by distinguishing between a profession and a discipline, it would seem more logical to conclude that administrative theory is a professional concern. Certainly, administration is a very practical sort of endeavor. I suppose it could be argued that a course in administrative practice would be part of professional preparation whereas administrative theory is for those who wish to study the process of administration without regard to its applicability. However, my own bias tells me that because administration is what it is, the subject of administrative theory can only be studied in terms of potential applicability.

Then, too, an argument might be raised against the idea of including history, philosophy, and comparative sport under one specialty. History has its own methodology. The methodology of philosophy is different from that of history and fraught with certain potential pitfalls, as noted in the first chapter. Comparative sport, even though it is a noteworthy subject, presents another kind of problem with respect to disciplinary investigation because it really has no particular mode of inquiry. It utilizes the methodology of other disciplines.

But whether or not one agrees with the initial specialties or subdisciplines outlined by the "Big Ten" group may be beside the point. At least they have attempted to do something other than just talk about the methodology to be employed. Since the earlier meetings concerned with planning, the Body-of-Knowledge Project has now developed into a series of symposia, each focusing on one of the specialties or subfields aimed at disciplinary status. The pioneering effort occurred at the University of Wisconsin November 18–20, 1968, when the symposium on the sociology of sport was held. The proceedings of this symposium have been published.[14]

In view of the debates over the methodology to be employed and the number and kind of subfields which might be included, I feel that it is absolutely necessary to begin somewhere. Otherwise, the entire enterprise is likely to remain mostly in the talking stage. From my perspective, I see two subfields

---

[13]*Ibid.*, p. 82.

[14]*Aspects of Contemporary Sport Sociology*, Proceedings of Committee on Intstitutional Cooperation. Symposium on the Sociology of Sport, ed. Gerald S. Kenyon (Chicago, Ill.: The Athletic Institute, 1969).

emerging; they are exercise science and sport studies or the theory of sport. The former is outside the scope of this text, so we will examine in more detail that which may be involved in the latter. Four components seem to be evident at this time.

HISTORY OF SPORT

The history of sport is certainly not a new subject. What is new is the suggestion that it may be developed as a subdiscipline. For example, the work in the history of physical education and sport has been largely an attempt to paint with a wide brush. In other words, there has been a strong tendency to blend the historical with the philosophical.

If the history of sport is to have disciplinarylike status as one of the distinct components of sport studies, a consortium, I propose that the frame of reference for the history of sport must be that of historicism:

The basic thesis of historicism is quite simple: The subject matter of history is human life in its totality and multiplicity. It is the historian's aim to portray the bewildering, unsystematic variety of historical forms—people, nations, cultures, customs, institutions, songs, myths, and thoughts—in their unique living expressions and in the process of continuous growth and transformation. This aim is not unlike the artist's; at any rate, it differs from the systematic, conceptual approach of the philosopher. The abstract concepts employed in philosophy are not adequate for rendering the concrete realities of history. Such abstract concepts are static and catch the common properties of things and people, not their specific differences. . . . Thus the special quality of history does not consist in the statement of general laws or principles, but in the grasp, so far as possible, of the infinite variety of particular historical forms immersed in the passage of time. The meaning of history does not lie hidden in some universal structure, whether deterministic or teleological, but in the multiplicity of individual manifestations at different ages and in different cultures. All of them are unique and equally significant strands in the tapestry of history; all of them, in Ranke's famous phrase are "immediate to God."[15]

Basically, what is called for is an in-depth approach if the history of sport is to emerge as a body of knowledge which is identifiable as such. There is nothing wrong with more global efforts, such as pointing out trends and persistent problems which may be evident in the history of physical education and sport. But such efforts may better be left to the sport philosopher. The sport historian has the obligation to present things as they were, be they bewildering or unsystematic. In other words, the sport historian is not searching for the "common properties." If he happens to come across such common properties, he obviously will not ignore them. But, his basic frame of reference must be that of looking for the particulars wherever they may be found.

---

[15]From *The Philosophy of History in Our Time* by Hans Meyerhoff, p. 10. Copyright © 1959 by Hans Meyerhoff. Reprinted by permission of Doubleday & Company, Inc.

When the historism mode of inquiry is employed, the history of sport largely becomes a history of sports. This may sound altogether too simple and even ridiculous, but it appears to be a point which is often overlooked. To begin by writing the history of sport is akin to writing the history of western civilization without first having available the data on the history of France. All sports do not neatly fit into the generalizations which have been made regarding the history of sport. There indeed may be certain gestalt features regarding the history of sport, but these cannot really be arrived at in a valid sort of way unless one first of all probes the particulars in the various sports.

By the way, this idea of applying historicism to the history of sport is not completely virgin territory. Some notable pioneering work has been done in recording historical features of the various sports. As one example, the work of Guy Lewis clearly demonstrates the effort to, in Meyerhoff's words, "portray the bewildering, unsystematic variety of historical forms." One of the popular, historical myths is that President Theodore Roosevelt issued an ultimatum in 1905 which saved the game of football. After studying the circumstances in depth, Lewis came to the conclusion that Roosevelt's role "was a significant but not a crucial one. His action did determine the direction of football, but he did not save the game, because its existence was never threatened; nor did he bring about reform in either rules or conduct by issuing an ultimatum."[16]

It would make for more interesting reading to state or suggest that Roosevelt saved the game of football. For one thing this would be consistent with the overall image of the man as a challenging, heroic kind of leader. However, the historicist does not engage in speculation. His mission is rather clear-cut: to present the facts as and wherever they can be found. The history of sport can emerge as a disciplinary endeavor whenever there are sufficient number of scholars who are capable of and willing to apply their efforts to this type of specialization.

SOCIOLOGY OF SPORT

From one standpoint, the sociology of sport is the most logical subfield to pursue if one is interested in developing a body of knowledge in relationship to sport. The reason should be rather obvious. Almost everyone knows that sport is an extremely significant institution in this culture. Sociologists are concerned with the study of social institutions. So, what could be more natural than to study the sociology of sport? Furthermore, there seems to be an intrinsic appeal in this subject matter which may be beyond precise description but which is nevertheless evident.

Even though it might not yet be appropriate to designate the sociology of sport as an established, disciplinarylike, subfield, much spadework has been

---

[16]Guy M. Lewis, "Theodore Roosevelt's Role In The 1905 Football Controversy," *The Research Quarterly*, Vol. 40, No. 4, Dec. 1969, p. 724.

done. In his opening remarks before the Committee on Institutional Cooperation Symposium on the Sociology of Sport, Lüschen summarized the state of the art:

The present state in the field of sociology of sport may be characterized by the fact that, by my rough estimate, if you do not define the field of sociology of sport too rigidly, you may count as of today something like 3,000 related publications internationally; a recently published selected bibliography lists something like 1,000 titles with the emphasis on those works appearing since 1965, with the remainder included to characterize the earlier development of the field. If we look at the topics that have been tackled in these publications, most prominent are programmatic discussions. These have been quite numerous recently coming from scientists in sociology and in physical education, and point to topics that should be discussed or point to the magnitude of the problem, or the benefits that come out of proceeding with this discipline. Such articles have appeared in many parts of the world in professional journals, whether they be for physical education or for sociology. If, however, you then look at the different subject areas you will find that the topic of sport in society, on the one hand—the structuring of sport through its affiliation with particular types of societies or to particular cultures—stands out quite prominently in publications. On the other hand, attention has also been given to the role that sport plays, i.e., the function that sport fulfills for societies at large.[17]

What is the potential for studying the sociology of sport? In other words, what topics might be researched in the future if this area is to emerge as a disciplinary subfield and thus to contribute to the cognitive dimension of sport?

1. *The Small Group in Sport:* This basically includes studies of group dynamics in sport. Specific topics might include leadership, conflict, cohesiveness, team morale, effects of achievement on group structure, and group motivation.

2. *Relationship Between Sport and Other Institutions:* Sport should be studied in relationship to the government, family, school, church, and the industrial establishment.

3. *Sport and Racial Relations:* Within recent years, this has been a topic which has evoked a great deal of philosophical speculation. A few descriptive studies have been conducted. There is need for much more scientific investigation.

4. *Sport and Social Status:* Racial relations is obviously a part of this topic, but there is more involved. Studies may range from those concerned with social mobility through sport to an analysis of social stratification resulting from sport.

---

[17]Günther Lüschen, "Some Recent Developments in the Sociology of Sport," *Aspects of Contemporary Sport Sociology*, Proceedings of the C.I.C. Symposium on the Sociology of Sport, ed. Gerald S. Kenyon (Chicago, Ill.: The Athletic Institute, 1969), pp. 2–3. Reprinted by permission of The Athletic Institute.

5. *The Socializing Effect of Sport:* This actually falls in the area of social psychology. Studies would be largely concerned with effects on the personality through group involvement with sport.

6. *Sport and Culture:* This broad area permits many possibilities. Unfortunately, the speculation has also far out-distanced the scientific work on this topic. Studies might include those involving age factors in sport, the role of the sexes, community life, sport as a leisure time activity, and the relationship between sport and politics.

PSYCHOLOGY OF SPORT

Among the subfields under consideration, sport psychology is the one which probably best bridges the gap between sport studies or the theory of sport on the one hand and exercise science on the other hand. The reason for this is both very natural and logical. It is to be found in the nature of psychology. The discipline of psychology, even though it has a focus, the individual, runs a gamut of scholarly investigations. Largely, the range extends from those studies which tend to be more physiologically based to those which are concerned with personality or attitudinal characteristics. Thus, it is not at all surprising that the purported subfield, psychology of sport, should reflect the enigma of the parent field. Studies which have been conducted to date in the psychology of sport fall roughly into two groupings: those concerned with motor learning and those which somehow or another focus on personality characteristics in relationship to sport. Because motor learning is more closely related to the exercise science consortium, for our purposes here we will only discuss the potential cognitive values which might be derived from a study of sport and personality characteristics.

The situation is very closely akin to that found with regard to the sociology of sport. Much fine spadework has been accomplished. However, if the psychology of sport is to achieve disciplinarylike status, more in-depth studies are needed. The following are suggested as possible areas to be explored:

1. *Aggression in Sport:* This involves another one of those two-headed considerations, both of which cry for more research. As mentioned earlier in this book, it has frequently been hypothesized that man is attracted to sport, particularly certain sports, because of his aggressive tendencies. If there are valid tools with which to measure aggression, they should be applied to both athletes and sportsmen in a large variety of athletic and sporting activities. On the other hand, it has also been hypothesized that sport is a medium for sublimating aggression. The assumption seems to be here that aggression should not be confused with conflict and competition. Longitudinal studies might be conducted to determine the effect of athletics and/or sport on aggressive-like behavior over a period of time.

2. *Motivation in Sport:* Several facets of motivation should be considered.

First of all, there is the question of what motivates man to participate in sport. The subject of aggression may be considered in this context. Secondly, there is the question of what motivates continued participation in sport. Thirdly, what are the factors which motivate one toward better performance in sport? Other motivational problems could also be considered, but the three just mentioned rank among the priority considerations.

3. *Personality Traits in Relation to Sport:* Again some overlap can be seen between this subject and that of aggression because the latter is one of the personality traits which should be considered. Much has been suggested concerning the possible personality traits of the athlete, such as the idea that he tends to be extrovertish. More comparisons should be made between the athlete and the casual sportsman. Several studies have focused on the athlete vs. the non-athlete. Relatively little allowance has been made for the vast majority who are not athletes but who do participate in sport on a fairly regular basis. Furthermore, there is great potential for studying personality traits in relationship to leadership in sport. This brings us again to the area of social psychology. Much has been made of the leader in sport, but he has been studied in a very minor sort of way. It is doubtful whether the leader can be determined by paper and pencil tests. Psychologists tell us that the peer rating is the only instrument which approaches having validity in determining the leader. But, how often has some form of peer-rating instrument been utilized in studying sport groups? The peer-rating instrument has been found to be particularly valid when combined with an assessment of personality traits. For instance, as a starting point it would be reasonable to hypothesize that the leader in sport might be characterized as having the following among his personality traits: he may be mature, well-motivated, socially poised, cooperative, and independent-minded.

The three examples cited above are obviously but a sample of what can be done to explore the personality phase of sport psychology. For instance, the relationship between sport and emotional stability or neurosis could also be mentioned. Needless to say, the realm of speculation still holds sway. But the potential is there for the researcher who desires to apply his cognitive attributes to the subject of sport psychology.

PHILOSOPHY OF SPORT

We now turn to the area which is the subject of this text. I have saved it as the last of the subfields to be discussed for several reasons. At least I am convinced that it should be either the first or the last for reasons which I will not go into here.

In the first chapter we looked briefly at the nature of philosophy. There it was noted that philosophy may be better known for what it isn't than for what it is. Philosophy is an elusive sort of field. This seems to trouble certain people who are searching for the handle for philosophy. It really shouldn't trouble them because even the scientists are inclined to philosophize from time to time. What seems more appropriate is to merely take the stance that philosophy begins where science leaves off. There are certain gaps in the knowledge of any field which should be brought to the foreground. A major role of philosophy, then, is to analyze what has been done and to point out those questions which remain unanswered.

Reid has offered a frame of reference for philosophy which I think is most appropriate for describing what can be done in the philosophy of sport if it too is to achieve disciplinarylike status:

Philosophy includes digging up and criticizing one's assumptions, one's experiences and one's judgments in all the main fields of human enterprise. Traditionally, for example, philosophy has examined the assumptions underlying the sciences, assumptions which are not in themselves the subject of scientific scrutiny. All this involves an examination of ideas and of the language (and languages) in which they are expressed, scrutinizing for ambiguity, exploring meanings. These things are included, broadly speaking, in the work of critical *analysis*. . . . The proper function of analysis is the better understanding of the wholes which are analysed; it is servant and not master. And analysis itself is strictly impossible without implicit relating: if it entirely loses the sense of the whole it ceases even to be intelligent analysis. Analysis is, in fact, one moment, one emphasis, in the strictly indivisible life of philosophy; synthesis is the other moment.[18]

What topics might be explored if this kind of philosophic temper is to be applied to the study of sport? The answer is that there are numerous possibilities; in this text I have attempted to outline some of these possibilities. Each one of the chapters from two through 11 might be viewed as a beginning attempt to analyze. In Chapter 12 our attention is directed toward synthesis. There we attempt to pull together the many loose ends which have emerged from the analyses throughout the book. However, considerably more can and must be done in the way of in-depth analyses if the philosophy of sport is to achieve disciplinarylike status along with the other subfields in the consortium. Among the concepts which should be probed and explicated are the following:

1. *Play:* What does it mean to play? Is play a universal need? If so, why? When does play become work? What are the forms of play? Are they of equal significance?

2. *Games:* What is a game? Of what significance are games? What is the relationship between games and play? Is there anything unique about games of sport?

3. *Human Movement:* What is meant by this concept? Why has it been associated with the idea of a discipline? Is it more meaningful than the concepts of physical education, sport, or exercise?

---

[18]L. Arnaud Reid, "Philosophy and the Theory and Practice of Education," *Philosophical Analysis and Education,* ed. R. D. Archambault (New York: The Humanities Press, 1965), pp. 23–24. Reprinted by permission of the publishers.

4. *Physical Education:* What caused the concept of physical education to emerge? What are some of the inherent limitations of the concept? Why has it been associated with a profession? What are the possibilities for eliminating the concept?

5. *Competition:* What does it mean to compete? What is the difference between competition and conflict? Is there a negative valence with regard to competition? Is sport competition different from other forms of competition? Is competition a primal drive in man? What is the relationship between competition and the pursuit of excellence?

SPORT STUDIES

The tentative title for this consortium has been chosen with some care even though it may not be entirely descriptive and relatively unsatisfactory to some observers. I will be perfectly frank in saying that from one standpoint I would prefer to group the four subfields under the category of the theory of sport. However, that would be a bit presumptuous. One cannot rightfully call something a theory until there is a sufficient body of knowledge to warrant the label. A theory does not emerge merely by proclamation. I suppose that there could be some argumentation over the question as to what is sufficient. That can probably only be answered by suggesting that sufficiency would appear to be evident when a field of inquiry can more or less stand on its own merit. For example, in studying the psychology of sport, if one has to rely primarily on psychological sources, rather than those dealing specifically with sport, chances are that studies in the psychology of sport have not as yet reached the theoretical stage.

Our hope is that sport studies will lead to or result in a theory of sport. In other words, sport studies might be assessed as an intermediate stage in which disciplinelike efforts are employed. The controversy then goes back to the consortium. Would it not be better, for instance, to work toward the development of four separate and distinct fields of sport studies, each of which would work toward the development of its own theory? From one standpoint, the answer is yes. It would certainly be more convenient that way. And, in essence, this is what is likely to happen. The idea of a consortium does not imply a complete merger. There is no intent to "water down" sport sociology by infusing it with sport history or vice versa. On the other hand it is also reasonable to expect that students in any one of the four subfields might benefit from at least an exposure to the content of the other three. This would be particularly true at the undergraduate and master's degree levels where there is still more need for breadth in approach and knowledge.

At least one other merit of the sport studies idea can be noted. It has the effect of taking the focus away from the parent disciplines and placing it on sport. Were this not the case, sport psychology might just as well be considered as a branch of psychology. There would be an advantage to that, but there is also a good probability that the study of sport would get lost in the shuffle. Thus, I would prefer to see historians, philosophers, psychologists, and sociologists converge their interests and talents on the study of sport. The consortium of sport studies would offer a framework for cross-fertilization without detracting from the in-depth pursuits of each subfield.

A parallel to this suggested arrangement can be found in the current interest in ecology. The latter is certainly not a discipline per se. However, today we find scholars from several disciplines combining their efforts to arrive at a clearer understanding of the mutual relations between organisms and their environment. Similarly, the knowledge of sport can be enhanced if qualified and interested scholars are willing to forego other pursuits and concentrate on sport.

This brings us back to our original proposition that two features emerge when one considers the cognitive values to be derived from sport. These features are fairly independent of each other. The first encompasses the idea that an individual may acquire knowledge through his participation in sport. Such knowledge tends to be supportive and incidental. It can scarcely be singled out as the raison d'etre for participating in sport. The other feature offers far greater potential for cognition. However, participation is not a necessary condition for acquiring this kind of knowledge. Either participants or nonparticipants may study sport from a historical, philosophical, psychological, or sociological frame of reference as well as any combination thereof.

BIBLIOGRAPHY

Aspects of Contemporary Sport Sociology, Proceedings of C.I.C. Symposium on the Sociology of Sport, ed. Gerald S. Kenyon. Chicago, Ill.: The Athletic Institute, 1969.

Contemporary Psychology of Sport, Proceedings of the Second International Congress of Sport Psychology, Washington, D.C., 1968. Chicago, Ill.: The Athletic Institute, 1970.

Daniels, Arthur, "The Potential of Physical Education as an Area of Research and Scholarly Effort," *Journal of Health, Physical Education, and Recreation*, XXXVI, No. 1, January 1965.

Fogelin, Robert, "Sport: The Diversity of the Concept." Paper delivered at the 13th Annual Meeting of the American Association for the Advancement of Science, Dallas, Texas, December 28, 1968.

Frankena, William K, *Ethics*. Englewood Cliffs, N.J.: Prentice-Hall, Inc., 1963.

Henry, Franklin, "Physical Education: An Academic Discipline," *Journal of Health, Physical Education, and Recreation*, XXXV, No. 7, September 1964.

Kenyon, Gerald, "On the Conceptualization of Sub-Disciplines Within an Academic Discipline Dealing with Human Movement," *Proceedings*, 71st Annual Meeting, National College Physical Education Association for Men, 1968.

Lewis, Guy M, "Theodore Roosevelt's Role In The 1905 Football Controversy," *The Research Quarterly*, Vol. 40, No. 4, December 1969.

Lüschen, Günther, "Some Recent Developments in the Sociology of Sport," *Aspects of Contemporary Sport Sociology*, Proceedings of the C.I.C. Symposium on the Sociology of Sport, ed. Gerald Kenyon. Chicago, Ill.: The Athletic Institute, 1969.

Meyerhoff, Hans, *The Philosophy of History in our Time*. Garden City, N.Y.: Doubleday Anchor Books, 1959.

Philosophical Analysis and Education, ed. R. D. Archambault. New York: The Humanities Press, 1965.

Schmitz, Kenneth, "Sport and Play: Suspension of the Ordinary." Paper delivered at the 13th Annual Meeting of the American Association for the Advancement of Science, Dallas, Texas, December 28, 1968.

Weiss, Paul, *Sport: A Philosophic Inquiry*. Carbondale, Ill.: Southern Illinois University Press, 1969.

Wittgenstein, L., *Philosophical Investigations*. New York: The Macmillan Company, 1953.

Zeigler, E. F., and K. J. McCristal, "A History of the Big Ten Body-of-Knowledge Project in Physical Education," *Quest* IX, *The Nature of a Discipline*, December 1967.

10/Why Sport?
Attitudinal Values?

After one considers the possible physical and cognitive values that may be derived from sport, there is only one broad area left to be considered if the justification is to be external. That area is embodied in the realm of attitudes. Of course, it is also entirely possible that sport requires no external justification; the idea of sport for sport's sake can be postulated. However, that is a topic which will be reserved for the next chapter. In the meantime it remains to be determined what is included under the subject of attitudes and how sport might be associated with this subject.

Throughout the 20th-century many attempts have been made to justify programs in sport and physical education on the grounds that participation in these programs contributes in some way to the development of positive attitudes. Most frequently, these claims have manifested themselves in the suggestion that sport builds character. However, the idea of character education is not as popular as it was at one time, and in recent years the same concept has been expressed in different ways. Generally speaking, attitudinal development has also been associated with the concept of education through the physical. The reason for this is rather obvious. If one is searching for other than physical values, the two remaining choices are cognitive and attitudinal. We previously noted that sport somehow or another doesn't seem to be very cognitive, so that left the speculators with attitudes.

Unfortunately, the scientific data which either refutes or supports these claims has been sparse. It has been much more convenient and/or attractive to explore the possible physical values which may accrue from participation in sport. However, the relatively few studies which have been done serve at least two purposes. First of all, they tend to cast doubt on many of the speculative claims which have been made. Secondly, they point out those areas which need to be further researched. Because the subject is attitudes there will always be some room for speculation, but, hopefully, the speculation will be handled with caution and future efforts will be directed toward the attempt to obtain more facts.

If one begins to analyze the broad scope of subject matter, he soon finds that three broad categories emerge. These are knowledge, skill, and attitudes. The subject matter of sport is no exception. In sport, too, one may acquire knowledge, skill, or attitudes, or any combination thereof. This has provided the basis for the possible values to be discussed if one is defending or attempting to justify a sport program from an external frame of reference. What, then, can be said about attitudes which will assist in understanding this third type of subject matter?

It is much easier to describe both knowledge and skill than it is attitudes. To know something is to have facts and/or understanding. When one has skill he is able to perform or do something. An attitude relates to feeling. Attitudes are not always expressed. Likewise, those expressed may not be the true or actual attitudes held by any given individual. In other words, attitudes are not easily assessed or measured. Furthermore, and more significantly, they cannot be directly taught. We can teach knowledge of subject matter, and we can teach skills; attitudes are acquired through teaching knowledge and/or skill. This poses special challenges for the teacher because it means that the students' attitudinal realm is not directly under his control. An example might help to clarify this point.

As a tennis instructor, one is first and foremost engaged in teaching the various skills of tennis. In so doing, he also teaches certain aspects of knowledge about the game of tennis. While this teaching is taking place, the students acquire not only skill and knowledge but also attitudes. These may be attitudes about the game itself, sport generally, the instructor, other students, or any combination of these. Unfortunately, the attitudes acquired are not always those which the instructor might hope would be acquired. Attitudes tend to be a very individual or personal matter, much more so than either knowledge or skill.

Another characteristic of attitudes is that they tend to be less specific than is noted with regard to knowledge and skill. Earlier reference was made to the specificity of motor skills and esoteric knowledge. Sometimes, attitudes are also quite specific or esoteric. But, more frequently, people carry their attitudes with them from one situation to another. This, in itself, poses a special problem for the teacher. When it comes to attitudes, he is seldom, if ever, starting from scratch, so to speak. The concept of predisposition probably best describes the dilemma of the teacher who wishes that each of his students would take a "fresh look" at the issues and problems which face them in the immediate teaching-learning situation.

Motivation is also an important concept in understanding attitudes. We know that when one is motivated, something or someone causes him to pursue a task or tasks with diligence and sincerity of purpose. Frequent reference is made to so-called positive attitudes. When a person has a positive attitude, he is able to transfer this attitude to more than one situation. On the other hand, positive attitudes are not always transferable. Individual X may have a positive disposition toward situation Y, but there is something about situation Z which causes him to approach it with less enthusiasm. Experience is an important factor in both attitudes and motivation. The teacher may often be aware of general experiences which predispose his students, but, more frequently, there is no way in which he can determine those particulars which result in the transfer of negative attitudes and lack of motivation.

As noted earlier, there has often been a tendency to associate attitudes with character. The thought seems to be that the person with "good" character is one who possesses the "right" attitudes, which, in turn, bring about "proper" conduct. There is very definitely a moral connotation with regard to character. Quality of character is evaluated in terms of standards which have been set by the culture or a group within that culture. Thus, when people refer to building character or character education, they are suggesting that attitudes should be shaped to conform with the ideals and standards which have been established by a group.

Jay B. Nash was perhaps the most eloquent spokesman for the idea of character education within the field of physical education:

Character education may be defined as the behavior of an individual upon which the society in which he moves places a stamp of "good." It must always remain a relative term as the qualities which the community pronounces "good" will vary with the community and will develop with the ages. The particular point to be noted in this connection is that character is one of the desirable outcomes of education and hence is one of the desirable outcomes of physical education. . . .

Character may properly be judged as the accumulation of the effects of these various situations upon the individual. Each act in itself is minor—taken together, major. At the Great Divide in the Canadian Rockies drops of water fall from the glacier under the rays of the sun. They flow gently down a little stream. In this stream is placed a very crude partition, the water that goes to the right forms one of the great rivers of the West, the water that goes to the left becomes one of the great rivers of the Mississippi Valley. The drops of water make the stream, the stream makes the river, and the river makes the ocean. In some such manner, the accumulation of minor social influences makes a character ocean. No phase of education offers so many opportunities for the guiding of this conduct as does physical education.[1]

One of the most interesting features of Nash's conception is that he begins with a recognition of the relativity of character, but he then proceeds to defend the idea that character can be developed. In other words, he would support the concept of character as being a composite of desirable attitudes and traits. Within recent years, the concept of character is not employed in the same way due to a recognition of its relative nature. In many ways the situation is analogous to

---

[1] Jay B. Nash, "Character Education as an Objective," *Mind and Body*, Vol. 38, May, 1931, pp. 497—499.

the problems involved in speaking of physical fitness and intelligence. Questions can always be raised concerning physical fitness for what or intelligence for what. Similarly, one might ask: character for what? For instance, can desirable attitudes in sport be compared with desirable attitudes in teaching? Even though attitudes are highly transferable, the same attitudes may not be appropriate for all situations. In other words, one might have the right attitudes for participating in sport, but these same attitudes could be quite inappropriate for a teacher.

It would seem more appropriate to suggest that many attitudes tend to be somewhat specific in terms of their desirability. At the same time, as noted earlier, this does not negate the fact that considerable transfer of attitudes may take place when one moves from one situation to another. That is, the individual is likely to transfer an attitude whether or not it is desirable. This can hypothetically be put to the test by randomly listing certain attitudes and then comparing the applicability of these attitudes to various situations. Some attitudes which may be commonly observed are:

cooperative
competitive
aggressive
introversive
extroversive
complacent
relaxed
intense
frivolous
gallant
reticent

An argument can be waged as to the difference between an attitude and a trait, but that is not particularly germane for our purposes here. Suffice it to say that a trait is a distinguishing feature of a person whether it be an attitude, a physical characteristic, or an act which that person customarily performs. Actions frequently reflect attitude. In other words, an individual may be aggressive in attitude as well as in actions.

An analysis of some typical situations will readily reveal that the above listed attitudes are not equally applicable. Following are examples of various situations found in life on a day-by-day basis. They are situations in which these attitudes may serve either as positive elements or deterrents.

a ground of casual golfers
a bridge club
a group of children at play
professional football players
adult bible study group

a group of "golden agers" at an afternoon tea
a group of college librarians
young men at a formal dance
a group of navy chief petty officers on liberty
a meeting of stockbrokers
a meeting of the board of trustees of a state university

It should be fairly obvious that it would be difficult to group the attitudes listed above and apply them to these situations while arriving at an assessment of what constitutes good character. At the same time, there seems to be little doubt that attitudes which are formed or caught in any one of these situations do not remain in isolation. Thus, we again conclude with the realization that attitudes are an extremely individual matter, depending primarily on the composite of experiences of each individual. If attitudes are to be categorized and assessed in relationship to something called "character," this can only properly be done with the full realization that strong value judgments prevail. Character becomes a composite of expectations for a group based on previous experiences of those who either direct or lead the group.

Attitudes have also been strongly identified as well as confused with the matter of social acceptability. A careful analysis will reveal that the relationship here is very closely akin to that found in comparing attitudes with character. Even though attitudes are very much an individual matter, the individual is constantly faced with the dilemma that he cannot merely express his attitudes, conduct his life accordingly, and expect that all his actions will be well received. Just as a group of people may arrive at a collective opinion of what constitutes "good" character, so too social acceptability is a group decision.

Each group establishes its own means of functioning. This includes both what is to be said and what is to be done. Sometimes the protocol for a group closely resembles that of other groups or the culture of which the group is a part. Social acceptability within the group is evaluated in terms of this protocol. In some cases the protocol very closely resembles character because definite standards are established and everything is judged in accordance with conformity to these standards. There are definite criteria for what is right and what is wrong. On the other hand, social acceptability is not always gained by following the generally accepted standards of conduct. The individual who follows this pattern may be referred to as a "square" by the young or as a "bore" by his adult peers.

Thus the individual, particularly the young and immature individual, is frequently faced with the dilemma that two kinds of attitudinal demands are simultaneously placed on him. There are demands on character, based on the generally accepted mores of the culture and/or institution within that culture, and the demands of social acceptability, based on peer group criteria. Sometimes there is no conflict between these two sources of demands; the individual's peer group is in accord with the generally accepted mores. Unless the individual is a complete nonconformist, there is a strong probability that his attitudes will be developed along a certain line and without a great deal of confusion or disturbance. However, more commonly, the individual is likely to experience some tension from time to time as he attempts to reconcile his attitudes with the contrasting, external forces which would desire to "shape" his attitudes.

This leads us to conclude that there is also a strong relationship between attitudes and goal orientation. Psychologists tell us that people differ markedly from one another in the extent or degree to which they are goal-oriented. This is not to suggest that many people are lacking in goals. It merely points to variance in kind, amount, and intensity of goal-orientation.

Attitudes are, at least in part, a by-product of the individual's goal orientation (or relative lack of it). This fact is recognized by either those who attempt to build character or those who strive to enhance the social acceptability of their students. A goal or goals are presented to the students with the hope that this may assist in developing positive attitudes.

Even though he does not hold to the traditional conception of character education, Paul Weiss is one who suggests that attitudes may be shaped in relationship to a goal. In his case the goal for all would be that of pursuing excellence in some form.

It is sometimes contended that athletics not only builds bodies but character. Character, it has long been known, is best forged by making men face crises in the little; by being pushed up against limits they define themselves. If they are made to do this again and again in the same areas, firm habits are established, enabling the men to act without much reflection and yet with surety and precision. Properly trained, the men gradually learn how to act quickly and yet successfully; properly aimed, their action will be productive of what enriches while it satisfies. As a result of their athletic activity the men will become more alert to the insistence and rights of others, both those with whom they play and those against whom they play. If athletic training will lead to such outcomes as these more expeditiously than other means allow, it will provide a strong justification for sport programs.

To support this view, one should show that character is not or cannot be properly molded in childhood, much before there has been an opportunity to engage in athletic activities. Yet some children seem to be habituated to act well, and in ways that are appropriate to their age, size, aptitude, and promise for growth, long before they are able to participate in sports. . . .

Like many another important objective, character is most effectively achieved when attention is directed not to it but elsewhere—in this case to sport itself as a finality, serving no other end.[2]

---

[2] Paul Weiss, *Sport: A Philosophic Inquiry* (Carbondale, Ill.: Southern Illinois University Press, 1969), pp. 29—30.

Thus, Weiss does not reject the concept of character even though he might not agree with some of the ways in which this subject has been customarily treated. He suggests that an individual's fulfillment, including attitudes which enable him to meet crises, can be developed. There is no magic formula or exclusive means for this. Sport or athletics may be one of the means. For some people, it might be the most appropriate means. At any rate, sport participation would not be justified on that basis. The relationship to goal-orientation is clear-cut. The goal might be sport or athletics. In pursuing this goal, the right kind of attitudes may accrue. At the same time, other people, with different goals, are also being guided in the development of worthwhile and productive attitudes.

ANALYSIS OF CLAIMS FOR UNIQUENESS OF SPORT

The foregoing is in rather sharp contrast with the many claims for the uniqueness of physical education and sport which have pervaded much of the physical education literature during the past 50 years. As suggested earlier, I suspect that many of these claims arose from a felt need and pragmatic attempt to justify the establishment or continuance of physical education programs in the schools. People are usually forced to justification when their programs are not accepted or accepted with reservation. In other words, attempts at external justification arise from external sources. When physical training became physical education there was a felt need to justify the concept of education through the physical. A logical hypothesis, without considering it too seriously or putting it to the test, was that sport and physical education are unique because of their potential for building character or developing the right kind of attitudes. Let us randomly examine some of the typical claims in the cold light of analysis.

We will begin by examining Nash's claim concerning the contribution of physical education to character education because it has previously been mentioned. He blatantly stated that "no phase of education offers so many opportunities for the guiding of this conduct as does physical education." Earlier in his article he presented his rationale for this value judgment:

The application of this to physical education is obvious. We are dealing with activities that children want to do. . . . Children are interested in activities which conform to the following formula: The activity must challenge the individual—the individual must be within reach of success—social approval must go with success. . . . Every activity which is taught to children should be judged by this formula. Game elements are dead unless the child connects success in them to success in the game. Nature study, manual training, music, and all other activities are dead, unless the child sees the challenge. We, in physical education, are dealing with activities in which the child can easily see the challenge. Hence, there is a "want." There is integration. There is opportunity for the building of character traits.[3]

---

[3] Nash, *op. cit.*, pp. 498—499.

A few observations can be made regarding Nash's claim. To begin with, the means toward character education, as described here, seems to be inconsistent with his definition of character which he defined as "the behavior of an individual upon which the society in which he moves places a stamp of 'good'." It would appear that the motivation or challenge to the individual is frequently found in those activities upon which society has *not* placed the stamp of "good." However, even if we give Nash the benefit of doubt, his bold assumption is subject to further questioning. He can be granted the benefit of doubt by suggesting that children are desirous of doing those things which society deems to be good. These would be the activities which afford a challenge. But, who is to say that sport or physical education presents a greater challenge than other activities in life? On the other hand, Nash's hypothesis becomes somewhat more credible when he refers to those "activities in which the child can easily see the challenge." If there is any sort of uniqueness about sport it may reside in that thought. There is no doubt that sport is a very visible kind of activity. The challenges in sport are out in the open, there for all to see or experience. If challenges are instrumental in the development of positive attitudes, then it is entirely possible that sport may be at least initially attractive because of its concreteness and accessibility. However, at the same time, it seems rather tenuous to justify a sport program merely because it presents immediate and easily recognizable challenges. For instance, one might suspect that more subtle challenges would be more significant in the long run.

With his advocacy of education through the physical, Jesse Feiring Williams was another articulate pioneer in speculating that sport and physical education were unique in terms of their attitudinal values. Any one of several passages could be selected to portray the general orientation of Williams. I have selected the following because of his specific reference to selected attitudes or traits that might be associated with those who have been enriched through their participation in sport or physical education:

This recasting of the scene for physical education is no superficial move but a tendency toward deeper growth. It holds that we need to aim higher than health, than victorious teams, than strong muscles, than profuse perspiration. It sees physical education primarily as a way of living, and seeks to conduct its activities so as to set a standard that will surpass the average and the commonplace. There is in such a view something of the loftier virtues of courage, endurance, and strength, the natural attributes of play, imagination, joyousness, and pride, and through it all, the spirit of splendid living— honest, worthy, and competent—so much desired by each individual.[4]

In all fairness to Williams it is not entirely accurate to state that he stressed the uniqueness of sport or physical education. His claim was one of placing physical education on a par with other educational endeavors. Throughout his

---

[4] Jesse Feiring Williams, "Education Through the Physical," *The Journal of Higher Education*, Vol. I (May, 1930), p. 279.

writing one main stream is evident: we must educate for the whole man. He was violently opposed to any esoteric emphasis which stressed the physical or any particular mental phase of education. His focus on the whole man and "education for fine living" constantly led him to a discussion of attitudes which should be developed through physical education as well as through any other phase of education. This, in itself, was sufficient cause for his successors to extend the claim in either suggesting or boldly stating that physical education was without parallel in its potential for shaping the right kind of attitudes. Professional physical education students in the 1930s, '40s, and '50s were exposed over and over again to clichés which related participation in sport to the most splendid attitudes and attributes which one could imagine.

Williams may have had something in common with John Dewey. Both of these prolific writers obviously saw a need to remove some of the shackles from traditional education. In so doing, their tendency was to exaggerate other possibilities. In the case of Williams, he was beset with the temper of his day which was that of physical training. He was determined to move his profession beyond that narrow realm. What was more logical than to state that physical education contributed to the attitudinal virtues of education generally?

Among the many physical education texts which have been written in the Williams vein, the book by Brownell and Hagman is representative of what might be called an aspect of mid-20th-century thought in physical education. No one can doubt where they would stand with regard to the question of this chapter.

The Unique Role of Physical Education. The discussion now turns to the unique functions of physical education, the contributions that enable this program to stand out in juxtaposition with others. Every subject or department must have unique characteristics to justify its place in the curriculum. . . .

Shall physical education be regarded as a program to develop and strengthen the organs and systems of the body, or shall physical education use large-muscle activities as a medium for obtaining the best kind of complete education that the schools and colleges have to offer? In brief, is physical education primarily concerned with the training *of* the physical, or education *through* the physical?

No one can deny the importance of a strong, well-formed body from the standpoint of maintaining health or for reasons of social acceptance. On the other hand, physical education has a deeper meaning and significance when it is regarded as a medium of expression, as an instrument by which youth may learn many lessons of immediate and enduring benefit. In a sound program of physical education, such qualities as health, good posture, strength, and endurance flow as by-products to successful participation in activity. To this end the focus of attention in physical education must be education *through* the physical which, in turn, gives due emphasis to building and maintaining the kind of strong bodies required for citizenship in a democracy.[5]

---

[5] From *Physical Education—Foundations and Principles* by Clifford L. Brownell and E. Patricia Hagman, pp. 19–20. Copyright 1951 by McGraw-Hill Book Company. Used with permission of McGraw-Hill Book Company.

At least three points appear clear in examining the position of Brownell and Hagman. First of all, they definitely felt the need to justify physical education by relating it to something external. In other words, physical education or sport could not be defended for what it is without searching for values it might have for the rest of life; the value could not be found in sport or physical education itself. This brings up an interesting point that has been alluded to before in this book. As I see it, there never has been any particular need to justify sport; it seems to be accepted by most people in its own right for what it is. By contrast, the history of physical education has been one of leaders in that field constantly searching for justification. This may be primarily attributed to the efforts and problems in establishing physical education as a bona fide part of a school curriculum.

Secondly, Brownell and Hagman stressed the need for uniqueness if physical education was to be justified. The surprising thing is that in so doing they accorded second place to the one element of physical education which is indeed unique. That is the physical aspect. It would appear that if one felt the need for justification he would at least begin by pointing out that which he or his group had to offer which was not shared by other educators.

In the third place, the above authors chose to "hang their hat" on education through the physical by relating it to citizenship in a democracy. Now, citizenship in a democracy undoubtedly falls somewhere in the attitudinal realm, but it is a bit difficult to say where. This much can be said for certain. Brownell and Hagman were not alone in attempting to justify the role of physical education in regard to the contributions which it might make to democratic living. Unfortunately, the matter is not quite that simple. It could be that sport or physical education may assist in reaching toward the ideal which has been called democratic living. But, to begin with, we need much more scientific data before the claim can even be accepted with some degree of seriousness. Furthermore, it is virtually impossible to approach the task of either supporting or refuting the claim unless we first of all present a conception of democratic living as an initial frame of reference. One such conception, with its possible application for physical education, is presented by Bookwalter and Vander-Zwaag.[6] This, in turn, may be an unsatisfactory frame of reference for many, but it is an attempt to conceptualize democracy without leaving it as a completely nebulous construct. Others may have other conceptualizations as to what is meant or implied by reference to democracy. I would suggest that they be postulated if attitudinal claims for sport are to be identified with that concept.

Delbert Oberteuffer is another who championed the cause of relating physical education and sport to the development of the right kind of attitudes. Even though he did not reject the idea or the possibility of accruing physical values through participation in sport, he felt that physical educators had overlooked much of their educational potential by focusing only on the physical outcomes.

---

[6] K. W. Bookwalter and H. J. VanderZwaag, *Foundations and Principles of Physical Education* (Philadelphia: W. B. Saunders Co., 1969), pp. 186—199.

Oberteuffer expressed his principal concern in many ways through different sources, but the following is selected as being fairly representative of his claim:

Thus the activities of physical education may become a remarkable instrument for socialization. In games, and in sports, we learn to expect things of our friends and we know our friends are expecting things of us. We take on status; we become persons. We rise and fall as we try to meet these expectations. We learn to judge and to be judged and when a friend fails to measure up, lets us down in a tight foursome, or fumbles at a crucial moment, we, because others have expected things of us, are more tolerant of him. We recognize his weakness and his despair because we share them. We do, that is, if we have played, if our physical education has been a full one. It is usually the person whose physical education has been neglected who is intolerant enough to shout his abuse when players make mistakes.[7]

Although Oberteuffer's statements are not based on scientific facts, he presents a meaningful description of attitudinal reactions that have been experienced by those who participate in sport. He did not merely rest the case by blanketly stating that sport is a positive influence in shaping socially acceptable attitudes. Also, he was somewhat more cautious about emphasizing the uniqueness of sport than others have been in writing on this subject. He does state that these activities "may become a remarkable instrument for socialization." However, that is quite different from stating that they *will* become or are *the most* remarkable instrument for socialization.

Of course, one can choose his words with care and remain overtly cautious while at the same time present a philosophical position designed to influence the thoughts of others. In my opinion, Oberteuffer's statements fall in that category. One could jump to the conclusion that sport is necessary for one to be judged or to be tolerant. These ideas are not stated as such, but they are implied in his remarks. He would probably be the first to agree that judgments and the need for tolerance can come from any one of several sources in life. On the other hand, maybe there is something different about the judgments and the tolerance required in sport. The jury is still out on that subject. If anything, this points to another area which requires scientific exploration, if that is possible.

The work by Voltmer and Esslinger also typifies that which is considered by many to be *the* physical education point of view. They begin by recognizing that physical educators may and should have several objectives. One of these is labeled as the "social development objective." Their discussion of this objective clearly reveals a strong claim for the attitudinal values that may be obtained from participation in sport of physical education:

---

[7]Delbert Oberteuffer, "Some Contributions of Physical Education to an Educated Life," Found in A. Paterson and E. C. Hallberg's *Background Readings for Physical Education* (New York: Holt, Rinehart and Winston, 1965), p. 115.

Physical education is one phase of school work that lends itself particularly to the development of character. Student interest prevails, activity is predominant, and relatively great authority and respect are accorded those in charge. The physical education class provides more than just a place to discuss character education theory; it furnishes a laboratory for actual practice. We develop character much more surely through experience than we do by hearing about what should be done or should not be done. It is one matter to decide upon the correct response to a tense situation when merely looking on, and an entirely different proposition to decide and act correctly when in the midst of heated combat. One contestant may foul another, unnoticed by the official, near the end of a close game and thus prevent an opportunity to score. The player fouled cannot get advice about his ensuing action and decide some time later what to do. He must decide at once and provide an immediate answer through action. This splendid educational laboratory demands actual responses to tense situations just as much as life in general does. The whole setup provides real rewards and punishments, which with proper guidance will serve to encourage sportmanship, cooperation, sociability, self-control, leadership, and other qualities of character and citizenship.[8]

The reader will note some similarities between this position statement and that made by Oberteuffer. They have in common the stress on attitudinal values that arise from the dynamics of specific situations in sport. Oberteuffer directed attention to the capacities to judge, be judged, and be tolerant. Voltmer and Esslinger have described a situation wherein the participant must react to pressure without the benefit of advice or the time to think through the circumstances. The common denominator would appear to be the experiential factor in sport, if it can be called that. This, in turn, brings us closer to the topic of sport for sport's sake, which will be examined in more detail in the next chapter.

In the meanwhile, it should now be fairly evident that claims for the attitudinal values of sport may be manifested in any one of several ways. No simple formula has been or is likely to be evident. The reason for confusion in this area should also be obvious. If one is seeking to relate sport to something other than the acquisition of physical skill or knowledge, he is faced with only one other large choice. That choice is what we have designated as the attitudinal realm. A particular writer or speaker may choose to refer to character; another may discuss social development; a third is oriented toward the concept of citizenship; still a fourth may get carried away with remarks about sportsmanship. But, in the final analysis, it seems evident that each one is referring to the attitudinal reactions which take place as the individual interacts with a group. More specifically, the group referred to in these claims is the sport group. The focus is not so much on what happens to the group as it is on what happens to the individual as he is faced with the dynamics of group involvement is sport.

---

[8] E. F. Voltmer and A. A. Esslinger, *The Organization and Administration of Physical Education.* Fourth edition, copyright © 1967 by Meredith Publishing Company. Reprinted by permission of Appleton-Century-Crofts, Educational Division, Meredith Corporation.

In light of the claims that have been set forth, the interesting problem is one of trying to determine what evidence is available. This is not said to cast a bad light on those who have been cited as examples in the above claims. Each of us is guilty at times of claiming more than is warranted by the facts. Promoters and supporters of sport have been most guilty in this regard. The authors cited above saw a need for justification. They reacted in an articulate manner. They, too, might have hoped for the availability of additional research findings. What is known at this time?

SCIENTIFIC STUDIES OF SPORT AND ATTITUDES

Actually, to attempt to answer the above question is very presumptuous. Within the scope of a few pages we cannot completely report on all studies that have been done to date on the subject of sport and attitudes. We can report on selectted studies which, hopefully, are somewhat representative of work in this area.

Richardson drew attention to the problems surrounding the concept of sportsmanship when he surveyed senior, male students who were majoring in physical education. Among the conclusions reached by Richardson are the following:

As indicated in observation No. 1, the respondents overwhelmingly approved the practice of taking advantage of a sports situation if they can "get by." It is an extension of the popular concept that the sin is in being caught. . . .

The problem of teaching good sportsmanship to major students becomes more complicated when the professional leaders can not themselves agree upon correct behavior. This was demonstrated by Brace who gathered the responses of 80 men and 20 women professional leaders in physical education. He stated, "it is worth nothing that certain actions considered unsportsmanlike were approved by ten to 25 percent of both men women."

The association between lower scores on sportsmanship tests and subsidized athletes in the "income" sports seems to be pretty well established. The results of this study corroborated the findings of Kistler. . . .

The author fails to observe any gain in increasing the level of sportsmanship in the college athletic program.[9]

If anything, Richardson's findings tend to lend strong support to James Keating's thesis, which was discussed earlier in this book. It is perhaps pure

---

[9]Deane Richardson, "Ethical Conduct In Sport Situations," *Proceedings*, 66th Annual Meeting, National College Physical Education Association (Washington, D.C.: American Association For Health, Physical Education, and Recreation, 1963), pp. 103–104. Reprinted by permission of the NCPEAM.

nonsense to talk about sportsmanship with respect to the behavior and outlooks of an athlete. The hard, cold truth of the matter is that the athlete is not concerned with sportsmanship. To associate him with the conduct of a sportsman only adds to the confusion and hypocrisy which already permeate most discussions on this topic. Consequently, this undoubtedly points out one of the major problems concerning the generalizations and hypotheses that have been advanced with regard to the influence of sport on attitudes. The attitudes of the casual sportsman can reasonably be expected to be quite different from those of the dedicated athlete. Therefore, the label of "right" or "wrong" cannot be universally and equally applied to those attitudes that are derived from participation in both sport and athletics.

Kroll and Petersen also studied attitudes in relationship to athletic participation. They administered a study of values tests to six collegiate football teams. Among the points raised in the discussion of their findings, the following are pertinent to the central question of this chapter:

It seems perilous to attempt drawing any parallel between the outcomes of this study and educational outcomes in athletics, but the situation that exists seems to be the reverse of what one might expect with fruition of the objectives commonly ascribed to athletics. For example, a high score on the social variable is associated with personality motives consistent with love of people, kindness, sympathy, and unselfishness. These values could well represent the outcomes of a sportsmanlike attitude toward life. The present result shows that the successful teams score low rather than high on this variable. . . .

The attitudes toward life demonstrated as contributing to significant discrimination among the teams studied represent a discordant image of the high ideals typically associated with sportsmanship and athletics. The results are highly suggestive of compatibility with Richardson's (7) findings that the sportsmanship standards possessed by athletes were considerably different from that advocated by the profession, with football players on athletic scholarship ranking lowest in sportsmanship [10]

It would be interesting to compare the results if the same test instrument was administered to sport groups, in the true meaning of that term. Unfortunately, studies of this type have tended to focus more on athletic teams for a couple of logical reasons. Athletic teams offer fine opportunity for study because of their structure and availability. Also, athletics is the activity which is constantly in the public eye. Researchers will be more inclined to probe that which reflects the public demand.

Singer sheds considerable light on the problems of relating sportsmanship to athletics. He summarizes the studies of Kistler[11], Richardson, and Kroll.

---

[10] W. Kroll and K. H. Petersen, "Study of Values Test and Collegiate Football Teams," *The Research Quarterly*, 36, No. 4, December 1965, p. 446.

[11] Joy W. Kistler, "Attitudes Expressed About Behavior Demonstrated in Certain Specific Situations Occurring in Sports," *Proceedings, College Physical Education Association*, 60, 1957, pp. 55–58.

Then, he calls attention to a study by McAfee[12], which might be classified in the sport realm as contrasted with a study of athletics. Singer's summary of this study in comparison with related studies again reveals the difficulties of generalization:

There is some indication of the changes that occur in sportsmanship attitudes during the maturing years. McAfee (1955) administered the Sportsmanship Preference Record to 857 sixth, seventh, and eighth-grade boys. . . . McAfee found that the attitudes became progressively lower from the sixth to the eighth grades. Pictured with Kistler's results on college students reported earlier, we get the impression that sportsmanship attitudes become less idealistic and more materialistic with increasing age. Athletes who are faced most often with competitive situations involving the pressures to win perhaps feel that need to moderate and sacrifice their ethics and morals. Whatever the case, there is a definite need to discover the impact athletics and physical education classes have on the participants on the development of sportsmanship.[13]

Thus, it would appear that as boys mature they become less sportsmanlike and more athletic. From one standpoint this could be summarily dismissed as something entirely natural because athletics connotes a higher skill level than does sport. Consequently, as boys mature, they improve their skills and become more athleticlike. However, the entire matter is not quite that simple. The emphasis on winning, which is associated with athletics, extends beyond the matter of skill level.

When it is reported that "the attitudes became progressively lower from the sixth to the eighth grades," a very definite value judgment has been inserted into the research findings. This statement is based on the assumption that athletic attitudes are on a lower scale than are attitudes of sportsmanship. Earlier, Singer draws a comparison between values and attitudes which is germane in understanding why McAfee found what he did and why he might be inclined to affix the label of "lower" to the eighth-grade results.

Our feelings toward something, our dispositions to evaluate and/or act in a certain way to certain stimuli are learned and develop with experience and maturity or even from tradition. These attitudes or ways of regarding something become more pronounced with age. . . . Extremely young children do not display the prejudices older children do, and adulthood brings fairly well-established attitudes. With age comes a greater awareness of social expectancies and pressures and a desire to conform to the value system of a culture or subculture.

The introduction of the word *value* in the previous sentence serves to place it in the context of our discussion and to point out its relationship to an attitude. The value system of a society establishes certain standards that provide direction to an attitude and

---

[12] Robert A. McAfee, "Sportsmanship Attitudes of Sixth, Seventh, and Eighth Grade Boys," *Research Quarterly*, 26, 1955, p. 120

[13] Robert Singer, *Motor Learning and Human Performance* (New York: The Macmillan Company, 1968), pp. 317–318.

account for its persistence. Attitudes are conditioned by values; they are not inseparable. Our attitude to make a choice from a number of alternatives is mediated by personal values. Some psychologists think of values as generalized attitudes, since attitudes supposedly have fairly specific objects.[14]

In other words, the eighth graders in McAfee's study were merely reflecting the prejudices of the culture in which they live. It has long been recognized that the concept of athletics has dominated the thinking of school leaders and parents in the United States. Consequently, it is not surprising that the value structure of eighth-grade boys should be predisposed toward athletics. When McAfee labeled these attitudes as "lower," he, too, was reflecting a value judgment.

Webb is another who has studied the change in attitudes that occurs as a result of age. More specifically he refers to the increasing "professionalization of attitudes." In so doing, he reinforces the idea that sport is an extension of play and that athletics is an extension of sport. "Thus the transition from 'child's play' to games, and then to sport, involves increasing complexity and rationalization of the activities and increasing professionalization of attitudes. By 'professionalization,' of course is meant the substitution of 'skill' for 'fairness' as the paramount factor in play activity, and the increasing importance of victory."[15]

His study consisted of a survey of students in grades 3, 6, 8, 10, and 12. A random sample of 920 public school students and 354 parochial school students were administered a questionnaire to determine their attitudes toward the physical education program. One of the items in his survey asked the students to indicate that which they considered to be most important and least important in playing a game. The respondents were to choose among the following: "to play as well as you can, to beat the other player or team, to play the game fairly."

In his discussion of the findings, Webb more or less concluded that attitudes toward play are influenced by other social factors such as economic background and religion. However, he also noted that the play sphere was a determinant in shaping attitudes at this age range. There was a tendency for the play attitudes to become more "professionalized" as the student grows older. Play might be considered significant in shaping values at this age level because it precedes the age in which attention is directed to participation in other activities. Webb's final point of discussion is perhaps most significant in terms of the topic at hand.

Thus to continue the sophomoric and even moronic insistence on play's contribution to the development of such "sweetheart" characteristics as steadfastness, honor, generosity, courage, tolerance, and the rest of the Horatio Alger contingent, is to ignore its structural and value similarities to the economic structure dominating our institutional

---

[14] *Ibid.,* p. 314.

[15] Harry Webb, "Professionalization of Attitudes Toward Play Among Adolescents," *Sociology of Sport* (Chicago: The Athletic Institute, 1969), p. 164. Reprinted with permission of the Athletic Institute.

network, and the substantial contribution that participation in the play arena thus makes to committed and effective participation in that wider system.[16]

Overall Webb leaves us with the thought that any claim for the uniqueness of sport in shaping attitudes has to be treated with extreme caution. Every child, adolescent, or adult has a composite of attitudes derived from a multitude of social factors. Sport may be a more significant social factor at one age than at another, but even that is difficult to isolate. His study points to another short-coming which has characterized much of the speculation about sport. Too frequently, we are inclined to generalize regarding sport without taking into consideration differences in age level. The attitudinal values of sport for the adolescent are undoubtedly quite different from those values which may accrue for the adult. Altogether too frequently, the proponents of sport have argued for it as a universal to be equally promoted for all ages in all situations.

For the reader who is interested in a single reference as to what we know to date about sport and attitudinal values, I would refer you to the *Proceedings of the Second International Congress of Sport Psychology*.[17] This congress was held at Washington, D.C. in 1968. I will not attempt to summarize the entire content of this 878-page volume, but results of the following studies are certainly pertinent to the question that has been raised in this chapter.

Kinji Ikegami, "Character and Personality Changes in the Athlete."

The influence of the length of athletic experience upon personality traits seems to be a reality, but it is not easy to determine experimentally the cause—the physical exercise—the act—the changes of emotion—because the influence upon personality usually appears gradually. But by this research changes effected by the length of exercise experience cannot be denied. Nevertheless, one cannot say it brings some changes to everybody because it differs according to the "quality" of people who receive the stimulus though they are put in the same circumstances ... and the influence effected by sport on personality traits is probably peculiar to each sport. (p. 59)

Jack Schendel, "The Psychological Characteristics of High School Athletes and Nonparticipants in Athletics: A Three Year Longitudinal Study."

The ninth-grade and twelfth-grade profiles for the athletes show the same general kinds of change as described for the nonparticipants in terms of the areas of greatest and most consistent change.... However, it is apparent that the *amount* of change in the athlete's profile is not as great as that of the nonparticipants; i.e., the margin of difference between 1963 and 1966 profiles is less for the athletes than for the nonparticipants. Very little change has taken place in the Class II scales, including such characteristics as responsibility, socialization, self-control and good impression....

---

[16] *Ibid.*, p. 178.

[17] *Contemporary Psychology of Sport*, ed Gerald Kenyon (Chicago: The Athletic Institute, 1970). Reprinted with permission of The Athletic Institute.

It is apparent that the athlete group has a high sense of personal worth and self-acceptance, significantly higher than that reflected by the nonparticipant group ... at both the ninth-grade and twelfth-grade levels. Again, it seems that whatever factors produced these differences, they had effected their major influence prior to the senior high school years. (pp. 86–89)

Erwin Hahn, "Performance in Sports as a Criterion of Social Approach in School Classes: A Sociometric Investigation."

For analyzing the effects of sports on socialization, a class of ten to twelve year old boys from a primary school in West Germany was investigated. The class consisted of three sharply differentiated subgroups. For a period of five months sociometric investigations were conducted. ... After great success in the sporting events, the social distances and the social roles in the group began to transform. Through the sport success a deepened and quicker fusion of the class was begun.

In all social areas the contacts changed. The heroes of the playground gained greater influence. Performance in sports seemed to be of great social value, independent from any intellectual factors. In the social order of boys between ten and twelve years old, physical fitness and sports play a significant role. Thus, sports activities are of great importance in the social approach of boys in primary school. (p. 403)

Roscoe Brown, "The Relationship between Physical Performance and Personality in Elementary School Children."

Data on the intellectual, physical performance, physical growth, and social and emotional development of 193 elementary school boys and girls were collected over a four year period. The data were analyzed using the factor analysis technique and the factor structure was examined to determine the extent to which physical performance and personality (emotional development) were related.

It was found that physical performance and emotional development were discrete factors and had negligible reciprocal loadings and thus are not related. The data revealed that the sociometric variable had moderately low relationship with physical performance and emotional development. ... The results of this study suggest that any relationships that may exist between physical performance and personality are more complex than ordinary descriptive studies indicate. (pp. 442 444)

John Kane, "Personality and Physical Abilities."

However, there is much more confidence to be placed in the relationship between Sports Participation and the combined personality measures. In order to support participation in sports and games an individual would seem to need certain basic physical abilities and his Sports Participation rating will reflect the achieved level in a number of appropriate physical abilities. The Sports Participation variable was therefore considered the most appropriate single physical measure to represent general physical ability, and it was for this reason that it was utilized as the criterion in the multiple correlation analysis in which the sixteen personality traits were the predictor variables. Highly significant correlations were obtained between Sports Participation and the combined personality measures for both the Total Men and Total Women groups of subjects. . . .

The conclusions reached on the basis of these multiple correlation and regression analyses are that Sports Participation and personality are significantly related in a meaningful way in that a high rating in sports participation is linked with low ergic tension (Q4-), dominance (E) and group-dependence (Q2-). (pp. 137—138)

CURRENT BASIS OF SPECULATION

To what extent is sport participation a determinant in shaping attitudes? This is the question under consideration. We began by attempting to describe that which might be called an attitude. We then noted some of the strong claims for the contributions of sport to the development of positive attitudes (character, personality) as set forth by pioneers in American physical education. This was followed by a brief summary of selected research findings which relate to the general question. This brings us to the point of trying to determine where we now stand. What is the current basis for speculation? it is fairly obvious that the claims of Williams, Nash, and others, as appropriate as they might have been at that time, will no longer stand up under the cold light of analysis. On the other hand, the speculative territory is still wider open than one might prefer. Possibly this will always be somewhat the case because of the nature of the subject, namely attitudes. At any rate, I will conclude this particular point of discussion with a few observations that represent my speculative thoughts at this juncture. These might be viewed as tentative generalizations or hypotheses which await the challenge of those who desire to uncover additional facts.

1. Attitudes toward sport and attitudes derived from sport, as well as any other attitudes, are inextricably linked to the process of socialization. The cliché that "no man is an island unto himself" is most appropriate in this context. Thus, even though each individual has his own composite or collective set of attitudes, the social milieu of the individual is an extremely important factor in determining the nature of these attitudes. Each individual is exposed to and is part of several social situations. Most people are sometime or another exposed to sport as one of the social situations. Many of these people also become part of, if not an integral part of, one or more sport groups. Therefore, it seems reasonable to conclude that sport does influence the participant's attitudes toward other people. If the sport experience has been a rewarding one (the participant attains some measure of success), it might further be hypothesized that sport assists in the development of favorable attitudes (kindliness) toward other persons.

2. Studies of personality must ultimately be reduced to study of attitudes. Personality is a gestalt; it defies precise definition; therefore, it cannot be investigated as a whole. Consequently, it is relatively useless to make value judgments regarding the influence of sport on personality. Whoever is to put the matter to

a test will soon find that he is forced to deal with specifics. Eventually, several specific conclusions may be combined to arrive at a more general assessment of attitudes. However, the collective notion of "personality" will always remain somewhat of an intangible. This may be one of the reasons why some proponents have been "carried away with the program" in their proclamations about sport. They recognize that sport is an area which readily portrays a variety of attitudes in a viable manner. This leads them to jump to the conclusion that sport is the most significant factor in molding personality. Unfortunately, whatever social or personal significance sport has may be lost amidst such efforts and utterances.

3. Any reference to sport in relationship to character is relatively meaningless unless character is more carefully defined in the context in which it is being discussed. As noted earlier, character is very much a relative term. The use of the term implies a value judgment. This is not to say that a group has no right to delineate their conception of "good" character. What is wrong is to arbitrarily associate sport with the conception. In a previous chapter we made the observation that a group may promote sport in an effort to enhance the internal cohesion among its members. If such a group also has a conception of what constitutes "good" character for its members, it is logical to assume that sport will be viewed as a positive element in contributing to the development of character. In essence, this is another way of stating that sport will likely contribute to socializing purposes, whatever the specific nature of those purposes might be.

4. Specific attitudes attained from participation in sport vary considerably from one age group to another. Studies completed to date would reinforce this suggestion. Unfortunately, there is a paucity of studies concerned with the adult age group. One might suspect that socializing attitudes would be at least one stream which is evident from one age group to another. The adolescent age is one in which many attitudes emerge as significant. Therefore, it is not surprising that sport also has a marked effect on attitude formation at this age level. In addition, most adolescents are not yet faced with the many demands of work, aside from their schoolwork which is often not taken as seriously as it might be. For many, sport occupies a considerable part of their time. Thus, it is not surprising that sport should be associated with attitudinal development among adolescents.

Adult attitudes regarding sport would appear to be first and foremost related to more general attitudes toward recreation and use of leisure time. Sport is an attractive form of recreation for reasons previously stated. I would expect that adult attitudes derived from sport are not too different from those which emanate from any form of recreation, if it has truly been recreation. Occasionally we are all inclined to assume that we are recreating when we are not working. From one standpoint, recreation may be more passive than active if one is thinking only of physical activity. On the other hand, to be truly recreation some form of activity must be involved. Recreation, in its fullest sense, carries away the individual from his usual concerns and problems. The attitudes derived from this are those involving feelings of relaxation. Contentment, not complacency, might best describe an attitude which is product of a recreative experience.

Adult attitudes derived from the sport experience are perhaps different in only one respect from attitudes that accrue through other recreational experiences. The difference is to be found in the physical characteristic of sport. I am not attempting to make any claims with regard to physical fitness. Rather, I am suggesting that a sense or an attitude of physical well-being may be one of the more significant effects which follow adult participation in sport. The feeling of physical improvement may be only imaginary, but it should not be disregarded or taken lightly. We know enough about the psychosomatic make-up of man to realize that the imaginary can often be as significant as the real. So, even if the physical changes resulting from sport participation are more imaginary than real, the accompanying attitude of physical well-being may be extremely important, especially for the adult who is becoming concerned about his physical state.

5. It would seem that the attitudinal values of sport are also somewhat specific to the particular sport. That is, the attitudinal values of playing golf may be quite different from those of playing basketball. A similar observation has been made in other contexts earlier in this book. There appears to be far too great a tendency to speculate or to draw generalizations about sport without consideration of variances within the broad gamut of sport. For instance, there is the difference between team play and one individual competing against another. Contact sports would likely produce attitudes which do not result from participation in other sports. I have heard the skiing experience described as being unique. It could well be that the game of football has as much in common with a game of chess as it has with skiing. We may never know the answers to these particular points of speculation, but, until we do, I feel the obligation to hypothesize that the specificity of sport skills is also applicable to any considerations concerning the potential values of sport as related to attitudes.

6. If I were forced to single out one specific attitude that characterizes all those who engage in sport, I guess that the attitude would be that which revolves around and emanates from the concept of *interaction*. There is one problem here; interaction is not an attitude; it is a process. However, the process of interaction in sport and through sport results in a collective feeling (attitude) that may be most significant, intangible as it is.

There are several features of interaction in sport which contribute to attitudinal development. To begin with, there is the interaction with other participants. This brings us back to the idea of socialization through sport. Such interaction may be with teammates, opponents, spectators, or any combination thereof. This form of interaction includes both competition and cooperation. The sportsman finds that he has a need to blend and harmonize his competitive and cooperative instincts in a variety of ways. If he fails to do so, he cannot properly interact to the situation at hand.

The sportsman is also required to interact with his environment. By environment here I am including both natural forces and manmade facilities. The skier must adjust to new slopes and the varying conditions of any given slope. A basketball player experiences the strange feeling of playing on an opponent's court. A football player battles the adversity of a driving wind and snow. Tennis players find it necessary to adjust their style of play as they move from one type of playing surface to another. A bowler finds that the ball does not react the same on all alleys. The baseball player must learn to cope with the problem of catching the ball with the sun in his eyes. Almost every sportsman or athlete finds that there are certain problems in interacting with his environment.

That which may be the most significant aspect of interaction in and through sport is also the most difficult to describe. Basically, it involves the demands imposed by the tatics of a game. The sporting game is a dynamic situation. It is filled with unpredictable elements. Strategy may be well planned; this will help. But the history of games of sport dramatically reveals that the unexpected will often occur. The participant in sport soon finds that he is forced to make many on-the-spot decisions. He has to interact with the move of an opponent or an unusual bounce of the ball. A chain reaction may also occur; a whole series of unexpected happenings places him in a spot where he must radically adjust his plan. All this is part of interaction.

It is a bit difficult to claim that any of these forms of interaction in sport will necessarily be transferred to other activities of life. On the other hand, who is to say that some transfer does not take place? One would almost have to suspect that there must be some kind of cumulative effect as any individual encounters new challenges and meets these challenges by interacting with an appropriate response. Life is filled with unusual occurrences. We frequently hear people comment that they do not know what is going to happen next. Yet, most of us proceed at the same time with some sort of expectation that we can chart the course ahead. Sport is but a replica of this twofold recognition. We plan our strategy for the upcoming contest. But, at the same time, we realize that several alterations will have to be made along the way as we encounter surprises. This causes us to interact without forethought and meditation.

7. Perhaps the one factor which makes the area of attitudes most difficult to research is that it is virtually impossible to isolate attitudes with regard to any particular activity. When we attempt to evaluate the attitudes an individual has attained from sport, we can never be completely certain what other factors also contributed to these attitudes. Each person accrues his own attitudes as a result of cumulative experiences. This brings us back to the fact that attitudes are first and foremost an individual matter, but the individual reacts to and interacts with his entire social environment.

Of course, a similar problem is present when one attempts to evaluate the physical values that may be obtained from sport participation. Other activities also may contribute to the improvement of physical attributes. Nevertheless, the problem is accentuated in the attitudinal realm due to the complexity of the gestalt or total attitudinal framework of each individual.

For this reason, I am let to believe that a certain amount of speculation will always have to characterize our discussions of sport in relationship to attitudinal values. This does not mean that we should forego our efforts to research the topic. To the contrary, every effort should be made to isolate the variables whenever possible. At the same time, there is a continuing obligation to challenge the presentation of supposed facts. This must be done with the full realization that all may not be as clear-cut and as factual as it sometimes appears.

8. As to future possibilities for attempting to know more about the influence of sport on attitudes, everything we do know about attitudes points in the direction of the need to employ peer evaluations. This stems from the recognition that attitudes are bound in with the process of socialization. Peer assessments are actually measures of social acceptability. There is good reason to believe that if sport does affect the attitudes of an individual, his peers are in the best position to evaluate those changes which have occurred. Unfortunately, the use of peer rating instruments in sport has been minimal in comparison with the use of paper-and-pencil tests. In spite of purported claims for the validity of paper-and-pencil tests in evaluating attitudes and personality, I find it difficult to imagine that such tests can favorably compare with peer ratings. To express an attitude on paper is markedly different from the attitude which is conveyed through interaction with peers. Of course, it could be argued that an individual does not always reveal his "true" attitudes. But, by the same token, there is no assurance that these "true" attitudes are measured by responses to items on a written test.

The limitation to peer rating, if there is one, may be a result of the need for longitudinal study. It certainly seems to be an important consideration to recognize that peer assessments have to be seriously questioned if they are based on limited observation. Researchers in all fields find that there are many practical limitations in conducting longitudinal studies. The time factor deters many. On the other hand, it is only reasonable to assume that individual reactions to the sport experience, or any other experience, can only be determined when viewed over a span of time.

Numerous research studies in the general area of psychology indicate that a combination of nominating technique with descriptive personality traits is the most valid instrument for indicating peer assessment. While evaluating personality traits of the peers, the rater is actually judging revealed attitudes. Because of the numerous forms of interaction in sport, the sportsman who rates his peers is in a very good position to observe revealed attitudes (personality traits). Such ratings should be made at all age levels in all sports over an extended period of time. When this has been done we will probably still be speculating about sport in relationship to attitudinal changes, but at least we should be proceeding on a firmer ground than that which still pervades the thought on this subject.

BIBLIOGRAPHY

Bookwalter, K. W., and H. J. VanderZwaag, *Foundations and Principles of Physical Education*. Philadelphia: W. B. Saunders Co., 1969.

Brownell, Clifford L., and E. Patricia Hagman, *Physical Education—Foundations and Principles*. New York: McGraw-Hill Book Company, Inc., 1951.

Contemporary Psychology of Sport, ed. Gerald Kenyon. Chicago: The Athletic Institute, 1970.

Kistler, Joy W., "Attitudes Expressed About Behavior Demonstrated in Certain Specific Situations Occuring in Sports," *Proceedings, College Physical Education Association*, 60, 1957.

Kroll, W., and K. H. Petersen, "Study of Values Test and Collegiate Football Teams," *The Research Quarterly*, 36, No. 4, December 1965.

McAfee, Robert A., "Sportsmanship Attitudes of Sixth, Seventh, and Eighth Grade Boys," *Research Quarterly*, 26, 1955.

Nash, Jay B., "Character Education as an Objective," *Mind and Body*, Vol. 38, May 1931.

Oberteuffer, Delbert, "Some Contributions of Physical Education to an Educated Life." Found in A. Paterson and E. C. Hallberg's *Background Readings for Physical Education*. New York: Holt, Rinehart and Winston, 1965.

Richardson, Deane, "Ethical Conduct In Sport Situations," *Proceedings*, 66th Annual Meeting, National College Physical Education Association. Washington, D.C.: American Association for Health, Physical Education, and Recreation, 1963.

Singer, Robert, *Motor Learning and Human Performance*. New York: The Macmillan Company, 1968.

Voltmer, E. F., and A. A. Esslinger, *The Organization and Administration of Physical Education*. New York: Appleton-Century-Crofts, Fourth Edition, 1967.

Webb, Harry, "Professionalization of Attitudes Toward Play Among Adolescents," *Sociology of Sport*. Chicago: The Athletic Institute, 1969.

Weiss, Paul, *Sport: A Philosophic Inquiry*. Carbondale, Ill.: Southern Illinois University Press, 1969.

Williams, Jesse Feiring, "Education Through the Physical," *The Journal of Higher Education*, Vol. I, May 1930.

11/Why Sport?
For Sport's Sake?

One need not necessarily search for or find a justification for sport other than sport itself. This viewpoint particularly has merit when sport is considered outside the scope of the school. Proponents of the idea of sport for sport's sake hold that the values of sport are intrinsic rather than extrinsic.

There is a close relationship between this idea and David Riesman's suggestion that maybe it is best to forego research into the nature of play. Because sport is an extension of play, a similar point could be made with respect to sport. Yet, on the other side of the coin, one of the characteristics of sport is that it does tend to be structured in one form or another. It is possible that when something is organized and structured with an intent in mind, it can no longer merely be accepted for what it is.

Physical educators have traditionally not been the spokesmen for the idea of sport for sport's sake, although in more recent years there have been a few notable exceptions, such as Howard Slusher. The reason why most physical educators have sought other justification may be fairly obvious. They have frequently been placed in a position where they were required to defend their program. The demand for justification was imposed on them before they had the chance to think through the argument for intrinsic value.

At any rate, the possibility of accepting sport for what it is should not be overlooked. I will attempt to analyze that which seems to be involved if one accepts this proposition. As with previous chapters concerning the question "why," I assume that the reader will be weighing the pros and cons and assessing his own position as we move along.

AN EXISTENTIAL POINT OF VIEW

Aside from the question concerning the "how" of sport, we have for the most part refrained from referring to the "isms" for reasons noted earlier. It now seems desirable to discuss an ism which really isn't an ism. Existentialism is not a systematic philosophy or an organized body of beliefs. In fact, many so-called existentialists prefer not to be known as such because they reject the premise that one should think in terms of a systematic philosophy.

Some people have suggested that existentialism is an extremely negative philosophy because it seems to be opposed to many things and leaves other questions unanswered. This may be partially true, but it does not really do full justice to the existential stance which influences the ideas of many people in the contemporary world. Let us begin, then, by delineating a few characteristic features of existential thought. This should reveal that the concept of sport for sport's sake is actually an existential point of view.

Perhaps the most outstanding feature of existentialism is the acute interest in the individual. The existentialist begins with the assumption that man, the individual human being, is at the center. Everything else in this world should be subordinate to and evaluated in terms of the "human condition." The existentialist desires to bring this idea to the focus of attention because he feels that "modern" man has become depersonalized amidst the conditions of the world today.

Much has been made of the existentialists' claim that "existence precedes essence." This accounts for the coining of the term "existentialism." The suggestion that existence precedes essence fits in perfectly with the existential stress that man should be at the focus of all considerations. Existence precedes essence only insofar as man is concerned. For everything else in the world, essence precedes existence. Kaplan describes this point very clearly:

And so with regard to anything and everything in the universe—with one exception, namely, man. With regard to anything else whatsoever, *its essence precedes its existence*. That is to say, I can conceive of a thing of a particular kind even if nothing of that kind in fact exists. If a thing of that kind comes into existence, it does so by being cast, as it were, into a predetermined role: it plays the part of a character which preceded the casting. Existence fills, so to speak, a position in logical space available before the particular existent came to be. In Los Angeles we might describe this as the view that the parking place is created before the car—for everything except man, that is; and trying to find a place to park is just the sort of thing that drives a man to existentialism.[1]

This in part explains the assumption that sport for sport's sake is an existential point of view. The essence of sport preceded the existence of sport. Man conceives of sport and then proceeds to establish the sporting activity. It might almost be more accurate to state that it is sport for the individual's sake. No further attempt at justification is actually required. When we attempt to rationalize the sport experience, we are actually detracting from the true existence of man.

---

[1]Abraham Kaplan, *The New World of Philosophy* (New York: Random House, Inc. 1961), p. 103. Reprinted by permission of Random House, Inc.

An extremely important consideration for the existentialist is that every man should have full opportunity to make choices in life. Without the opportunity to make legitimate choices man loses some of his existence. Life becomes prefabricated when alternatives for thought and action are no longer present. In this frame of reference it can easily be seen that there would be no recognition of external values. Thus, an existentialist would contend that there are no values of sport other than sport itself when the individual makes the decision to engage in sport.

The decision-making process goes hand in hand with the capacity and freedom to make choices. Sport has value only when the individual decides that sport is for him. If any group proceeds to claim the values of sport, the individual has already lost some of his opportunity to make a decision. Values are specific to each individual, and they grow out of the experiences of each person. There are no eternal values so to speak. The only real aspect of permanence is to be found in the need for each man to work out his own destiny. Consequently, nothing could be worse than to require people to participate in sport. Sport is not for everyone any more than is any other activity in life.

Man's freedom by no means negates his responsibility. Furthermore, man is responsible not only for himself but also for his fellow man. In a way this seems like a circular argument until it is more carefully examined. The responsibility for others does not mean dictating to others or attempting to limit their freedom in any way. It does mean that one's decisions must be made with the full conscience that such decisions will also influence and affect others. When I choose to participate in sport or a particular sport, the matter does not necessarily rest there. If I choose to play golf my neighbor may also decide to play that game, or he may decide that golf is not the game for him. Furthermore, there is also the distinct possibility that my decision to play golf will deter other members of my family in their desire to pursue other choices. As a result, the concept of responsibility always remains paramount in existential thinking. It causes this philosophical stance to be less liberal and carefree than it first appears. To the contrary, the existential concept of responsibility places a burden on man which is almost unmatched in any other philosophy. In many respects it would be much easier to say that I have no freedom or that I have no responsibility for my fellow human beings.

Another key concept in existential thought is that of authenticity. However, this concept is inextricably linked to the focus on individualism, as it has been outlined. The authentic person is one who does not permit various forms of essence to define what he is; rather, he is guided by his own existence. In simplest terms, the authentic individual is truly an individual; he is not a role-player. I might add that the concept of authenticity is one of the more difficult to reconcile with the idea of sport. The very nature of sport is such that a certain amount of role-playing occurs. For instance, it could be argued that I am playing a role as soon as I enter a game. This might lead one to believe that there is an essence about sport which always works contrary to the participant's existence.

An existentialist may be able to explain this apparent dilemma by suggesting that the individual need not be governed or molded by the essence of sport. If I am unable to detach myself from the role which I play in sport, then I have probably lost my authenticity. On the other hand, it is entirely possible that I can thoroughly enjoy sport and still recognize it for what it is—nothing more or less than a form of game. The very nature of a game is such that it is prefabricated. Role-playing is part of that particular essence. The individual who makes the decision to participate in sport recognizes that he will be playing a role. When he is unable to leave his role-playing with the sport, he has yielded to an essence which may be a handicap to his existence.

For this reason it is difficult to imagine that an existentialist could ever be a proponent of athletics, as we have earlier described that concept. The athlete is required to be so completely absorbed in his activity that he would probably find it impossible to stop playing the role when he leaves the athletic realm. The football hero imagines that he is still the hero when he enters the business world. The fact is that he may still be in the eyes of some, but the existentialist would say that he is less than he might otherwise be; he is not an authentic person if he extends his football role to his business pursuits. Again, we can see the consistency with the theme of sport for sport's sake. When sport becomes something more than sport, the existentialist would say that something has been lost. The individual has sacrificed part of his existence at the expense of an essence.

It should be fairly clear by now that an existentialist is just as much, if not more, concerned with psychological questions than he is with those having philosophical import. I suppose the same thing might be said about certain other philosophical positions, but the philosophical/psychological blend in existentialism is particularly noteworthy due to the extreme focus on the individual. The concept of sport for sport's sake is also consistent with the psychological inclination of the existentialist. He is not looking for any universal causes or explanations in his effort to describe sport. Sport is there for those who desire it. Differences in extent and kind of participation are accounted for by noting individual differences in psychological make-up.

Many people suspect that an existentialist is first and foremost desirous of ignoring tradition. This is not necessarily true. It is true that he does not expect any man to rely solely on tradition. In fact, tradition should be only one of several factors taken into consideration when man makes his choices. To reject the past without looking into the merits of what has been done is just as bad as a blanket acceptance of a pre-established pattern. In either case, an individual has forfeited his right and obligation to make a legitimate choice. Again, the implications for proponents of and participants in sport should be obvious. The conduct of sport certainly exemplifies many tradition-laden practices. It is only recently that strong voices have been heard in protest of the status quo which has been with us for some time.

The current protest is much more against athletics than it is against sport per se. Leaders of the "life" movement, such as Jack Scott and Harry Edwards, are expressing an existential point of view, whether or not they call it that. To them, athletics as it has been traditionally conducted in this country represents a "death" cause with an emphasis on winning and the accompaniment, losing. Life should not be viewed as a matter of winning and the losing. Scott and Edwards suggest that coaches symbolize those who are blinded by tradition, a tradition which glorifies the end, while overlooking the means. The net result is that boys are herded and molded into the athletic prototype without really having the opportunity to be authentic. Particularly, they point out that the black athlete has been exploited. He has been treated like a "nigger" in athletics because the history of western culture has been one of considering him to be a "nigger."

Therefore, the idea of sport for sport's sake is much more than a mere matter of accepting sport for what it is; first of all, we much accept the individual for what he is and not for what tradition says he should be. When we do that, we will have taken a major step forward in accepting sport as one of life's activities in which the individual may experience selfhood. From the existential frame of reference, athletics tends to be prefabricated, just as many of the institutions in western culture are prefabricated. Athletics may be a mirror; it may be reflecting a valid image. But, the existentialist tells us that the image must be changed.

At least one other concept is germane in understanding the existential frame of reference. This is the concept of *ambiguity*. Existentialism itself might be called ambiguous, but ambiguity has a special meaning for those who share this philosophical viewpoint. Kaplan also brings across this point in a succinct but descriptive manner:

Existentialism emphasizes not only constraints but also possibilities. There must be alternative possibilities of action, or choice would be meaningless; and there must be alternative possibilities of existence, or it would be predetermined by essence. This manifold of possibility gives rise to the final basic existentialist category: *ambiguity*, what Jaspers calls "the endless ambiguity of all existence and all action." We live, he says, "in a seething cauldron of possibilities." No single choice defines once and for all the nature of man and thereby of the world significant for human existence. Choice is continuous as we go through life, and with each choice some possibilities vanish forever while new ones emerge for the next choice. We are continuously making something of life, but we can never make it out: life is inescapably ambiguous.[2]

The meaning of this for those interested in sport is twofold. To begin with, the most obvious consideration is that the final boundaries of sport cannot be defined in terms of what might be accepted as a sport. Priorities among sport should give way to fresh insights. For instance, in recent years college physical education directors have witnessed growing student interest in such activities as yoga, tai chi, and aikido. If the trend continues we could witness the day when

---

[2] *Ibid.*, p. 117.

an activity such as basketball will no longer occupy a treasured spot among sports. This would represent a mark of progress as far as the existentialist is concerned. It is not that he is against basketball. That particular sport should sit side-by-side with all other sports as among the choices for the individual. What the existentialist deplores are cultural pressures which would shove basketball or any other sport to the foreground. When that is done, there is a tendency for the sport to become less sportlike. The shift along the continuum from sport to athletics almost immediately begins to take place.

The second meaning of ambiguity for sport is probably more significant in the final analysis. Ambiguity connotes the idea that one should not even attempt to justify sport. The reason for this is simply that sport is nothing more than an essence. Furthermore, it is an essence that is constantly changing. Those who strive to justify sport are really doing notheing more than jumping on a "bandwagon." Today, the bandwagon may be physical fitness; at one time it might have been character education; tomorrow it may be cognition through movement education. All such esoteric attempts are fraught with the potential pitfall that they may cause people to lose sight of sport as an essence. The sport experience is actually a personalized matter. The individual who enjoys sport may not even be conscious of the reasons for his enjoyment. This is where the notion of ambiguity comes most clearly into the picture. Life is ambiguous, and sport as part of life is also ambiguous. We will never completely understand sport because the possibilities within the realm of sport are constantly changing.

Therefore, we find that the question "why" is not a particularly significant question for the existentialist. This may further help to explain the opinion held by many that existentialism is really not a philosophy. In the first chapter we noted that "why" is ultimately the most significant philosophical question. An existentialist appears to shun the question "why" because it suggests that the question can be answered. To provide an answer would eliminate some of the choices that should be left open for every individual. Two questions are of importance for the existentialist. They are the questions "what" and "how." These are questions which lead to descriptive answers. When the answers are received they do not force the individual to pursue a particular course of action. If I know something about what sport is and how it is conducted, I am still free to reject it. Likewise, description of the status quo may stimulate me to either accept this situation or attempt to make a change. I am still left with one or more choices.

CONFLICT WITH EDUCATIONAL PHILOSOPHY

A few attempts have been made to compare existentialism with philosophies of education. The effort may be a noble one, but the results have not been particularly enlightening. If existentialism is to be questioned as a philosophy, the possibility that there can be an educational philosophy of existentialism becomes even more remote. The reason I make this assumption is that educational philosophies have, in general, been even more prescriptive than have systematic philosophies of life. If we look into some of the bases for educational philosophy, it should become clear that there is an inherent tension between that form of philosophizing and existentialism.

When all the frills have been removed, philosophers of education are concerned with one principal question: what is education? Initially, that would seem to be a very simple question, but, as we all know, it is a question of great complexity. During the years since it was first raised, the question has never been answered in such a way as to satisfy large numbers at any given time. However, the paradox is that neither educational philosophers nor laymen have been inclined to hedge the question or their answers. To the contrary, the records are replete with bold answers. This, in itself, is enough to cause conflict with the existentialist's position. One is led to believe that there are no legitimate alternatives if he is to be educated.

This seemingly simple question is also misleading in another respect. It sounds like a question involving the end or goal to be reached, but it inevitably becomes a question involving means. I made this point earlier in considering the question of the "how" of sport. As mentioned there, differences in philosophies of education primarily revolve around that question. Education is a process; so, in attempting to define education, one gets caught up in an effort to describe what the process should be.

Now, at the outset it would appear that the existentialist could live quite comfortably with the intent to describe the process of education because he prefers to cope with the questions "what" and "how." But, again the matter is not as simple as one might wish it would be. The question "how" ultimately results in the question "why" because educational philosophers cannot agree on the former. Eventually, they end up debating why one method is preferable to another. The answers are generally unacceptable to the existentialist because they tend to be prescriptions in which there are relatively few choices.

This is not to say that an existentialist finds all educational philosophies to be equally repulsive. With respect to the two major constellations of educational beliefs, essentialism and progressivism, the former undoubtedly represents the major source of conflict with existentialism. In fact, about the only thing the two groups share in common is the conviction that life is a very serious matter. There is an air of optimism about progressivism which is not present in other philosophical positions.

Progressivists and existentialists find considerable common ground in stressing such concepts as freedom and ambiguity. However, there is a social/psychological characteristic of progressivism which leaves the existentialist wondering whether the individual is not once again being swept up in a current, without real choices. The progressivistic idea of social self-realization is an answer to the "why" of education which is at cross-purposes with the concept of the authentic person.

One of the most basic issues in educational philosophy is that which revolves around the role of the school in society. As is true of most issues, extreme positions can be noted, and the majority of people fall somewhere in between. That is, they are not inclined to say that the matter can be resolved by saying it is either this way or that way. On the one extreme, we find those who boldly state that the school is a mirror of society; it is an arm of society; it should reflect the societal image. In sharp contrast, particularly today, we hear strong voices urging that the school must assume leadership in bringing about social change. The majority are inclined to hedge in regard to this debate. They are vacillators; that is, they stand here today and there tomorrow. An existentialist finds it very difficult to accept any one of the three positions. The entire issue is quite contrary to his very nature. The basic problem as he sees it is that the issue revolves around the role of an essence which should not even be an issue. Schools should be designed with only one purpose in mind—that is to serve the individual. When one accepts that basic premise, it becomes purely an academic question whether the school reflects society or attempts to change society. Chances are that it is not an either-or situation. On the other hand, a given individual is forfeiting his claim for existence if he does not make his choices with regard to more specific issues that evolve from the role of the school in society.

An example from sport can be used to illustrate that an existentialist would make his choice apart from any broader considerations in educational philosophy. I will begin by assuming that football is a popular American sport. That is, people in this society generally like football and consequently support it in many ways. Now, I will further assume that Mr. X is a believer in the idea that the school should reflect society. To be consistent with this overall belief, he would work toward the promotion of football as a popular sport in the schools. Of course, that is predicated on another assumption that he considers sport to be an integral part of a school program. This entire line of thinking is foreign to an existentialist because in his opinion it all proceeds from a false premise. The premise is that one's overall educational philosophy should determine his choices when faced with various alternatives. According to the existentialist, such a premise places essences before the individual's existence. Once again, the concept of "ambiguity" helps to explain why an existentialist reacts to these matters in the way he does.

Another favorite topic in educational philosophy is the curriculum for a school. What should be taught? What should be required? Both of these questions "turn off" an existentialist before he can even get started in seriously considering them. The reason for his rejection of these questions is that he would contend they are virtually impossible to answer. When one answers the question what should be taught he sets forth a prescription for prospective students. If he sets forth requirements, he merely adds to and further specifies the prescription. An essentialist will do both these quite freely because he is confident that he has the answers that have been imparted to him through tradition. A progressivist, on the other hand, will reject the idea of requirements and will be inclined to leave the door open for students to decide that which should be taught. Either alternative and most of the predetermined eclectic suggestions cause the existentialist to agonize. Life is not that simple. One cannot sit down and arbitrarily decide the content for a curriculum. By the same token, it is just as foolish to leave the matter entirely flexible for the students to decide. Remember, says the existentialist, each of us shares a responsibility for our fellow man. It is a bit difficult to say exactly how an existentialist would arrive at a curriculum. About as close as I can come is to suggest that a teacher would decide the content after surveying the background, needs, and interests of the prospective students. It certainly would not be acceptable to have students vote on the matter because the needs of the minority could be overlooked through the wishes of the majority.

An existentialist is faced with a similar kind of perplexing situation when he hears educational philosophers discuss the topics of methodology and administration for the school. All that seems to be so much waste of time because we really don't know what is suitable in the way of methodology and administration until we assess the needs and interests of those people with whom we are working. The focus should always be on individuals, not on institutions or systematic philosophies.

Needless to say, from an existentialist's frame of reference, the most objec-tionable feature of educational philosophy is the discussion of aims, objectives, goals, and anticipated outcomes. Education, as an essence, has no aims. People, as an existence, do have aims. Their aims or objectives for education are about as diverse as there are number of people. The concept of "ambiguity" particular-ly applies here. Everything around us is constantly changing. Consequently, my educational goals today may be quite different from what they were five years ago. To speak or write of the aims for education is virtually useless. Aims grow out of the dynamics of a situation.

In terms of the three forms of educational philosophizing, only one could be generally acceptable to an existentialist. Ironically, it is the form which has been least evident in the writings of educational philosophers. I am, of course, referring to philosophical analysis. This can be accepted because it is relatively free from prescriptions. A true analysis attempts to present all sides of an issue and leaves the matter open to be decided by each individual. Most educational philosophizing has been of the normative variety. Numerous statements of educational principles have been set forth. Some of these have been so vague and "flowery" that one could scarcely question or oppose them. Others have been pure dogma, reflecting an essentialistic bias. Still others have been more cautious and even with some scientific bases, but the whole idea of principles is contrary to existentialistic thought.

Speculative philosophizing is probably just as much of an anathema for the existentialist, although he may not be as directly concerned about it for a couple of reasons. In the first place, there has been relatively little speculation, as such, in the realm of educational philosophy. The speculation has been done by philosophers, and, then, educational philosophers have set forth principles based on the speculation. Secondly, speculation can remain relatively harmless until one begins to elicit principles or guidelines for action derived from the speculation.

The meaning of all this for sport becomes rather clear when one considers the concerted effort which has been made by many people during the past 50 years to establish the idea that sport is but part of physical education. This is an attempt by educational philosophers to rationalize sport by placing it under the educational banner. Such people were unable to accept the idea of sport for sport's sake. In their defense, they were often forced into this position by other people who considered sport to be frivolous and noneducational. Thus, the drive to justify by placing it under the umbrella of physical education proceeded apace and has continued more or less to the present day.

This attempt to relate sport to the process of education has been manifested in what might be called the "implications" approach. The person who utilizes this approach begins by outlining certain principles of education. From that point he deduces or draws implications for physical education. The assumption always is that physical education is part of education. Physical education shares the purposes of education generally. For the most part this has been the approach taken by those professional physical educators who have written textbooks on the philosophy, curriculum, methodology, and curriculum of physical education. They have begun by examining these topics in education generally. This leads them to infer the particularized meaning for physical education. Sport always ends up being considered as a part of this thing called physical education.

Although a case can be made for this line of reasoning, it certainly is contrary to the orientation of an existentialist. He is not necessarily concerned about the matter of whether an activity is or is not educational. We cannot actually define education. What is education for me may be something different for you. To say that sport is part of physical education and that physical education is part of education really adds nothing to our understanding and appreciation of sport. That is merely an intellectual exercise for someone who feels the need to relate sport to other essences.

That in itself might not be too bad if it did not lead to other practices which work at cross-purposes to the authenticity of the individual. The biggest problem is that students are taught these principles and subsequent clichés as though they were the "gospel" truth. In other words, an existentialist feels that educational philosophy is frequently used as a tool to indoctrinate those students who are about to enter the profession.

Even though an existentialist may reject the methods employed by an educational philosopher, he does not disregard the need for *a* method. As a matter of fact, he stresses a method which he refers to time and time again. The method is called phenomenological analysis. Erwin Straus[3] is among those who have

---

[3]Erwin Straus, *Phenomenological Psychology* (New York: Basic Books, Inc., 1966).

advocated the phenomenological approach. Although the phenomenological method is not easily and readily described, it appears to be what might be called experiential description. This much can be said for certain about phenomenology: it is a long way from speculation, on the other end of a continuum. Those who employ the phenomenological method make a concerted effort to present things as they are or at least as they are perceived. The focus is supposed to be on objectivity. On the other hand, there is an open recognition that the results of experiential description are never completely objective. They represent an attempt to portray the way things seemed to the person who underwent the experience. Description will never present the experience exactly as it was. It will attempt to present the experience in such a manner that the true significance of the experience may be grasped. I think it should now be evident that phenomenological analysis really has nothing to do with educational philosophy, as that subject has been traditionally conceived. Education is something one must experience before he describes it. Even when it has been experienced, my description of the experience is likely to be quite different from yours. Educational philosophers are too inclined to talk and write about education as though it were a universal quality: we should begin to seek and experience education as a series of particular experiences. Each experience has a certain meaning for you and me which may be part of our education.

Among professional physical educators, Seymour Kleinman is one who has displayed a keen interest in phenomenology. During the past few years, he has presented several papers and articles on the subject. His rejection of a theory of sport vividly reveals his particular philosophic temper:

I suggest that engagement in game, sport, or art, whether it be as participant or spectator, and a description of this kind of engagement enable us to come to know what game, sport, or art is on a level that adds another dimension to our knowing. Phenomenological description does this. While Weitz and Wittgenstein tell us to look and see how the word sport or art is used in the language, the phenomenologist tells us to look and see how sport or art is experienced and to describe it in that fashion. . . .

It should be obvious by now that phenomenology's objective is to go directly to the experience and take if for what it is. Sport does not exist in a vacuum, and theorizing about it has a dangerous tendency to present it in that light. The phenomenologist tells us not to regard experience with suspicion, but to accept it as a valid and meaningful aspect of being or existing in the world.[4]

Those who have an interest in developing a theory of sport would find greater compatibility with educational philosophers. In fact, the latter group often purport to be presenting a theory of education. It seems that a theorist is one who would be inclined to place an essence before existence. In the case of sport, as a possible essence, that would amount to an effort of beginning with a

---

[4]Seymour Kleinman, "Toward a Non-Theory of Sport," *Quest*, X, May 1968, pp. 31—33.

study of sport as a collective social phenomenon. From there one proceeds to an analysis of the individual's experience in sport.

The entire discussion of sport in relationship to theory is further complicated by the recognition that scholars are not in complete agreement on a definition of theory. Scientists, especially those in the natural science vein, insist that theory can only be derived from the gathering and treatment of quantifiable data. However, other scholars, with a more humanistic bent, would allow philosophic inquiry as a form of theory. In either case, it appears that an existentialist, with his phenomenological orientation, desires experiential description in preference to theory-building. Again, I will cite Kleinman, this time as an example of one who stresses the need for more than scientific exploration:

Science, because of its enormous impact on contemporary civilization, has caused us to treat experience and behavior as significant only when they are reduced to quantifiable data. But any attempt to reduce the descriptions we have quoted to quantitative analysis or explanation would render them sterile. Phenomenological description, on the other hand, brackets out inference and hypothesis. These are regarded as irrelevant to the ongoing nature of the act.[5]

Although an existentialist may not be as enthusiatic about science as are most of his contemporaries, I suggest that there may be a compatibility between existentialism and science which is not found between science and certain other philosophical positions.

COMPATIBILITY WITH SCIENTIFIC THOUGHT

In the first chapter we noted a comparison of science with philosophy. To restate the main point, science has gradually reduced the scope of philosophy. More specifically, the field of speculation has been limited. For the most part, philosophers have turned to analysis, in one form or another, as a mode of inquiry which does not conflict with scientific investigation. Among the various forms of philosophical analysis, logical description is perhaps the one that can most easily be reconciled with scientific findings. Yet, there may also be room for the phenomenological analysis of the existentialist. My reason for saying this is that one cannot help but note that existentialism continues as a pervasive influence amidst our scientific advances. What is there about existentialism which will permit this compatibility? Kaplan offers an initial key in attempting to answer this question.

Existentialism, moreover, is a philosophy which does not content itself with a mere description and evaluation. It returns to the classical philosophical tradition in insisting

---

[5] *Ibid.,* p. 33.

that philosophy is quite different from other intellectual pursuits in a very fundamental way—namely, that its goal is not merely to arrive at a certain system of propositions, however logical the system and however true the propositions of which it is composed. A philosophy is not a body of propositions but a way of life. This is precisely what a great many people in this muddled world are searching for. We want to know, not just what propositions to accept, but what kind of life to live, and on what basis. Any philosophy which addresses itself to these questions begins with an enormous presumption in its favor: at least, it is talking about the things that people want to hear talked about.

Because of this conception of philosophy, existentialism sets itself quite firmly against any system or school—so much so, indeed, that existentialists don't like to be identified as "existentialists." Such an identification implies that they agree with other philosophers who share the label, but who, they may feel, are talking nonsense.[6]

The critical reader will raise a pertinent question at this point: does not the statement that existentialism involves more than mere description and evaluation conflict with the suggestion that existentialists employ the phenomenological method of experiential description? I think the answer is "no" if one realizes that experiential description also involves more than mere description and evaluation. At least it involves more than description. Whether experiential description also extends beyond the evaluation phase depends on one's interpretation of evaluation. Experiential description does include an attempt to convey the significance of the experience. This can be positively related to Kaplan's suggestion that existentialism is involved with a way of life. When one reveals the personal significance of his experience he is indirectly offering possibilities for a way of life.

The compatibility of existentialism with science is most evident in the recognition that an existentialist assiduously avoids presenting a set of propositions. If he did present these, he would be taking a major step toward a proclamation of universals. Generally speaking, science and philosophy do not conflict if those involved with the latter refrain from the presentation of propositions and universal statements.

When the idea of sport for sport's sake is analyzed, it does not involve propositions or a statement of universals. No particular claims are made for sport other than the fact that it is sport. If the scientist wishes to study sport, he is free to do so without being faced with prejudices and *a priori* judgments. Sport is there to be experienced by those who desire to experience it and to be studied by those who wish to study it.

The study of sport may lead to the conclusion that there is more involved than just sport for sport's sake. In other words, a theory of sport may be developed. Carnap describes what is involved when a scientist develops a theory:

---

[6]Kaplan, *op. cit.*, p. 99.

The activities of a scientist are in part practical: he arranges experiments and makes observations. Another part of his work is theoretical: he formulates the results of his observations in sentences, compares the results with those of other observers, tries to explain them by a theory, endeavors to confirm a theory proposed by himself or somebody else, makes predictions with the help of a theory, etc.[7]

If scientific investigation revealed that there is more involved with sport than just sport, this should not be upsetting for an existentialist. It does not refute any claims which he might have made because he has not made any claims. At the same time, he would hasten to add that this in no way negates the significance of the sport experience just as an experience for the individual. It might be proven, for instance, that sport does contribute to the development of physical attributes. An existentialistic response would be to say well and good, but let us not stop there. For a given individual, the total sport experience may far surpass any specific values that have been demonstrated through research.

There is still another basis for suggesting that the concept of sport for sport's sake is not actually an unscientific point of view. This is related to the methodology involved in explaining sport for sport's sake—the method of experiential description. A common denominator of the scientist and the phenomenologist is that they both firmly believe in the need to get fully engrossed in the experience. Neither can be criticized for approaching things superficially or in a casual manner. Total immersion is an expression which aptly describes the efforts of each. The scientist is totally involved because of his felt need to exercise the necessary controls and rigors. One pervading thought constantly hovers in his mind: his conclusions will be accepted as fact. The person with the existential or phenomenological frame of reference realizes that he cannot experience the sport unless he completely accepts the sport for what it is and concentrates on it as a sport experience. If he is thinking about his work or other experiences while participating in sport, he will not have experienced sport in the existential meaning. This is one of the reasons why the propositions of external values of sport are hostile to the thinking of the existentialist. Such propositions tend to distract from the core of the sport experience.

THE SPORT EXPERIENCE

This now brings us to the central topic of this chapter—the sport experience. When someone says that he participates in sport for sport's sake, he is actually stating that the sport experience is the significant thing for him. The qeustion then becomes: what is the sport experience? This question is almost impossible to answer because of two variables which determine the answer. The most im-

---

[7]Rudolf Carnap, "Foundations of Logic and Mathematics." Found in *The Structure of Language*, by J. A. Fodor and J. J. Katz (Englewood Cliffs, N.J.: Prentice-Hall, Inc., 1964), p. 419.

portant of these variables is the individual. If two people participate in the same sport, even at the same time, each will not have the same experience. Common denominators may be found in their experiences, but the existence of the individual outweighs any essence in the sport. The second variable is to be found within sport itself. From one standpoint it is improper to speak of *the* sport experience. It would be more accurate to refer to sport experiences. My experience in golf will not be the same as my experience in basketball. I cannot generalize from my experiential description of participating in any particular sport. The description and analysis will be limited to that sport. There is even a further limitation as to time and space. One's experience in playing golf today will not be identical with that of playing golf yesterday or some time before. In other words, the sport experience is specific to the individual, the activity, time, and space. Thus, description of the sport experience becomes a description of a given individual's sport experience in a particular sporting activity at a certain time in a specific location. In an unpublished paper, Drew Hyland clearly describes an athletic experience:

The particular experience I wish to relate involves the last basketball game I played for Princeton, in fact the last four minutes of that game. . . . With about five minutes left, Artie committed his fourth foul, and the coach sent me in to take his place. I reported to the scorer and knelt along the sideline, awaiting a pause in the game so that I could go in. As I waited, the pressure relaxed a bit, and my thoughts wandered, not definitely, but vaguely, over my whole experience of basketball that year, and all years. . . .

I reflected, vaguely as I say, on these people, and on this game, as I awaited a pause. These reflections, and especially this game, were given a deeper sense of urgency and meaning by the realization that the four remaining minutes were probably to be the last four minutes I was to play with this team, these people. Yes, I would continue to live with them, probably know some of them all my life, even play basketball with them in pickup games; but not like this; not with the peculiar unity and closeness that had gone with playing on an organized team, where more, it seemed, was at stake. If I had time to continue reflecting, I might have become sad; but the whistle blew, and I entered the game. . . .

The past, present, future were all drawn into my activity, into the action of the game. I remember that we began to catch up, that we stole the ball again and again, scoring each time, so that the pandemonium of the spectators made more forceful still the excitement of knowing that we were catching up. . . . As St. Joseph's was coming down the court I ran to deflect a pass, turned to throw the ball to a teammate alone for any easy shot, when the referee's whistle blew. . . . I looked at the scoreboard for the first time since I had entered the game. There were twelve seconds left. We were losing by one point, one point which, if the referee had not blown his whistle, would have been our margin of victory instead of defeat.

It was not really sadness that pervaded the locker room as we sat there, mostly glancing at each other and back to the floor. Nor was it depression, bitterness, anger. There was something simple, a sense of oneness between us all, which both had to terminate, yet would always be; a silent calmness that bespoke a deep realization; something had come to an end.[8]

Even though Hyland has described what I would call an athletic experience, rather than a sport experience, I included several details of his description here because it is a beautiful example of what is meant by and intended through experiential description. If someone were to quiz Hyland concerning the specific values of that experience, he would probably be hard-pressed to come up with definitive answers. Yet, the total experience left such a vivid impression with him that he can accurately describe the details. Furthermore, his description brings out the significance at the same time. It may even reveal potential significance for others.

Hyland discusses the relevance and significance of this experience in terms of the concepts of space and time. With regard to space he points out that the spatial relations within the game are the all-important considerations for the experience. Where the game was played is relatively insignificant. Likewise, the time significance cannot be measured according to clock time. He was virtually unconscious of clock time. His past, present, and future were all brought together in a focus on time that had little to do with the clock. In fact, he was not particularly aware of game time until he looked up at the scoreboard with 12 seconds left to play. His overall description parallels a point made earlier in this book that a game has its own contingencies of space and time.

I am not certain that Hyland's experiential description of his last intercollegiate athletic contest can be directly compared with sport experiences. As a matter of fact, to be consistent, I would have to venture that such a direct comparison cannot be made. But, the difficulty of pinpointing the sport experience does not stop there. The truth of the matter is that *the* sport experience cannot be approached from an objective point of view. *The* sport experience is the personal experience of a given individual under very specific circumstances. Thus, there are as many possibilities for describing *the* sport experience as there are people who have had an experience in sport. By the way, an existentialist would be quick to add that having an experience in sport would not be the same as participating in sport. One can participate merely by going through the motions of playing the game. To experience is to gain a feeling or insight which transcends the superficial conditions of the game.

With this as a background, I will now venture to do something which an existentialist would never attempt or probably never permit. To put it more strongly, it almost seems like heresy to set forth the potential for sport experiences when we know that *the* sport experience is a personal, contextual matter. It should be rather clear by now that I am not in complete accord with the existential viewpoint. On the other hand, it is entirely possible that I have not grasp-

---

[8]Drew A. Hyland, "Strange Bedfellows: Playfulness, Heidegger, and Philosophy." Unpublished paper. Reprinted by permission of the author.

ed the meaning of the existential experience. If the presentation that follows serves no other purpose, it may stimulate those with phenomenological leanings to demonstrate the fallacy of our approach. What I intend to do is to outline some possibilities (a framework) from which *the* sport experience may be described. It should be very clear that none of these suggestions represents experiential description. They merely indicate a limited source from which a given individual may gain value from his experience in sport for no other reason than the sport itself.

GOLF

There is a satisfaction to be gained from hitting a long, straight drive in golf that cannot be appreciated by someone who has not played the game. Even the so-called "hacker" may have had this experience. For some reason or another, he finds that he "can put it all together" on a given swing. His next shot or succeeding shots may be horrible, but the one "good" shot remains in his memory. He can still see the ball in the air as it sailed over the fairway. This is the thing that "keeps him coming back." He tells himself that if he did it once he can do it again. Part of this experience for the sporting golfer is that he temporarily projects himself into the world of fantasy. He may imagine that he will become a "par" golfer with sufficient practice. Or, he may even stretch his imagination further to compare his drive to those of professional golfers whom he watched on television. Part of this experience is also likely to include the discussions which follow the actual play. On the "19th hole" or at work the next day, the casual golfer describes "his" drive to anyone who will listen. His 225-yard drive is suddenly stretched to 275 yards.

A similar kind of experience may occur when the occasional "weekend" golfer plays a "par 4" hole. He hits a fairly decent drive down the fairway. Prior to his second shot he methodically studies all the pertinent conditions—the wind, terrain near the green, position of the pin, and the situation of his opponent. He then carefully selects the club from his bag and takes his time in hitting. After he hits his five-iron shot, he sees it head straight for the pin. The ball lands on the green just short of the pin and rolls a few feet beyond. The golfer is now in position for a "birdie" putt. As he approaches the green to line up his putt, a feeling of immense satisfaction overtakes him. He says to himself and maybe to others that the game was designed that way. Actually, in many cases it may even be relatively insignificant whether or not he sinks his "birdie" putt at this point. Most importantly, he has had the experience of playing the hole according to the model for that hole. The experience was not a unique one in comparison to that of other golfers, but it was unique and thus a meaningful experience for that particular "duffer."

On succeeding holes, the golfer is more than likely to return to his usual form. He hits a reasonably good shot and then proceeds to "top" the next one or "spray" the shot. However, the memory of the well-played hole remains with him. That particular sporting experience has left an impression with him that cannot be measured in terms of externally determined physical, cognitive, or attitudinal values.

BASEBALL

Many American boys have sometime or another experienced the satisfaction of "giving the baseball a ride." However, the most meaningful baseball experience is more than likely to occur under very specific circumstances. Therefore, permit me to engage in a bit of fantasy by hypothesizing a particular case which may represent *the* sport expewience for a young man.

A boy grows up in a small town where most of the boys in the town spend their leisure time during the spring and summer playing baseball, not as part of a little league organization but on an informal, sandlot basis. Our imaginary boy joins in the baseball playing and enjoys it immensely even though he is not among the more physically gifted. When he enters high school, he goes out for the team and manages to "make the team." For two years, he is a substitute, entering the game for brief appearances either as a pinch hitter or an outfielder during the last inning when his team is either way ahead or way behind. In his senior year, our boy manages to "crack" the starting line-up as a center fielder. However, during the first few games he is so tense over the situation of being a starter that he makes several blunders. In one game he drops an "easy" fly ball. He strikes out several times, swinging at bad pitches. Consequently, he is "benched" by the coach and makes only occasional appearances in the games until the last game of the season. In that game the rival is a traditional opponent from a neighboring town which has already won the conference championship for the season. The coach of our boy's team decides to start him in this last game becuase he is a senior, has been a faithful team member, and the conference championship is not at stake.

The game proceeds along rather routinely to the ninth inning with the opposing team leading 3 to 1. In that inning our team gets a runner on second and third with two out. Our boy comes to bat, facing a pitcher with a blazing fastball. Everybody on both sides expects a pinch hitter, but the coach permits our boy to bat. On the first pitch he lines a "screaming" hit to right field. Unfortunately, the ball was hit so hard that the runner on second is thrown out at home plate and the game ends 3–2.

Now this may not sound like a very exciting baseball story. The truth of the matter is that it is fairly routine. Similar occurrences can be noted almost every day during the baseball season. However, for our hypothetical boy it was far from routine or without significance. For him, it was a "real" experience. It was an experience which he would probably never forget even though it was just another game and another loss for his teammates and his coach. This again reveals that the sport experience is first and foremost a personal matter. The experience may be shared with others, but, more often than not, two or more people may participate together in the same sport and have an experience different from one another.

TENNIS

The tennis experience, generally speaking, is different from both golf and baseball in one important respect. A person who has had a sport experience through tennis is less likely to recall a specific shot or hit which earmarked the significance of the experience. He may remember a crucial point which decided the contest, but even the most sensational tennis shot is not likely to leave the impression which results from the long drive in golf or the baseball which was hit hard in the "clutch." Tennis is a game in which a whole series of shots mark the contest. It is a game of rhythm.

Perhaps the novice tennis player has his first real opportunity to experience tennis when he is able to perform all the routine shots with some degree of consistency. When he first begins to play the game he finds that he spends most of his time chasing the ball, resulting from a poor shot by him or his opponent. Likewise there is constant frustration in attempting to serve the ball. He may frequently "double fault." If not, he may miss a hard first serve and then "punch" the second ball over the net to get it in the service area. Someone has told him that he should "take the net" whenever possible, but when he does so he finds that he always loses the "point" for some reason or other. In short, he cannot experience sport through tennis until he gets beyond certain obstacles.

Even though the transformation is not instantaneous, the tennis sportsman eventually reaches the stage where he can go on the court and play the game with some degree of consistency. He also finds one or more opponents who play at approximately his level. The play is not at championship or even tournament level, but the game can be played without distractions and frustrations. When he is able to serve the ball with some consistency, rally with regularity, and take the net when appropriate, the tennis player has reached the potential for a sport experience. The kind of experience he has might be described as a cumulative satisfaction of being able to put together a series of strokes which are impossible for the beginner.

HANDBALL

The sport experience need not be limited to one experience. That is, it need not necessarily be a particular happening at a specific time. The tennis example above partially brings out that point. Hyland's athletic experience was a dramatic one. In a five-minute span of time it seemed to him as though the past, present, and future were all brought together. I will use handball as an example of a kind of sporting experience which may be just as significant as other more dramatic, instantaneous experiences, but it is an experience that occurs repeatedly.

For our example, we will hypothesize that there is a middle-aged business-man who enjoys playing handball. He is a former athlete in high school and college, although he never dedicated himself to the pursuit of excellence in the athletic realm. He now belongs to a private sport club located in the business section of the city. The club is located close enough to his office that the business-man can walk the distance. Most of the other members of the club have a similar life style. They enjoy playing handball or squash three or four times a week, if possible. Usually, the businessman will attempt to play during the noon hour. His primary reason for this is that he feels much better in the afternoon when he has had the opportunity to play handball at noontime. This "good" feeling cannot be measured in terms of physical or attitudinal values. Needless to say, the cognitive values have also been minimal, if any. *But*, the businessman has had a sport experience. To repeat, it is not an experience which represents a single event or happening. It is a continuous experience in that it is repeated time and time again.

Our hypothetical man always tries hard to win. But the experience is not drastically affected by wins and losses. It might be if he always lost, but our businessman wins some and loses some. On a given day, he realizes that he is playing against a "tougher" opponent. With that in mind, he may even put forth a little extra effort on that day. But, the cumulative effect of the sport experience in this case is not measurable in terms of the number of victories.

After each handball match, there is a feeling of exhilaration and satisfac-tion as the businessman showers, dresses, and proceeds with the business of the day. When he misses his handball match because of a luncheon engagement or out of town business, there is a sense of temporary loss. His sport experience has been interrupted. Overall, I am striving to bring out the point that the sport experience may be a continuing, integral part of a way of life.

SKIING

I suspect that skiing is the one sport which has been cited most often as an example of having an experience in and through sport. There seems to be something unique about the skiing experience that sets it apart from experiences in other sports and other activities in life. Howard Slusher, who reveals a dis-tinctly existential flavor in his book, utilizes an experiential description of skiing to illustrate the potential relationships between "sport and being." The description is by Miss Becky Parks. Following is the concluding paragraph of that quotation as found in Slusher's book.

Suddenly I saw the final gate and the finish line beyond. Momentary relief spread through me as I realized the race was almost over. Quickly, though I forced the pleasant thoughts from my mind as I dutifully repeated my silent instructions and fought to gain speed. Three more gates behind me, and I was nearly upon the poles which marked the final gate. Now, fighting madly for extra speed, I thrust my poles into the snow and shoved myself forward. As I pulled my poles back to my sides, I realized that the push had been a bit overdone and had cost me my balance. My next sensation was a horribly delightful feeling of tumbling over and over as I rolled down the hill. Mixed with my joy at such complete freedom of movement was the sickening realization that this fall had cost me the most important race of my life: the Winter Olympics. (Parks, 1966)[9]

Of course, once again it is important to note that Miss Parks was describing a highly competitive experience—an athletic experience. Even though the circumstances were altogether different, there are similarities between the experiences of Hyland and Parks. The weekend skier is more likely to experience part of that described by Parks—the delightful feeling of complete freedom of movement. Skiers often remark that they have a feeling of liberation as they move down the slope. Almost paradoxically, this feeling may be blended with a feeling of satisfaction resulting from an obstacle which has been overcome. Each contour of a difficult slope poses a challenge to the skier. As he approaches the next challenge, the skier senses the peculiar blend of liberation and concentration. He realizes that he cannot afford to take his attention away from the task at hand. Yet, at the same time, he is aware that he must relax. If he "tightens up" he will increase the probability of falling.

There is also a totality about the ski experience which cannot be measured in terms of the accumulation of specific happenings. Many elements contribute to this experience—part of it may be merely the fact that the skier spent a day outdoors, when this is not his usual routine. The scenic beauty of the ski area may contribute to the overall feeling of satisfaction and relaxation. The total setting of the ski area tends to take the skier away from problems and other endeavors in his life. Suspension from the ordinary is an apt expression for describing the activities and outlook of the weekend skier.

BASKETBALL

Thus far, with the exception of baseball, our examples have focused on what might be called "individual" sports. The word "individual" has to be used with caution because these sports may also have a team basis. Nevertheless, there is some validity and merit in classifying some sports as individual sports because they are sports in which the participants may either engage alone or against another individual. It is perhaps not accidental that one should first of all think about individual sports when he considers the sport experience. Because the sport experience is a personal experience, the natural inclination is to begin by looking at the individual in sport.

However, there are many people who may find that their most meaningful personal experiences are those which emanate from a team organization. Those

---

[9]Howard Slusher, *Man, Sport, and Existence: A Critical Analysis*, (Philadelphia: Lea & Febiger, 1967), p. 5. Reprinted by permission of the publishers.

who adhere to the "social theory" would undoubtedly argue that meaningful personal experiences in sport can only be derived from affiliation with a group. The existentialist, by contrast, would suggest that the team experience is but one of many and that it may be *the* experience for certain individuals.

Hyland's basketball experience, an athletic experience, was one in which he gained personal meaning from his relatively long association with a group — the university team. In the realm of sport, the significant experience may well be of a different nature. For a given individual it may be just the fact that he makes the team. The single experience of for the first time being part of an organized basketball team, regardless of the level of competition, could be a most instrumental factor in a boy's self-realization.

It is a bit difficult to single out one particular element in the game of basketball and suggest that it alone has the potential for being *the* experience, such as the long golf drive or the baseball which was really "tagged." Basketball is a game of many moves and executions. I imagine that one would be most inclined to cite the long shot which drops through the basket at the closing buzzer. But, by the same token, a blocked shot, a clean rebound, a perfectly timed pass, and a well-executed dribble all present their own satisfactions to the individual who enjoys this particular sport.

I am continually amazed about one fact with regard to basketball. It may be a fact that stems from the American cultural demand for basketball. However, at this point I am not primarily interested in probing the reasons for or the source of this fact. The fact is that millions of American boys and young men continuously and regularly are attracted to playing basketball on an informal, pick-up team basis. Seldom have I gone into a high school, college, or YMCA gymnasium and not found a group playing basketball when there was not a scheduled gym class or athletic practice session. Boys and young men do not have to be encouuaged to play basketball on this basis for the most part. Rather, they seem to more-or-less naturally gravitate toward this form of sport on a spontaneous basis.

What is there about the pick-up basketball game which might make it a meaningful experience? I must admit that I cannot really provide the answer. It is doubtful whether the answer can be found in purported physical, cognitive, or attitudinal values, as discussed earlier. At the same time, such an experience lacks the glamor of skiing or playing golf. Of course, it could be argued that those who play pick-up games of basketball would ski or play golf if they had the opportunity. However, the record would indicate that, when the choice is there, this is not always the case.

Once again this points to the suggestion that it is very difficult to generalize regarding the reasons for various people's participation in various sports. The existential explanation for this is that the experiences are different from one another. The basketball experience cannot be compared with the ski experience or the golf experience. Likewise, the experience in the pick-up basketball game is markedly different from the varsity basketball experience.

In the "postscript" to his book, Howard Slusher offers an excellent frame of reference for anyone who prefers to accept sport for what it is—sport for sport's sake. At the same time, he clearly reveals that sport for sport's sake is inextricably related to the concept of sport for the individual's sake.

Throughout this book I maintained my belief in the dignity of man. It was my contention that both the individual and sport existed. Both could be experienced. Sport began and ended with man. *Being* was not at the center of sport but rather it was deduced from sport by man. Through this process sport and man could be viewed within a relational context....

I have little doubt that far too many participants in sport did not question the meaning of their involvement within the sport experience. One came to accept his environment in the best of the stoic tradition.... In fact, it had been my impression, in athletics, that strongly self-imposed forms of dogma were often used to contain the encroachment of existential doubts. Why did I run? What was the meaning of my participation in sport? These questions, and others like them, have plagued many a performer. Sport was real. Abstractions have little place in the world of action. It was not infrequent that the former was superimposed on the latter. In this way thought was repressed and man came to learn of the pragmatic advances of his efforts. He replaced *meaning* with achievement. If one tried "hard enough" he could even come to the point of unification of thought and action.[10]

In my opinion, Slusher's reflections typify the thoughts of those who reject the manner in which sport has customarily been promoted and defended. Many people, particularly professional physical educators, seem to feel that sport cannot be accepted in its own right. Slusher would agree with this only in part. His idea is that sport is meaningful when viewed in relationship to man. It is not necessary to disguise sport amidst something called physical education or human movement if what man desires is sport. Furthermore, the value of sport is to be found within sport. When one begins to attach external values to sport, it loses some of its meaning. People often find it difficult to enjoy sport because they are searching for a meaning which may not be present.

It seems quite evident that the idea of sport for sport's sake is contrary to the developments which can be noted in the United States throughout the 20th century to date. People are constantly told from many sources why they should participate in sport. Sport contributes to physical fitness. One acquires friendships through sport. Sport participation is a worthy use of leisure time. Lessons in courage, adversity, can be learned through sport. These are among the more common, popularly advanced reasons for joining in the sport arena. Seldom, if ever, does one hear the suggestion that sport is there for whoever desires it without regard to justification. Hyland, Slusher, and others with an existential frame of reference (even though they may not be self-proclaimed existentialists) wish to call attention to another possibility. They would probably compare

---

[10]*Ibid.*, pp. 215–216.

sport to art in this respect. Those who appreciate art seem to do so without regard to the external value of such appreciation. If one seeks sport and enjoys sport, why not accept that fact as it is?

BIBLIOGRAPHY

Carnap, Rudolf, "Foundations of Logic and Mathematics," found in *The Structure of Language* by J. A. Fodor and J. J. Katz. Englewood Cliffs, N. J.: Prentice-Hall, Inc., 1964.

Hyland, Drew A., "Strange Bedfellows: Playfulness, Heidegger, and Philosophy." Unpublished paper.

Kaplan, Abraham, *The New World of Philosophy.* New York: Random House, 1961.

Kleinman, Seymour, "Toward a Non-Theory of Sport," *Quest*, X, May 1968.

Slusher, Howard, *Man, Sport and Existence: A Critical Analysis.* Philadelphia: Lea and Febiger, 1967.

Straus, Erwin, *Phenomenological Psychology.* New York: Basic Books, Inc., 1966.

12/A Scenario for Sport

Throughout the first 11 chapters of this book I have attempted to take a somewhat neutral stance with regard to the various issues that have been presented. Of course, I would have to be the first to admit that the stance was not as neutral as it might be; biases were revealed, and value judgments were inserted along the way. For instance, the reader cannot help but note that the concept of physical education has been presented and discussed in a negative light. Likewise, there has been a concerted effort to cast serious doubt on the manner in which physical education has customarily been organized and conducted in the schools. The focus has been on sport because the book is about sport wherever it is found and in whatever form it appears. Some readers will undoubtedly feel that I have already committed an act of heresy while others will dismiss the whole matter as a mere statement of the obvious.

Be that as it may, I will not even make an attempt at being neutral in this chapter. It seems to me that every author, particularly in a book concerned with ideas, is somewhere along the way entitled to "let his hair down a bit." For the most part, the thoughts expressed in the following pages have been presented earlier, possibly in a more indirect and subtle form. The effort here is partly one of synthesis in that most of my personal reflections about sport are brought together.

Before we turn to sport, a few observations about philosophy seem in order. Philosophy is a strange subject because it is at the same time shunned, abused, and exalted. People are often accused of being philosophical rather than scientific or practical in their approach. This causes many would-be scholars to state that they avoid philosophy like the plague. At the same time, philosophy is a term which is used very loosely. It is not uncommon to hear reference to a philosophy of most anything or everything. Paradoxically, philosophy is sometimes held in reverence. This is the exalted stage. Scholars may become philosophical after they have explored other possibilities of a more concrete nature. In fact, it is a rare person who doesn't reveal a philosophical bent somewhere along the way, even though he makes a concerted effort to avoid the same.

This book has been written under the title "Toward a Philosophy of Sport" because it does not represent an attempt to present new facts with regard to sport. A few facts have been presented. However, for the most part, the discussion centers around those matters which extend beyond or outside the factual realm. The effort was directed toward the probing of concepts and issues. Hopefully, more than one side of the coin was presented. If not, maybe that which was left unsaid will prompt someone to fill in the gaps.

At any rate, here it is; this is the author's conception of what sport should be. I must begin with a confession at the outset. A change in thinking has occurred while the book was written. This does not represent a complete change of thought but certainly an alteration of a major idea. At the outset, the question "why" was postulated as the most significant philosophical question. It may be, the question "what" is a prime determinant in attempting to answer the question "why." The confession is that the book was approached with the hypothesis that the "why" of sport is the paramount issue. I was searching for a reasonable hypothesis as to why people participate in sport. At the same time, the idea of sport for sport's sake seemed to lack appeal. However, the more carefully one examines the thesis of sport for sport's sake, the more reasonable it seems to be. This is particularly true when it is coupled with the recognition that sport is a stimulating form of recreation. The conception of sport for sport's sake does not conflict with the hypothesis that sport is a stimulating form of recreation. People are attracted to sport for what it is   a stimulating form of recreation. Those factors which tend to make sport stimulating have been discussed earlier.

At least two concepts and subsequent programs have caused people to be confused in their thinking about sport. They are physical education and athletics. It is unfortunate that the concept of physical education ever emerged. The concept has plagued the profession and served as an irritant to the public. Sport has been more or less submerged within the concept and programs of physical education. Many professional physical educators have constantly suggested that physical education is more than sport. That in itself might be acceptable but with it goes an insinuation that there is something inferior or degrading about sport. At the same time, the public has placed sport in an exalted position. Thus, it is no small wonder that physical education has not always achieved the kind of acceptance that might be possible. To put it bluntly, physical educators have failed to capitalize on the one component which interests the public. In education we constantly talk about the interest principle and then proceed to violate that principle again and again.

An example may serve to illustrate the point. In recent years movement education or movement exploration has become the fad among teachers of physical education at the elementary-school level. There may well be a place for this teaching approach, but it has been overdone and sometimes works contrary to the sport interests of older children. I suspect that movement exploration is most appropriate at the early elementary level where the interest in sport is generally not as fully developed. There, movement exploration can be employed as a lead-up to later participation in sport and dance. However, in the upper elementary grades many children would prefer to play games of sport. Instead, they are forced in their gym classes to engage in various forms of movement exploration. The net effect is that they have a negative reaction toward their physical education experience. At the same time, they will clamor for their parents to provide them with swimming lessons at the local swim club or golf lessons at the country club. Under these circumstances, can it be said that physical educators are meeting the needs and interests of students?

The concept and programs of athletics have hindered the cause of sport in a different sort of way. There is nothing wrong with the concept of athletics. It is a well-conceived idea, and athletic programs are legitimate in the same way that big business is legitimate. What is wrong is when athletics is purported to be something other than what it is. There is a great deal of hypocrisy surrounding athletic programs in colleges and even high schools. For the most part, the coaches are not guilty of this. They are more inclined to "call a spade a spade." That is, if you ask a coach, he will likely tell you that winning is the name of the game. However, most school officials and much of the public like to have it both ways. To begin with, they loudly proclaim all the sweetheart characteristics and clichés ascribed to athletics over the years. Then, they bemoan the fact when "their" team loses. Frequently, this is accompanied with a suggestion that the coach is incompetent and that he should be fired. Seldom does one hear the statement that a coach should be fired because he failed to build character. If those who desire to replace the coach had begun with a recognition that winning is all important in athletics, the inconsistency would not be present.

Sport is affected by this sort of irrational attitude and behavior because the confusion surrounding athletics also permeates sport. Some people would be inclined to use sport merely as a "feeder system" for athletics. Coaches are often guilty of this. They would transfer their athletic bent to the realm of sport. School officials and the public are often inclined to overlook sport altogether because they seem to feel that athletics serves all purposes. The needs of the majority for a stimulating form of recreation (sport) are overlooked in favor of offering interschool competition for a few.

An example will reveal some of the cloudy thinking which pervades opinions about athletics. The same people who favor athletic scholarship programs will be very critical when a college basketball player today decides to sign a contract with the ABA before he has completed his college eligibility. Once again, they would prefer to have it both ways. They expect that a college athlete can be recruited through all sorts of enticements. Then, once he is recruited, they expect that this same athlete will forget about the idea that athletics is big business. Why should he? The basketball player who signs the ABA contract or some other contract is honest with himself and with others. He recognizes that he is merely moving from one business enterprise to another. Any person in the business world might be expected to accept an offer from another concern if such an offer is presented to him. So, why shouldn't the talented athlete accept a lucrative offer to move from the business of college athletics to full-time employment in athletics?

For those who find this viewpoint to be too abrasive and unnecessarily realistic, I have only one suggestion. Let everyone involved with athletics make his decision as to how he would have it be. An athletic director, a faculty board of control, a principal, or a school board need not subscribe to the concept of athletics. But they must make a choice. If they chose to promote athletics, this is defensible and possibly even commendable. Athletics can serve as an excellent public-relations medium. Students, faculty, alumni, and public supporters tend to rally around the cause of a winning athletic team. On the other hand, the decision to promote athletics also represents a gamble just as any business enterprise is somewhat of a gamble. Not everybody can be a winner. It is even more difficult to be a winner in many different activities. Thus a school might do well to select a particular activity as the focus for the pursuit of excellence through athletics. At the same time, they can offer a complete program of sport for all the students in the school.

In my opinion, nothing is worse than the gray area. There are many schools in this country which purport to offer what is called a well-rounded athletic program. What this usually amounts to is fielding as many athletic teams as possible. Some colleges sponsor as many as 15 intercollegiate teams in different activities plus junior varsity and freshmen teams in most of these activities. It is a rare school today which can afford such an enterprise. The result is a situation in which the school neither pursues excellence through athletics nor offers a complete sport program for all students. Coaches are expected to be winners when they do not have the resources to be a winner. Students are frustrated because of insufficient opportunity to participate in sport and identification with athletic mediocrity. If the school officials make the decision that they would like to promote athletics as well as sport, they might do better to select one or two athletic activities in which they can actually pursue excellence. Examples of this have been observed for some time and continue to be evident. A school becomes known as a basketball school, a gymnastics school, or a swimming school. The similar kind of situation can be noted in academia. One school acquires a reputation as having an outstanding history department, whereas another is known for the quality of its botany department.

At the same time, it would be a pleasure to see more schools proclaim and demonstrate that they are dedicated to the idea of sport. This would be particularly desirable at the high-school level, but there is also room for such an approach in college. For a school, athletics serves primarily a public-relations function. However, this function can be of either a positive or a negative nature.

It might be better not to have an athletic program than to have one which operates in the gray area. Above all other considerations, we must eliminate the hypocrisy that exists. To be more specific, school officials should stop making glib statements that they offer a complete sport program for all students and then proceed to offer a program which is only of an athletic nature.

More attention should be given to intramural sport programs at all levels. Some people seem to hold the opinion that intramural sport emerged as the stepchild of physical education. The situation could just as well be reversed, but that wouldn't make any sense either. To distinguish between intramural sport and physical education only serves to confuse the issue. I assume that such a distinction is intended to contrast a competitive program in sport with an instructional program in sport, dance, and other forms of exercise. However, when the distinction is employed it frequently leads to overlapping functions and programs which work at cross-purposes with each other. Sport is competitive by its very nature. Thus, it is redundant to refer to a competitive sport program. Sport instruction is nothing more than a lead-up to sport participation. An intramural sport program should be organized so as to offer instructional classes for those who desire and need instruction in sport skills. Required physical education or gym classes should be eliminated.

The intent to focus on sport often seems to be upsetting to those who have a primary interest in dance. This is certainly understandable if they sense that the sport emphasis will work contrary to their interests as dancers. As a result, umbrella concepts such as physical education and human movement emerged and have been promulgated by those who wish to make certain that all related programs receive adequate attention and support. The cause may be a noble one, but, unfortunately, the umbrella concepts have not brought about the intended purpose. Within recent years more and more dance specialists have sought to be administratively identified with fine arts rather than physical education. This is a reasonable move and should be facilitated whenever possible. If not, there is no reason why dance cannot and should not be accepted in its own right just as sport would be accepted for what it is. In large schools there can be a department of sport and a department of dance. Smaller schools would have a department of sport and dance. If necessary, it is better to sacrifice brevity at the expense of specificity. At least people will have some idea of the functions of a department if it is designated as sport and dance.

Exercise is another concept which has confused many scenarios of sport. Although exercise is a meaningful concept, it is often employed in a manner which clouds the issue. First of all, exercise is a "work" concept as contrasted with play. People frequently do exercise in their play, but when they do so, exercise is subsidiary to the overall idea of play. An exercise program is just that. It is purely a program of exercise; it is work. The conduct of exercise and the study of exercise are legitimate in their own right just as the conduct and study of sport and dance have their own boundaries and dimensions.

Personally, I prefer to exercise through the medium of sport whenever time and facilities permit. But this does not negate the fact that an exercise program per se is a more efficient means of exercising if the individual wishes to first and foremost have an exercise experience. The sport experience is a sport experience; the dance experience is a dance experience; and the exercise experience is an exercise experience. From an administrative perspective, departments organized according to function should be designated as departments of sport, dance, and exercise science. If the overall size of the institution is too small to permit the establishment of three such departments, it would again be preferable to be specific rather than brief and abstract.

Even though I am attempting to move away from the concepts of physical education and human movement toward the concepts of sport, dance and exercise, I suspect that I am somewhat of a "lone voice in the wilderness" at this jucture. For instance, in spite of increased talk about the latter three concepts, the following is a statement in a position paper for college physical education which was written by a group of national leaders in physical education and published very recently:

Physical education is the study and practice of the science and art of human movement. It is concerned with why man moves; how he moves; the physiological, sociological, and psychological consequences of his movement; and the skills and motor patterns which comprise his movement repertoire. Through physical education, an individual has the opportunity to learn to perform efficiently the motor skills he needs in everyday living and in recreational activities. He can develop and maintain sound physiological functions through vigorous muscular activity. He may increase the awareness of his physical self. Through expressive and creative activities, he may enhance his aesthetic appreciations. Physical education provides situations for learning to compete as well as to cooperate with others in striving for the achievement of common goals. Within the media of physical activity, concepts underlying effective human movement can be demonstrated and the influences these have on the individual can be better understood. Satisfying and successful experiences in physical education should develop in the individual a desire to regularly participate in activity throughout life. Only through enjoyable and persistent participation will the optimum benefits of physical activity be derived.[1]

This may well be an entirely defensible statement of the nature of physical education. Any questions which are raised here are not intended to be personal criticisms. But it would be interesting to hear answers to the following questions:

1. Why are sport, dance, and exercise not even mentioned in attempting to describe the nature of physical education? What is physical education other than program of sport, dance, and exercise?

---

[1]"Guide to Excellence for Physical Education in Colleges and Universities," *Journal of Health, Physical Education, and Recreation.* Vol. 42, Number 4, April 1971, p. 52.

2. Is human movement a science? If so, what is there about human movement which makes it a science?

3. Is it necessary to be concerned with why man moves? If man didn't move, he would probably be ill or incapacitated. A more significant question would seem to be why man chooses to move through a particular medium, such as sport, or dance, or exercise.

4. The physiological, sociological, and psychological consequences of man's movement covers an extremely broad territory. Would physical educators actually purport to be concerned with all that is involved? Much of what man does could be included under that category.

5. The motor skills which man needs in everyday living include such things as pounding nails, typewriting, sewing, and performing various mechanical tasks in a garage or factory. Do physical educators claim this as part of their domain?

6. What does it mean to increase the awareness of one's physical self? Most people would probably agree that man should learn to realize his physical potential and limitations. On the other hand, psychiatrists tell us that awareness of one's physical self may lead to emotional problems. The physical self is often not what man would desire it to be. It would seem more appropriate to suggest that sport, dance, or exercise may assist man in accepting his body. That is, these activities may enable him to become less concerned about his physical problems.

7. Life is a process in which people are constantly placed in situations which require them to compete and cooperate in striving for the achievement of common goals. Does it help to describe physical education by singling this out as something which is provided by physical education?

8. Is not the desire to regularly participate in activity throughout life a fundamental human need? Does it take a satisfying and successful experience in physical education to develop such a desire?

So, the long and short of it is that I would prefer to see people stop defending physical education programs by describing the nature of these programs in such a way that they seem to encompass all of life. Would it not be better to accept the fact that there is exercise, there is dance, and there is sport? Programs involving these activities exist for those who desire them. The individual's attraction to sport, dance, or exercise will primarily depend on two factors: (1) the innate characteristics of the individual (some people are not attracted to sport, dance, or exercise regardless of the availability or quality of programs), and (2) the quality of the programs (this includes facilities, organization, and teaching effectiveness). Nothing can be done about factor number one. That leaves us with quality programs as the variable.

Therefore, I wish to conclude this book with an outline of what I consider to be a quality program of sport, extending from the pre-school through the

Ph.D. level. This is not an intent to sell sport, because sport does not have to be sold. It becomes a matter of offering programs which are attractive so that people do not lose their interest in sport. The omission of dance and exercise programs in this scenario is not designed to negate the place of these programs or to relegate them to a lower order. This book is about sport, so someone else may offer scenarios for dance and exercise programs if they so desire.

PRE-SCHOOL SPORT

Sport at the pre-school level should be manifested more in the form of sporting skills than sport per se. This distinction is based on the characteristics of sport as noted earlier. Actually, the situation is basically one of degree. Participation in sport as an institutionalized game should not occur at the pre-school level. There is plenty of time for that. The pre-schooler may participate in sport when it appears as a modified form of an institutionalized game of sport. For the pre-schooler, sport should be a neighborhood and family affair. It is a pathetic practice when car pools have to be formed to bring pre-school children to various community sport centers so that they can get an early start on participating in the institutionalized game of sport. In this society we all too often seem to work on molding the organization man before he even enters school. There is nothing wrong with backyard and neighborhood sandlot sport, but one sometimes gets the impression that this is a thing of the past.

The above comments are not meant to preclude the need to make sport facilities and equipment available to underprivileged children who do not have a backyard or a neighborhood play area in which they can participate in sport. It may be highly desirable for someone to transport them to an area where they too can experience the spontaneous joys of sport. But that is quite different from bringing middle- and upper-class children to the athletic arenas so that they can be exposed to coaching methods and attempt to imitate their athletic heroes.

When money and time are available, family activities are an excellent medium for introducing the pre-schooler to sport. Swimming is perhaps one of the best examples for a variety of reasons, although others could also be cited. Croquet *is* a sport, be it at an elementary level, and because of the level is something which a four-year-old can enjoy. Shuffleboard is another similar possibility. Ice skating is another very fine possibility, but it need not include hockey sticks, pucks, uniforms, etc., in an effort to get them ready for the the "pee wee" league a year or two later. Some pre-school children are also able to benefit from skiing lessons when they accompany the family on a weekend trip to the ski slope. Overall I wish to convey the idea that the pre-school child should be exposed to sport as interests and maturation level permit. Whatever the exposure, it should remain relatively unstructured and fun for the child.

This brings up the subject of the place for that which is called a movement exploration program in preparing the child for later participation in sport. I have been informed by movement exploration exponents that one of the purposes of this approach is to offer a lead-up to sport. For instance, various ball skills can be and are used in movement exploration. As I understand it, the movement exploration concept is favored by some people because it supposedly extends the idea of movement beyond games and sport. Movement exploration is also designed to offer ample opportunity for creativity. The inference usually is that children need more than games in learning to move and to understand the significance of movement. If there is a place for movement exploration it is probably at the pre-school and early elementary levels. On the other hand, I oppose the inference that movement exploration is needed because games are not enough. Children enjoy games. If the concept of movement exploration is introduced in the nursery school, this too is likely to be viewed as a form of game by the children unless a concerted effort is made to eliminate the game-like characteristics. So, if movement exploration is presented as a form of game and because it demands some form of physical prowess, the sport dimension is already present whether or not one strives to avoid it. Therefore, I am led to believe that the lead-up to sport, even at the pre-school level, is almost inescapable in this culture. The situation becomes one of form and degree. Children should be introduced to a variety of sporting skills and lead-up games to sport when they appear to be ready for them. All this should be accomplished with as relatively little organization and structure as possible.

SPORT AT THE EARLY ELEMENTARY SCHOOL LEVEL

Most of the basic skills in the various sports can and should be taught in grades K through 3. Prior to this level many of the boys and girls are not ready for sport-skill instruction as such. Subsequent to this level the children may become more anxious to utilize their basic skills in a game situation. Thus the idea of required sport-skill instruction is most defensible at the early elementary-school level. This is also the age where the student takes required work in reading, mathematics, music, and art. Thus the sport-skill instruction at the early elementary level should be focused on required exposure to a variety of skills which might be used in later participation. Students in this age range are not yet prepared to select their sports because most of them have had limited exposure due to unavailability of facilities and maturation level which precluded earlier participation in certain skills.

Games should continue to be part of the experience at this level. In fact, the need for and the desirability of participating in games runs the gamut from pre-school through adulthood. Differences along the way are to be found primarily in the form of these games. Iona and Peter Opie, in an excellent treatment of children's games, offer a description which is most appropriate for the child in the five- to eight-year range.

Yet the belief that traditional games are dying out is itself traditional; it was received opinion even when those who now regret the passing of the games were themselves vigorously playing them. We overlook the fact that as we have grown older our interests have changed, we have given up haunting the places where children play, we no longer have eyes for the games, and not noticing them suppose them to have vanished. We forget that children's amusements are not always ones that attract attention. They are not prearranged rituals for which the players wear distinctive uniforms, freshly laundered. Unlike the obtrusive sports of grown men, for which ground has to be permanently set aside and perpetually tended, children's games are ones which the players adopt to their surroundings and the time available. In fact most street games are as happily played in the dark as in the light. To a child "sport is sweetest when there be no spectators". The places they like best for play are the secret places where no one else goes.[2]

I have included this quotation in an effort to reinforce the idea that sport-skill instruction should not replace the playing of games at the age level of the early elementary-school child. The truth of the matter is that this will not happen anyhow if the child is given the opportunity to play his games. This opportunity need not be during the school day. Based on the observations of the Opies, it might be found even better if the game-playing was not associated at all with the school except maybe to use the school playground as a place where the games could be played. On the other hand, brief but daily periods of sport-skill instruction can be defended as a legitimate educational experience in the early elementary school. The greatest deterrent to the child's natural tendency to play "his" games is when teachers, parents, and other adults feel the compulsion to get into the act. Those who attempt to organize sport too early are guilty of this mistake, even though their intentions may be good from another perspective.

SPORT IN THE UPPER ELEMENTARY GRADES

In this culture, at least, we have observed that the desire to participate in the games of sport increases at this age level. This is true of both boys and girls. They are no longer content to merely "play catch" or to hit the baseball or soft-ball thrown to them. They express a desire and a need to combine some of their fundamental skills in a game situation. At the same time, while they still have an interest in their "own" games of the street and playground, they are becoming increasingly interested in the adult games of sport. Again, this interest should be recognized and accommodated but not exploited. This can be accomplished by making available the time and space for them to organize their games of sport. Supervision may be desirable and sometimes even necessary, but it should not be the coaching form of supervision.

---

[2] Iona and Peter Opie, Children's Games in Street and Playground. (London: Oxford University Press, 1964), pp. 14–15, Reprinted by permission of the Clarendon Press, Oxford.

If instruction in basic skills is needed, this can be provided through the required sport-instruction program. Although there would still be a requirement at this level to receive sport-skill instruction five days a week, the requirement now takes on a new dimension. The student is permitted to elect within the framework of the requirement. Thus, he may choose to receive golf instruction in lieu of volleyball. The sport-game period would be distinct from the instructional period. However, there is nothing sacred about the times for either. From one standpoint it might be better to offer the sport-skill instruction during the regular school day and have the period for supervised games of sport after school, but the situation could just as well be reversed.

JUNIOR HIGH SCHOOL SPORT

If the job has been done at the elementary-school level, namely five periods a week of sport-skill instruction, there is no need to have required instruction in the junior high school or subsequent educational levels. However, all junior-high students should be required to participate in some form of sport. This is the age when the concept of intramural sport offers the greatest potential. A period should be set aside, probably at the end of the school day, when all junior-high students participate in sport. On the other hand, all need not fulfill the requirement at the same time. For instance, a particular student may choose to sign up for the intramural basketball league which plays its games in the late afternoon. Another student may choose to enter the tennis or golf tournament or to accompany the students who are bussed to the nearby ski slope. Above all other considerations, there should be something for every-body during every week of the school year. An effort should be made to have a qualified instructor available for each sport skill which can be offered, based on availability of facilities. Hopefully, a particular instructor might be qualified to teach two or three sports. If not, the matter should not be forced. An instructor should never be assigned to teach a sport skill just for the sake of offering instruction. Too much of this has been done in the past in the schools.

There is no need to offer interscholastic competition at the junior-high level. Some people have opposed competition at this level because of claims that it may be detrimental physiologically or emotionally. However, we lack evidence to support such hypotheses. Intramural sport is preferable at this level for one simple reason: more students are given the opportunity to compete. A critic might argue: why not offer both programs? Can we not offer inter-scholastic competition and still have a fine intramural sport program? Theoretically, the answer is yes. But it doesn't usually work out that way. When interscholastic competition is offered in junior high school, it tends to negate the possibility of offering a complete and well-conceived intramural sport program. Coaches too frequently are assigned intramural supervision as an additional duty. They view it as just that. Students are inclined to lose interest in sport if they do not make "the team." Interscholastic competition offers great possibilities, but there is no logical reason why it cannot wait for implementation at the high-school level.

SPORT IN THE HIGH SCHOOL

There is no need to add much in regard to a description of sport in the high school except to note it will mark the beginning of the transition from sport to athletics for some boys and girls. That is, interscholastic competition would be offered for the first time. The timing is consistent because this is the age when youth begin to realize and think about possibilities for the pursuit of excellence. For some, an athletic activity may loom as a distinct possibility as a result of earlier success in intramural sport. For most, intramural sport should continue to be the focus. It will be much more beneficial for them to participate in one or more sports of their choice than to sit on the bench for three years just for the sake of being on an interscholastic team.

Sport-skill instruction should continue to be part of the high-school program. However, as with the junior high school, it should be offered only on a voluntary basis. Particularly at this age level, boys and girls are likely to choose a sport for which they have not previously been prepared. It is not surprising to find high-school boys and girls choosing to play tennis or golf or to ski for the first time, even when these facilities and instruction were earlier made available to them. Thus, the need for sport-skill instruction does not diminish in spite of earlier programs that are well-conceived.

SPORT IN THE COLLEGE OR UNIVERSITY

I will attempt to delineate a complete program of sport at the college level, extending from the program for all students to undergraduate majors to graduate students who are interested in either sport administration or the theory of sport. This part of the scenario is, of course, set forth with the recognition that not all colleges or universities could or even should attempt to offer all the programs which might fall under the administrative framework of a department of sport. The only program which should be found in every school is sport activities— a program of application. Schools which have a professional as well as a disciplinary orientation might choose to offer a program in sport education. A program in sport studies or the theory of sport should be limited to a relatively few schools. There are two very obvious reasons for this. First of all, only a few schools can and will be willing to financially support professors and services for this specialized area. Secondly, the market for graduates will be somewhat limited. But this in no way negates the need for a few schools to explore that which has long been neglected. Thus, the following structure is set forth with the realization that one or more components may be found in any given college or university.

SPORT ACTIVITIES—A PROGRAM OF APPLICATION

This program could perhaps be labeled intramural sport except that would convey the idea of its being only a program of organized competition. Sport activities would include instruction, spontaneous participation, and organized competition, all integrated and under the same administrative control. Following are some of the procedures which I consider necessary if a program of sport activities is to serve the needs of all students.

1. As students enter college, they complete a questionnaire which provides information concerning their sport background and current interests in sport. This would include provision for signing-up for sport instruction, if such is desired by the student.

2. Schedules for sport-skill instruction are prepared for those students who desire instruction in one or more sports. This would not involve courses taken for credit. There is no need for students to receive academic credit for sport-skill instruction. Sport-skill classes would be scheduled at times which do not normally conflict with the scheduling of academic classes.

3. Facilities are made available throughout the campus for spontaneous participation in sport. This is the one part of the program which comes the closest to being play. As examples, a bowling alley might be built in the basement of a dormitory and backboards and baskets installed for basketball on paved surfaces near housing areas. Similarly, fields for touch football and softball as well as tennis courts would be spread around the campus. This helps to take away some of the organizational effects as when students must go to one particular location to participate in their sports. Such facilities will undoubtedly require some supervision to reduce the amount of property damage. However, scheduling is needed only when there is likely to be a conflict with other interest groups.

4. Individuals and teams register for organized competition, solely on an interest basis. At various intervals throughout the year, the Department of Sport announces that tournaments are planned. Entries are received, but the matter is not forced. Organized sport competition is highly desirable, but it should not be forced. Students should not feel any peer-group or administrative pressure to participate in sport on a structured basis. Some people more thoroughly enjoy their sport when it is not preplanned and established on a tournament basis. Others will eagerly await the tournament. Both groups can be accommodated.

SPORT EDUCATION—A PROGRAM OF METHOD

There are two aspects of this program. One involves an education for teaching. The other is education for administration. Both tend to focus more on methodological than on scholarly considerations. The preparation for teaching sport skills occurs at the bachelor's level. Sport administration is a master's specialization. I will briefly set forth my ideas concerning each of these.

The student who completes undergraduate work in any college or university should be first and foremost a liberally educated person. That is, the bulk of his course work should be taken in the arts and sciences, regardless of his career plans. Professional preparation is thus viewed as an addendum. In this case, professional preparation for the teaching of sport would include course work in sport studies or the theory of sport and apprenticeship in sport skills. The latter would not involve course work; the student would do his apprenticeship work outside the realm of the curriculum per se. Approximately one-fifth of the curriculum might be devoted to course work in sport studies or the theory of sport. It would be sport studies until such time as a theory of sport is actually established. As mentioned earlier in this text, the theory of sport is still virgin territory. Basically this includes scholarly work in the history, psychology, and sociology of sport. Efforts have been made toward developing a theory of sport. However, we are not yet at the point where sport studies can more appropriately be called the theory of sport.

In terms of the methodological aspects of the program, the most significant experiences for the student will be those involving the apprenticeship in sport-skill instruction. This would include observation of and work under coaches and master teachers of sport skills. Prospective teachers of sport skills can only be adequately prepared through apprenticeships of this type. Students will not adequately learn to teach sport skills by taking one or two courses in each sport with which they hope to be involved. A prolonged and intensive exposure to the sport is necessary. This can be accomplished by many hours of work under the careful guidance of a master teacher in the sport.

A program in sport administration should exist only at the master's level. The reason for this is to be found primarily in the market potential. Those holding only bachelor's degrees are less likely to have the opportunity to obtain a position in some phase of sport administration. Likewise a doctorate is not really necessary for most administrative positions in sport. Work at the doctoral level should be limited to those who have scholarly interests. An administrator is not usually a scholar, and a scholar seldom is a capable administrator.

Course work for sport administration should consist of sport studies or sport-theory courses and courses in business administration, journalism, speech, or education. Again, as with the teacher-education program, the methods of sport administration can best be learned through some form of internship. One course in sport administration may be offered, but it should be an effort to show how the knowledge of sport history, sport philosophy, sport psychology, and sport sociology may be used in administering a sport program. Administrative procedures will be learned through the internship wherein the student is assigned to work in an actual administrative setting under the supervision of a sport administrator, much as the prospective teacher of sport skills works under the master teacher of a sport. The administrative setting might be in the offices of a high-school or college athletic director, an intramural sport director, a professional team or league, a ski resort, a country club, or a community recreation program.

SPORT STUDIES—A PROGRAM OF THEORY

There is a variety of ways in which a curriculum focused on the social significance of sport might be structured. The following model is thus one of many which could be developed. It is strictly a doctoral program which is based on the assumption that all students who enter the program will have taken their bachelor's work exclusively in arts and sciences or in the sport-education program as just described. Students would be expected to complete 90 credits of course work beyond the bachelor's degree. A master's degree would not be required enroute to the doctorate. However, the student might be awarded the master's if he chose to terminate his study along the way. The 90 credits would be distributed somewhat as follows:

Course Content Areas	Credits
History Courses	12
Psychology Courses	12
Philosophy Courses	12
Sociology Courses	12
Sport History Courses	6
Sport Psychology Courses	6
Sport Philosophy Courses	6
Sport Sociology Courses	6
Independent Study	6
Dissertation	12
	90

It might be argued that the program suggested above has a weakness due to the fact that the student will not have sufficient study in any one of the four related disciplines. However, the corresponding advantage is that it will cause the student to regard sport as his primary interest. When students of sport and exercise are completely "farmed out" to a particular discipline, the natural tendency seems to be for them to gravitate more and more toward that discipline and away from their initial interest in studying sport. Furthermore, interdisciplinary work is becoming more and more widely accepted. The ecologist draws from several disciplines. So, too, the sport theorist would benefit from knowledge and understanding of history, philosophy, psychology, and sociology.

Before putting down my pen, I would like to add one final thought. Some people may consider it strange to conclude a book on the philosophy of sport with a chapter on a scenario of sport. A scenario is a skeleton libretto or the plot of a dramatic work. Thus, a scenario is not really philosophical although it may have philosophical overtones. When a scenario is philosophical it seems to be so in a normative sort of way. For the most part our effort in this book has been analytical. However, there is still the normative need which flows from analysis. For students of sport, philosophical analysis cannot remain in a theoretical vacuum. It may be nice to know what sport is or isn't, but the understanding of sport becomes meaningful when the conduct of sport programs is effected by this knowledge. The real problem is that sport programs have been conducted for years without an understanding of the basis for the teaching and administration. Hayakawa concludes his excellent work on language with a position statement that hopefully has served as a frame of reference for this book:

A few words, finally, need to be said on the subject of reading as an aid to extensional orientation. Studying books too often has the effect of producing excessive intensional orientation; this is especially true in literary study, for example, when the study of words—novels, plays, poems, essays—becomes an end in itself. When the study of literature is undertaken, however, not as an end in itself, but as a guide to life, its effect is extensional in the best sense.

Literature works by intensional means; that is, by the manipulation of the informative and effective connotations of words. By these means, it not only calls our attention to facts not previously noticed, but it also is capable of arousing feelings not previously experienced. These new feelings in turn call our attention to still more facts not previously noticed. Both the new feelings and the new facts, therefore, upset our intensional orientations, so that our blindness is little by little removed.

The extensionally orientated person, as has been repeatedly said, is governed not by words only, but by the facts to which the words have guided him. But supposing there were no words to guide us? Should we able to guide ourselves to those facts? The answer is, in the vast majority of cases, no. To begin with, our nervous systems are extremely imperfect, and we see things only in terms of our training and interests. If our interests are limited, we see extremely little; a man looking for cigarette butts in the street sees little else of the world passing by. Furthermore, as everyone knows, when we travel, meet interesting people, or have adventures before we are old enough to appreciate such experiences, we often feel that we might just as well not have had them. Experience itself is an extremely imperfect teacher. Experience does not tell us what it is we are experiencing. Things simply happen. And if we do not know *what to look for* in our experience, they often have no significance to us whatever.

Many people put a great deal of stock in experience as such; they tend automatically to respect the person who has "done things." "I don't want to sit around reading books," they say; "I want to get out and do things! I want to travel! I want to have experiences!" But often the experiences they go out and get do them no good whatever. They go to London, and all they remember is their hotel and the American Express Company office; they go to China, and their total impression is that "there were a lot of Chinamen there"; they may have served in the South Pacific and remember only their dissatisfaction with their K-rations. The result often is that people who have never had these experiences, people who have never been to those places, know more about them than people who have. We all tend to go around the world with our eyes shut unless someone opens them for us.

This, then, is the tremendous function that language, in both its scientific and its affective uses, performs. In the light of abstract scientific generalizations, "trivial" facts lose their triviality. When we have studied, for example, surface tension, the alighting of a dragonfly on a pool of water is a subject for thought and explanation. In the light of reading *The Grapes of Wrath*, a trip through California is a doubly meaningful experience. And we turn and look at migrant families in all other parts of the country as well, because Steinbeck has created in us new ways of feeling about a subject that we may formerly have ignored. In the light of the subtleties of feeling aroused in us by the literature and poetry of the past, every human experience is filled with rich significancies and relationships.

The communications we receive from others, insofar as they do not simply retrace our old patterns of feeling and tell us things we already know, increase the efficiency of our nervous systems. Poets, as well as scientists, have aptly been called "the window washers of the mind"; without their communications to widen our interests and increase the sensitivity of our perceptions, we could very well remain as blind as puppies.

Language, as has been repeatedly emphasized in these pages, is social. Reading or listening, writing or talking, we are constantly involved in the processes of social interaction made possible by language. Sometimes, as we have seen, the result of that social interaction is the sharing of knowledge, the enrichment of sympathies and insight, and the establishing of human co-operation. But at other times, the social interaction does not come out so well: every exchange of remarks, as between two drunks at a bar or between two hostile delegates at the United Nations Security Council, leads progressively to the conviction on the part of each that it is impossible to co-operate with the other.

We come back, then, to the judgments explicitly announced at the beginning of this book—the ethical judgments on which the argument has been based throughout—that widespread intraspecific co-operation through the use of language is the fundamental mechanism of human survival, and that, when the use of language results, as it so often does, in the creation or aggravation of disagreements and conflict, there is something wrong with the speaker, the listener, or both. Sometimes, as we have seen, this "something wrong" is the result of ignorance of the territory which leads to the making of inaccurate maps; sometimes it is the result, through faulty evaluative habits, of refusing to look at the territory but insisting on talking anyway; sometimes it is the result of imperfections in language itself which neither speaker nor listener have taken the trouble to examine; often it has been the result, throughout the history of the human race, of using language not as an instrument of social cohesion, but as a weapon. The purpose of this book has been to lay before the reader some of the ways in which, whether as speakers or listeners, we may use or be used by the mechanisms of linguistic communication. What the reader may wish to do with these mechanisms is up to him.[3]

---

[3] From *Language in Thought and Action*, Second Edition, by S. I. Hayakawa, copyright, 1941, 1949, © 1963, 1964, by Harcourt Brace Jovanovich, Inc., and reprinted with their permission.

Bibliography

Aldrich, V. C., *Philosophy of Art*. Englewood Cliffs, N.J.: Prentice-Hall, Inc., Foundations of Philosophy Series, 1963.

Alston, W. P., Philosophy of Language. Englewood Cliffs, N.J.: Prentice-Hall, Inc., Foundations of Philosophy Series, 1964.

Archambault, R. D., ed., *Philosophical Analysis and Education*. New York: The Humanities Press, 1965.

Aspects of Contemporary Sport Sociology. Proceedings of the C.I.C. Symposium on the Sociology of Sport, ed., Gerald S. Kenyon. Chicago, Ill.: The Athletic Institute, 1969.

Avedon, E. M., and Brian Sutton-Smith, *The Study of Games*. New York: John Wiley & Sons, 1971.

Beise, D., and V. Peaseley, "The Relation of Recreation Time, Speed, and Agility to Certain Sport Skills," *Research Quarterly*, 7, March 1963.

Beisser, Arnold, *The Madness in Sports*. New York: Appleton-Century-Crofts, 1967.

Betts, John R., "Organized Sport in Industrial America," Ph.D. Dissertation, Columbia University, 1951.

Betts, John R., "The Technological Revolution and the Rise of Sport, 1850–1900," *Mississippi Valley Historical Review*, 40:231–256, 1953.

Black, M., ed., *Philosophical Analysis*. Ithaca: Cornell University Press, 1950.

Bookwalter, Karl, and H. J. VanderZwaag, *Foundations and Principles of Physical Education*. Philadelphia: W. B. Saunders Co., 1969.

Boyle, Robert H., *Sport—Mirror of American Life*. Boston: Little, Brown and Co., 1963.

Broer, Marion, *Efficiency of Human Movement*. Philadelphia: W. B. Saunders Co., 1960.

Broudy, H. S., "How Philosophical Can Philosophy of Education Be?" *The Journal of Philosophy*, LII (October 27, 1955), pp. 612–622.

Broudy, Harry S., *Building a Philosophy of Education*. Englewood Cliffs, N.J.: Prentice-Hall, Inc., 1961.

Brownell, Clifford L., and E. Patricia Hagman, *Physical Education—Foundations and Principles*. New York: McGraw Hill Book Co., 1951.

Brubacher, John S., *Modern Philosophies of Education*. New York: McGraw Hill Book Co., 1962.

Caillois, Roger, *Man, Play and Games.* tr. Meyer Barosh. New York: Free Press, 1964.

Carnap, Rudolf, "Foundations of Logic and Mathematics," found in *The Structure of Language* by J. A. Fodor and J. J. Katz. Englewood Cliffs, N.J.: Prentice-Hall, Inc., 1964.

Chase, Stuart, "Play," in Charles A. Beard (ed.), *Whither Mankind.* New York: 1928, pp. 332–353.

Cole, Arthur C., "Our Sporting Grandfathers," *Atlantic Monthly* 150: 88–96, July, 1932.

Conant, James B., *The Education of American Teachers.* New York: McGraw Hill Book Co., 1963.

Contemporary Psychology of Sport, *Proceedings of the Second International Congress of Sport Psychology, Wash. D.C., 1968.* Chicago, Ill.: The Athletic Institute, 1970.

Cozens, Frederick W., and Florence Stumpf, *Sports in American Life.* Chicago: University of Chicago Press, 1953.

Cratty, Bryant, *Social Dimensions of Physical Activity.* Englewood Cliffs, N.J.: Prentice-Hall, Inc., 1967.

Cureton, T. K., "Aspects of Flexibility and Its Relationship to Physical Education," *Research Quarterly* 9, October 1938.

Cureton, T. K., *Improving the Physical Fitness of Youth.* Monograph of the Society for Research in Child Development, 95, 29.4, 1964.

Daniels, Arthur S., "The Potential of Physical Education as an Area of Research and Scholarly Effort," *Journal of Health, Physical Education, and Recreation*, No. 1, 32–33, 74, Jan. 1965.

Dawkins, Pete, "We Play to Win, They Play for Fun," *New York Times Magazine*, 34–36, April 24, 1960.

Demiashkevich, M. J., *An Introduction to the Philosophy of Education.* New York: American Book Co., 1935.

Dulles, Foster R., *A History of Recreation: America Learns to Play.* 2nd ed., New York: Appleton-Century-Crofts, 1965.

Elton, W., *Aesthetics and Language.* New York: Philosophical Library, Inc., 1954.

Falls, H. B., E. L. Wallis, and G. A. Logan, *Foundations of Conditioning.* New York: Academic Press, 1970.

Flath, Arnold W., *A History of Relations Between the NCAA and the AAU of the United States, 1905–1963.* Champaign, Ill.: Stipes Publishing Co., 1964.

Fleishman, Edwin A., *The Structure and Measurement of Physical Fitness.* Englewood Cliffs, N.J.: Prentice-Hall, Inc., 1964.

Fogelin, R., "Sport: The Diversity of the Concept." Unpublished paper presented at the 13th Annual Meeting of the American Association for the Advancement of Science, Dallas, Texas, Dec. 28, 1968.

Frank, J. D., "Recent Studies of the Level of Aspiration," *Psychological Bulletin*, 38, 1941.

Gould, Rosalind, "Some Sociological Determinants of Goal Striving," *Journal of Social Psychology.* New York: Macmillan Co., 1941.

Graves, H., "A Philosophy of Sport," *Contemporary Review*, 78 (Dec. 1900), 877–893.

"Guide to Excellence for Physical Education in Colleges and Universities," *Journal of Health, Physical Education, and Recreation*. 42, No. 4, April 1971, p. 52.

Hackensmith, C. W., *History of Physical Education*. New York: Harper and Row Publishers, 1966.

Harvard Educational Review, XXIV, Fall 1954.

Harvard Educational Review, XXVI, Spring 1956.

Hayakawa, S. I., *Language in Thought and Action*. New York: Harcourt, Brace and Company, 1949.

Henry, Franklin M., "Physical Education: An Academic Discipline," *Journal of Health, Physical Education, and Recreation*, XXXV, No. 7, 32–33, 69, Sept. 1964.

Hetherington, Clark W., "The Foundation of Amateurism," *American Physical Education Review*, Nov. 1909, 566–578.

Higdon, Hal, "Jogging Is an In Sport," The *New York Times Magazine*, Section 6, April 14, 1968.

Huizinga, Johan, *Homo Ludens—A Study of the Play-Element in Culture*. Boston: Beacon Press, 1955.

Hunsicker, Paul, "Myths About Fitness, "*Journal of Health, Physical Education, and Recreation*, XXXI, No. 2, Feb. 1960.

Hyland, Drew A., "Strange Bedfellows: Playfullness, Heidegger and Philosophy", Unpublished paper.

Kaplan, Abraham, *The New World of Philosophy*. New York: Random House, 1962.

Keating, James, "Winning in Sport and Athletics," *Thought*, XXXVIII, 149, Summer 1963, 201–210.

Keating, James, "Sportmanship as a Moral Category," *Ethics*, LXXV, No. 1, Oct. 1964, 25–35.

Keating, James, "Athletics and the Pursuit of Excellence," *Education*, 85, No. 7, March 1965, 428–431.

Keating, James, "The Heart of the Problem of Amateur Athletics," *The Journal of General Education*, 16, No. 4, Jan. 1965.

Keeler, L. B., "The Relation of Quickness of Bodily Movement to Success in Athletics," *Research Quarterly*, 13 (May, 1942), pp. 128–133.

Kenyon, Gerald S., and John W. Loy, "Toward a Sociology of Sport," *Journal of Health, Physical Education, and Recreation*, XXXVI, No. 5, 24–25, 68–69, May 1965.

Kenyon, Gerald S., "On the Conceptualization of Sub-Disciplines Within an Academic Discipline Dealing with Human Movement," *Proceedings*, 71st Annual Meeting National College Physical Education Association For Men, 1968.

Kistler, Joy W., "Attitudes Expressed About Behavior Demonstrated in Certain Specific Situations Occurring in Sports," *Proceedings*, College Physical Education Association, 60, 1957.

Knapp, Barbara, *Skill in Sport*. London: Routledge and Kegan Paul, 1963.

Kraus, Hans, and Ruth Hirschland, "Minimum Muscular Fitness Tests in School Children," *Research Quarterly* 25, 1954.

Kroll, Walter, and K. H. Peterson, "Study of Values Test and Collegiate Football Teams," *The Research Quarterly*, 36, No. 4, Dec. 1965.

Langer, S. K., *Philosophy in a New Key*. Cambridge: Harvard University Press, 1957.

Lee, Mable, "The Case For and Against Intercollegiate Athletics for Women and the Situation Since 1932," *The Research Quarterly of the American Physical Education Association*, Vol. 2, 93—127, May 1931.

Lewis, Guy M., "The Ladies Walked and Walked," *Sports Illustrated*, 27 (Dec. 18, 1967) R—3—4.

Lewis, Guy M., "Theodore Roosevelt's Role in the 1905 Football Controversy," *The Research Quarterly*, Vol. 40, No. 4, Dec. 1969.

Loy, John W., "The Nature of Sport. A Definitional Effort," *Quest* X, May 1968, 1—15.

Lüschen, Günther, *The Sociology of Sport*. The Hague Paris: Mouton & Co., 1968.

Madlem, Leo, "Athletics in a Young Man's Life," *Proceedings*, 39th Annual Meeting, American Football Coaches Association, Jan. 1962.

Mallet, Donald, "An Educator Views the Contribution of Campus Intramural Sport Programs," *Proceedings*, 64th Annual Meeting, College Physical Education Association, 1960, 95—96.

Mathews, Donald, *Measurement in Physical Education*. Philadelphia: W. B. Saunders Co., 1963.

McAfee, Robert A., "Sportmenship Attitudes of Sixth, Seventh, and Eighth Grade Boys," *Research Quarterly*, 26, 1955.

Metheny, Eleanor, "Are Sports Enough?" *Journal of Health, Physical Education, and Recreation*. XIV, No. 5, 1943.

Meyerhoff, Hans, *The Philosophy of History in our Time*. Garden City, N.Y.: Doubleday Anchor Books, 1959.

Mitchell, Curtis, "Run For Your Life," *The Healthy Life*, Time-Life Books Special Report. New York: Time Incorporated, 1966.

Murphy, Chet, "Principles of Learning with Implications for Teaching Tennis," *Journal of Health, Physical Education, and Recreation*, Feb. 1962.

Nash, Jay B., "Character Education as an Objective," *Mind and Body*, Vol. 38, May 1931.

Oberteuffer, Delbert, "Some Contributions of Physical Education to an Educated Life," Found in A. Paterson and E. C. Hallberg's *Background Readings for Physical Education*. New York: Holt, Rinehart, and Winston, 1965.

Opie, Iona and Peter, *Children's Games in Street and Playground*. London: Oxford University Press, 1969.

Oxendine, Joseph B., *Psychology of Motor Learning*. New York: Appleton-Century-Crofts, 1968.

Plato, *Gorgias*, trans. Helmbold, New York: The Liberal Arts Press, 1952.

Quest I, "Quo Vadis?" Physical Education, Dec. 1963.

Quest II, "The Art and Science of Human Movement," April 1964.

Quest IV, "Man — Culture — History," April 1965.

Quest V, "The Leisure Enigma," Dec. 1965.

Quest VI, "A Symposium on Motor Learning," May 1966.

Quest VIII, "Collage," May 1967.

Quest IX, "The Nature of a Discipline," Dec. 1967.

Quest X, "Toward A Theory of Sport," May 1968.

Quest XI, "Our Heritage," Dec. 1968.

Quest XII, "Melange," May 1969.

Richardson, Deane, "Ethical Conduct in Sport Situations, *"Proceedings,* 66th Annual Meeting, National College Physical Education Association, 1963.

Riesman, David, *The Lonely Crowd.* New Haven: Yale University Press, 1961.

Rooney, John F., "Up From the Mines and Out From the Prairies," *The Geographical Reviw,* LIX, No. 4 (Oct. 1969), pp. 471—492.

Root, Robert K., "Sport Versus Athletics," *Forum* 76 (Nov. 1924), 657—664.

Ryan, Dean, "Competitive Performance in Relation to Achievement Motivation and Anxiety," The American Association of Health, Physical Education and Recreation, Minneapolis, Minnesota, 1963.

Schiller, von Friedrich, *Essays, Aesthetical and Philosophical.* London: George Bell & Sons, 1875.

Schmitz, Kenneth, "Sport and Play: Suspension of the Ordinary," unpublished paper presented at the 13th Annual Meeting of the American Association for the Advancement of Science, Dallas, Texas, Dec. 28, 1968.

Shaw, M. E., "Some Motivational Factors in Cooperation and Competition," *Journal of Personality,* 27, 1958.

Singer, Robert, *Motor Learning and Human Performance.* New York: The Macmillan Co., 1968.

Spencer, Herbert, *The Principles of Psychology.* New York: D. Appleton & Co., 1873.

Sports Illustrated, "The Desperate Coach," Parts I—III, August 25, Sept. 1, and Sept. 8, 1969

Sports Illustrated, "The Black Athlete," Parts I—V, July 1, 8, 15, 22, and 29, 1968.

Staley, Seward, "The Four Year Curriculum in Physical (Sports) Education," *Research Quarterly,* II, No. 1, 76—90, March 1931.

Straus, Ewin, *Phenomenological Psychology.* New York: Basic Books, Inc., 1966.

Studer, Virginia, "The Historical Development of Human Movement Fundamentals for College Women in the United States," unpublished M.S. thesis, University of Illinois, 1966.

"The Golden Age of Sport," *Time,* June 2, 1967, 18—19.

Trow, William C., "The Psychology of Confidence," *Archives of Psychology,* 1923.

Tunis, John R., *The American Way in Sport.* New York: Duell, Sloan, and Pearce, 1958.

Tunis, John R., "Changing Trends in Sport," *Harper's Magazine,* 170 (Dec. 1934), 75—86.

Tunis, John R., "Sports Return to 1900," *Harper's Magazine*, 186 (May 1943), 633–638.

Ulrich, Celeste, *The Social Matrix of Physical Education*. Englewood Cliffs, N.J.: Prentice-Hall, Inc., 1968.

Voltmer, E. F., and A. A. Esslinger, *The Organization and Administration of Physical Education*. New York: Appleton-Century-Crofts, 1967.

Weiss, Paul, *The World of Art*. Carbondale: Southern Illinois University Press, 1961.

Weiss, Paul, *Sport: A Philosophic Inquiry*. Carbondale: Southern Illinois University Press, 1969.

Whyte, William F., *Street Corner Society*. Chicago: The University of Chicago Press, 1943.

Williams, J. F., "Education Through the Physical," *The Journal of Higher Education*, I, May 1930, 279–282.

Wind, Herbert W., *The Gilded Age of Sport*. New York: Simon and Schuster, 1962.

Wittgenstein, L., *Philosophical Investigation*. New York: The Macmillan Company, 1953.

Zeigler, Earle F., *Problems in the History and Philosophy of Physical Education and Sport*. Englewood Cliffs, N.J.: Prentice-Hall, Inc., 1968.

Zeigler, Earle F., and H. J. VanderZwaag, *Physical Education: Progressivism or Essentialism?* Champaign, Ill.: Stipes Publishing Co., 1968.

Ziff, P., "The Task of Defining a Work of Art," *Philosophical Review*, LXII, 1953.

Index

Index

A BCDEFGH798765432